W0259526

China-Pakistan Relations

A Historical Analysis

China-Pakistan Relations

A Historical Analysis

Ghulam Ali

OXFORD
UNIVERSITY PRESS

Oxford University Press is a department of the University of Oxford. It furthers the University's objective of excellence in research, scholarship, and education by publishing worldwide. Oxford is a registered trade mark of Oxford University Press in the UK and in certain other countries

Published in Pakistan by
Ameena Saiyid, Oxford University Press
No.38, Sector 15, Korangi Industrial Area,
PO Box 8214, Karachi-74900, Pakistan

First Edition published in 2017

ISBN 978-0-19-940249-6

Typeset in Adobe Garamond Pro
Printed on 80gsm Local Offset Paper

Printed by Kagzi Printers, Karachi

To

Muhammad Ahad
and
Wei-ling Chang (Fatima Ali)

Contents

Acknowledgements

My first and foremost acknowledgement of gratitude for the cooperation I received when writing this book goes to Professor Bruce Jacobs, Dr Joel Atkinson, the late Dr Dennis Woodward, Ms Sally Riley, Ms Jocelyne Mohamadally, Mr David Bell, Mr Colin Rose, and Ms Dennis Kishere; all affiliated with Monash University.

There are others too whose support has benefited me immensely. The University Services Centre, Chinese University of Hong Kong, gave me access to their resources while the Taiwan Fellowship enabled me to visit Taiwan to conduct research at the National Central Library, Taipei. My thanks also go to Professor Arthur Ding at the Institute of International Relations, National Chengchi University, Taipei.

Others to be acknowledged are my friends: Dr Wang Weihua from Shanghai Institute of International Studies (SIIS) for arranging contacts with Chinese scholars, Syed Adnan Ali Shah Bukhari and Dr Rajesh M. Basrur (both then based in Singapore), Dr Salma Malik, Mr Humayun Khan, Mr Mohammad Yasin, and Professor Zhou Rong, Chief Correspondent of the *Guangming Daily* in Islamabad. My special thanks go to Professor Hassan-Askari Rizvi, Dr Fazal-ur-Rahman, and Dr Ali Zaman for their comments on my manuscript.

I am also grateful to the Confucius Institute Headquarters (Hanban) for its generous grant which made my visit to China possible. Also to be thanked is Ms Mei Huang. A number of scholars at Peking University helped me in arranging my meetings with Chinese academia and in guiding my research. Also of invaluable help have been Professor Tang Mengsheng and his wife Professor Kong

Julan, Associate Professor Qian Xuemei, Associate Professor Han Hua, Associate Professor Zhang Jiamei, and Associate Professor Wang Xu.

I benefited a great deal from the interviews and am grateful to those who spared their precious time to share their views with me.

My family—especially my wife Wei-ling Chang (Fatima) and my brother Ghulam Murtaza Anjum—and friends and colleagues have been very supportive; needless to say, without their helping hand, I could not have completed the book.

Ghulam Ali
Beijing, 2016

Abbreviations

ASEAN	Association of Southeast Asian Nations
BCIM	Bangladesh, China, India, and Myanmar
BFA	Boao Forum for Asia
CATIC	China National Aero-Technology Import and Export Corporation
CENTO	Central Treaty Organisation
CGWIC	China Great Wall Industry Corporation
CNAMC	China Nanchang Aircraft Manufacturing Company
CNNC	China National Nuclear Corporation
CPC	Communist Party of China
CPEC	China-Pakistan Economic Corridor
EHP	Early Harvest Programme
ETIM	East Turkestan Islamic Movement
FAC	Fast Attack Craft
FDI	Foreign Direct Investment
FTA	Free Trade Agreement
GB	Gilgit-Baltistan
HEC	Heavy Electrical Complex
HIT	Heavy Industries Taxila
HMC	Heavy Mechanical Complex
HRF	Heavy Rebuild Factory
IAC	Islamic Association of China
IAEA	International Atomic Energy Agency
ICBC	Industrial and Commercial Bank of China
IISS	International Institute for Strategic Studies

IPI	Iran-Pakistan-India
IR	International Relations
IRBM	Intermediate Range Ballistic Missiles
ISI	Inter-Services Intelligence
JI	Jamaat-e-Islami
JIC	Joint Investment Company
JUI	Jamiat Ulema-e-Islam
KANUPP-2	Karachi Nuclear Power Plant-2
KKH	Karakoram Highway
KP	Khyber Pakhtunkhwa
KRL	Kahuta Research Laboratories
KSEW	Karachi Shipyard and Engineering Works
LAC	Line of Actual Control
MBT	Main Battle Tank
MFN	Most Favoured Nation
MoU	Memorandum of Understanding
MTCR	Missile Technology Control Regime
NCNA	New China News Agency
NPC	National People's Congress
NPT	Nuclear Non-Proliferation Treaty
NSG	Nuclear Suppliers Group
NWFZ	Nuclear-Weapon-Free Zone
OBOR	One Belt, One Road
OIC	Organisation of Islamic Cooperation
PAC	Pakistan Aeronautical Complex
PAEC	Pakistan Atomic Energy Commission
PAF	Pakistan Air Force
PCICL	Pak-China Investment Company Limited
PIA	Pakistan International Airlines
PLA	People's Liberation Army

PLAAF	PLA Air Force
PML-N	Pakistan Muslim League-Nawaz
PML-Q	Pakistan Muslim League-Quaid
PoW	Prisoners of War
PPP	Pakistan People's Party
PRC	People's Republic of China
ROC	Republic of China
SAARC	South Asian Association for Regional Cooperation
SC	Security Council
SCO	Shanghai Cooperation Organisation
SEATO	Southeast Asia Treaty Organisation
SUPARCO	Pakistan Space and Upper Atmosphere Research Commission
UN	United Nations
UNGA	United Nations General Assembly
UNSC	United Nations Security Council
WoT	War on Terror
XSLC	Xichang Satellite Launch Centre

Introduction

In spite of divergent socio-political systems, cultures, and ideologies, China and Pakistan have maintained a steady relationship since the early 1960s. Over this long period of time, a great deal has changed within the two countries, in the region, and in the world at large but their relationship has remained unaffected. Both the countries describe their friendship using terms such as 'all-weather', 'time tested', and 'sweeter than honey'. Analysts who have examined this relationship acknowledge its durability and some of its special features. An authoritative scholar in the field, John W. Garver, stated, 'There is a consensus among analysts who have studied Sino-Pakistan relations that this partnership has consistently been of a truly special character.'[1] He added:

> China's cooperative relationship with Pakistan is arguably *the most* stable and durable element of China's foreign relations. China's partnerships with other countries, both large (the USSR and the United States) and small (Albania, Vietnam, Algeria, and North Korea) have waxed and then waned into coldly correct relations at best. China's partnership with Pakistan, however, emerged during the mid-1950s, when China was trying to make friends with all developing countries, deepened during the radical anti-imperialist phase of Chinese foreign policy in the early 1960s, persisted unmolested under the direct protection of Mao Zedong during the upheaval of the Cultural Revolution, proved useful during the anti-Soviet hegemony phase of Chinese policy in the 1970s and 1980s, and continued with vitality after the dissolution of

> the USSR and the end of the Cold War. The Sino-Pakistan entente can be traced back to the heyday of Sino-Indian hostility and has continued as China and India restored a level of comity during the 1990s. It is, indeed, a remarkably durable relationship.[2]

These views are broadly shared by other scholars in the field such as William Barnds and Rajshree Jetly.[3] For instance, Jetly argued, 'Sino-Pakistan relations stand out as one of the few enduring friendships that have withstood the pressures of time and shifting geostrategic conditions.'[4]

In international relations, however, state-to-state relations are driven primarily by national interests. The old dictum, there are neither permanent friends nor enemies but national interests, retains its validity even today, and the Pakistan-China relationship is not an exception. This work attempts to answer the key question: what are those interests?

Most existing studies examine China-Pakistan ties from a geostrategic perspective. They argue that the theory 'the enemy of my enemy is my friend'[5] has been guiding this relationship. Since India, also referred to as the India factor, is a 'common enemy'; it holds these two countries in an enduring partnership. This argument carries some weight, especially if one looks at the origin of the 'special' relationship that Sino-Pakistan have. As discussed in Chapter 1, China and Pakistan only maintained limited ties until the mid-1950s, and were unfriendly, if not hostile, towards each other during the late 1950s. On the other hand, in the 1950s, China and India developed closer ties termed as *Hindi-Chini Bhai Bhai* (the Chinese and the Indians are brothers). An upward turn in China-Pakistan relations started almost parallel to the deterioration of Sino-Indian relations. Afterwards, Beijing and Islamabad found India to be a shared security concern which led them to devise mutually supportive policies. China started backing Pakistan on Indo-Pakistan issues, and soon emerged as a major and reliable arms supplier. It not only supplied conventional arms but also assisted Pakistan in strategic areas such as its nuclear and missile programme. Since India's territorial and political disputes with Pakistan and China have been sustained, they provide a constant glue to Sino-Pakistan amity.

Can two countries remain friendly due to the 'common enemy' factor, especially when their perceptions towards the 'common enemy' has undergone changes since the inception of their entente cordiale? No doubt, Indo-Pakistan rivalry remains constant but the nature of China's relationship with India has transformed from what it was in the early 1960s. Beijing-New Delhi ties have improved especially in the wake of Indian Prime Minister Rajiv Gandhi's visit to China in December 1988. Regardless of the media hype we witness from time to time, not a single bullet has been fired across their border while two-way trade crossed the US$70 billion mark in 2015.

Secondly, a state-to-state equation is a complex phenomenon which involves multiple actors. It seems hard to maintain a robust relationship for long, between two governments with divergent outlooks, merely on strategic grounds. This is more valid in a globalized world where economics and trade have assumed a considerably large role in international politics. Intense defence cooperation remains important and, over a period of time, China and Pakistan have expanded their cooperation in almost all conceivable areas. This has, according to Beijing and Islamabad, developed a degree of 'trust' and 'reliability' in their relationship.[6]

As a result of this durability, China and Pakistan have acquired an important place in each other's foreign policy. Pakistan is crucial to Beijing's Central, South, and West Asian strategy; and complements

China's modernisation of its western regions by quelling insurgency in the restive Xinjiang Uyghur Autonomous Region and maintaining a permanent check on India. Pakistan's clout provides China a natural ingress in the Muslim world. For Islamabad, on the other hand, Beijing has become the most reliable arms supplier, a source of defence technology in strategic areas, and a means of regular economic and diplomatic support. As a result, a consensus has developed among political parties and the army that good relations with China must be maintained. Finally, the recently formulated China-Pakistan Economic Corridor (CPEC) serves both the countries' economic and geostrategic interests in the short and long term. Given the relationship's durability, consistency, and implications, both the regional partners appear to regard it as vital. These features have led me to re-examine, in this book, the China-Pakistan relationship.

CHAPTERIZATION

The book has been divided into seven chapters and a conclusion. Chapter 1 'The Formative Phase (1950–62)' covers the period of limited relationship. Even though the two countries had established early diplomatic ties and had, from the mid-1950s onwards, initiated summit level contacts and exchange of visits, the relations could not move beyond a certain level. The chapter explains how inherited internal and external challenges pushed China and Pakistan into opposite security blocs, taking the alliance to their lowest ebb in the late 1950s. Interestingly, the relationship which became an entente cordiale emerged out of these cold beginnings.

Chapter 2 'Strengthening and Deepening of Relations (1963–77)' discusses the consolidation of this relationship. Pakistan and China perceived India as a common security threat. Partly due to this, both sides initiated mutually supportive policies, started defence cooperation, and began to support each other at multilateral forums. China extended a helping hand to Pakistan on Kashmir and other Indo-Pakistan disputes, and also provided economic, diplomatic, and military assistance.[7] In return, Pakistan resumed its support for China's seat in the UN and helped break China's isolation. This chapter also argues that disruption in US-Pakistan relations, with Washington's sanctions on Islamabad, pushed Pakistan even closer to the Chinese side.

In the late 1970s, China's second generation leadership, led by Deng Xiaoping, replaced the leaders who had headed the revolution. After assuming power, the new leadership introduced deep reforms internally and externally. It defined its economic development as a top priority, de-radicalized foreign policy, and began to normalise relations with other countries, especially those in the neighbourhood. Under this new policy, China began to distance itself from Indo-Pakistan disputes, especially on Kashmir, and began to improve ties with India. This chapter assesses the balance China struck between a policy of improving relations with India without affecting its traditional ties with Pakistan. Almost simultaneous with China's reforms and the opening up of policy, the Soviet Union invaded Afghanistan in December 1979. The invasion took place at the height of Sino-Soviet tension. In response to the Soviet move, a trilateral US-Pakistan-China cooperation emerged. Chapter 3 'China's Reforms and Modernisation, and Relations with Pakistan (1978–89)' studies how post-Mao reforms in China and the Soviet invasion of Afghanistan had an impact on Sino-Pakistan relations.

Chapter 4 'China's Policy of Balance and Stability (1990–2001)' examines the repercussions of certain developments such as the Soviet withdrawal from Afghanistan, China's improving relations with Russia (former Soviet Union), and America's partial sanctions on Sino-Pakistan nuclear and missile programme against the backdrop of China's improving ties with India.

Chapter 5 'China's Renewed Interest in Pakistan—Relations Post-9/11' analyses the Beijing-Islamabad relationship in light of the September 2001 terrorist attacks. Following these attacks, the US launched its War on Terror (WoT) which Pakistan joined. Once again, this revived US-Pakistan ties as US economic and military assistance began pouring into Pakistan. In addition, the US established a military presence in Central and West Asia. These developments cautioned China which expanded, as this chapter shows, engagement with Pakistan. High-profile two-way visits, strong defence ties with the initiation of counterterrorism measures, and a gradual improvement in economic and trade ties were the hallmark of post-9/11 Sino-Pakistan relations.

During Chinese premier Li Keqiang's visit to Pakistan in May 2013, the two countries decided to establish the China-Pakistan Economic Corridor (CPEC) to connect China's Kashgar with Pakistan's Gwadar Port through a network of roads, railway tracks, pipelines, and fibre optics. Later in April 2015, Chinese President Xi Jinping committed US$46 billion for the completion of CPEC which China termed as the flagship project of 'One Belt, One Road'.

Chapter 6 'China-Pakistan Economic Corridor' explains the aims, objectives, and scope of CPEC. Chapter 7 'Factors of Durability' identifies the factors upon which the Sino-Pakistan relationship is based. This is followed by the Conclusion.

Notes

1. Garver refers to three main authors who have written on Sino-Pakistan relations: J. P. Jain, *China, Pakistan and Bangladesh* (New Delhi: Radiant, 1974); Anwar H. Syed, *China and Pakistan: Diplomacy of an Entente Cordiale* (Amherst: University of Massachusetts Press, 1974); and Yaacov Vertzberger, *The Enduring Entente: Sino-Pakistan Relations, 1960–1980* (New York: Praeger, 1983). See John W. Garver, *Protracted Contest: Sino-Indian Rivalry in the Twentieth Century* (Seattle and London: University of Washington Press, 2001), 187. Also see footnote on page 409.
2. Garver, *Protracted Contest,* 187–8.
3. William J. Barnds, 'China's Relations with Pakistan: Durability Amidst Discontinuity', *The China Quarterly*, no. 63 (September 1975), 463–4.
4. Rajshree Jetly, 'Sino-Pakistan Strategic Entente: Implications for Regional Security', *ISAS*, Working Paper no. 143 (Institute of South Asia Studies, National University of Singapore, 14 February 2012), 1.
5. See, for example, Robert G. Wirsing, *The Enemy of My Enemy: Pakistan's China Debate* (Honolulu, Hawaii: Asia-Pacific Centre for Security Studies, December 2003).
6. The exponent of international relations may question the validity of 'trust' and 'reliability' in the practice of world politics. However, most officials and scholars of China and Pakistan who were interviewed referred to these terms. Some Pakistani scholars interviewed underlined the importance of 'trust' and 'reliability' in a country's relations with China too.
7. China's political support became more important for Pakistan once China acquired the permanent seat in the United Nations Security Council (UNSC) in 1971 for which Islamabad had also made a meaningful contribution. The first demonstration of such support came in August 1972 when Beijing exercised its first-ever veto in the UNSC to block Bangladesh's entry into the UN, and threatened to repeat it until Bangladesh and India resolved their war-related issues with Pakistan.

1

The Formative Phase (1950–62)

China and Pakistan claim that the people living on both the sides of the Himalayas have been interacting with each other since ancient times. According to a Chinese scholar, the term 'Western Paradise' in Chinese literature referred to the present-day South Asian subcontinent. Monks and scholars took the message of Buddha from Pakistan's Taxila and Ghandhara civilizations to China. In 126 BCE, the Han Dynasty sent Zhang Qian to areas that today constitute the northern parts of Pakistan and Afghanistan. In 400 CE, a famous monk, Faxian, arrived in Pakistan's Swat Valley. During the rule of the Tang dynasty (618–907), Xuanzhang visited Peshawar, Taxila, and Rawalpindi. In his travelogue, he described Taxila as a rich place with fertile soil, and friendly and prosperous people living under a central administration.[1] These travellers used China's Silk Route; the arteries of which passed through parts of Pakistan, especially the northern areas: Gilgit-Baltistan (GB) and Khyber Pakhtunkhwa (KP).[2]

There is no denying the fact that little interaction had existed between the two regions which later comprised of China and Pakistan. The mighty Himalayas, in the absence of modern means of communications, prevented frequent dealings between the two sides from happening. Pakistani and Chinese references to 'old historical' links, it appears, are intended to boost their effusive rhetoric. In reality, in the past, only limited contact existed which could not provide a strong base for a modern day relationship. As Kissinger stated, 'The two civilizations exchanged goods and Buddhist influences along the

Silk Road but were elsewhere walled off from casual contact by the almost impenetrable Himalayas and the Tibetan Plateau.'[3] Arguably, the Sino-Pakistan relationship is a product of modern times with its roots in the mid-twentieth century.

The struggle for the independence of the Indian subcontinent's people and China's revolution ran almost parallel to each other. They entered their closing stage at the time during the Second World War. When the UN Charter was being drawn up in 1945, China was in the grip of a civil war between the Nationalists led by General Chiang Kai-shek and the Communists led by Chairman Mao Zedong. The Western world, led by the US and involved in the formation of the UN, took into account China's large geographic size and population, and allocated it a permanent seat of the United Nations Security Council (UNSC). As the Nationalists had closer ties with the US, they were regarded as the legitimate representatives of China and were, therefore, invited to join the UN.

Two years later, in August 1947, Pakistan and India won their independence from British rule. The Nationalists' government of Chiang Kai-shek extended recognition to the newly independent states. India, which inherited British India's diplomatic privileges, established an embassy and consulates in China in 1947. Pakistan also developed certain economic and diplomatic links with the Nationalists,[4] including a Special Representative's office in Nanjing and a consulate in Kashgar.[5] Regardless, the overall relationship remained limited and no exchange of ambassadors took place.

In the short span of diplomatic ties with the Nationalists, Pakistan adopted an ambivalent policy towards the Chiang Kai-shek regime. As the Nationalists held a permanent seat in the UNSC with veto power, they could play a crucial role in the Kashmir issue, which was referred to the UN in December 1948. However, at the same time, the Pakistani leader was aware of their relationship with Indian leaders Mahatma Gandhi and Jawaharlal Nehru. Pakistan also knew of Chiang's displeasure with the partition of the subcontinent and the creation of two states.[6] In other words, General Chiang did not support the popular Muslim struggle for a separate homeland in the subcontinent. These aspects, along with the fact that Pakistan was deeply involved in inherited challenges, seemed to be the reasons behind Pakistan's restricted interaction with the Nationalists.

ADVENT OF THE COMMUNISTS

In late 1949, the civil war in China took a decisive turn; the Nationalists were defeated and fled to Taiwan (Formosa), while the Communists took control of the entire mainland. On 1 October 1949, the Chairman of the Communist Party of China, Mao Zedong, announced the establishment of the People's Republic of China (PRC), and Taiwan as an integral part. He invited other countries to establish diplomatic relations with the PRC based on this premise. He issued a warning, stating that China would not establish relations with states unwilling to endorse China's sovereignty over Taiwan, or wanting to treat them as two separate entities: China and Taiwan.[7] The unification of Taiwan became central to PRC's foreign policy objectives, and these have remained unchanged and unfulfilled since then. Mao stated that the Nationalist regime was defunct and had lost its legitimacy to represent the Chinese people. In November 1949, China's premier, Zhou En-lai, sent a message to the UN Secretary General, Trygve Lie, demanding an immediate replacement of the Nationalists by the Communists.[8]

The Communists' control over the mainland fundamentally changed China's internal and external politics. On the other hand, it posed a new challenge to the nascent UN by dividing the international community over the issue of who should represent China in the

UN; whether the Nationalists who had lost control on the mainland and were confined to Taiwan alone should continue to represent the Chinese people, or the newly established Communist government should be recognised as the lawful ruler. Different countries responded to the situation in various ways. Some accepted the Communists' claim and switched their recognition while others continued upholding diplomatic ties with the Nationalists. A small number of countries distanced themselves from the debate and did not recognise either side.[9] With the backing of the US, the Nationalists continued to hold a permanent seat in the UNSC while the PRC remained outside the international system until 1971.

The emergence of China was a vital development in the region. India took the initiative and recognised it on 30 December 1949 (becoming the first non-socialist country to do so), established diplomatic relations in April 1950,[10] and appointed its first Ambassador, K. M. Panikkar, in May 1950.[11] Pakistan also welcomed the end of the civil war and the establishment of a central government in China. For Pakistan, the rise of a fellow Asian nation, with a sizable Muslim population and sharing a common border, was a welcome development. Pakistan regarded China's overthrow of a long and humiliating foreign occupation as an 'original Asian revolution that had opened a new chapter in the history of Asia'.[12] These factors were enough to overshadow China's Communist orientation which at that time was the chief concern of the Western world.[13] Immediately after the emergence of the PRC, the daily *Dawn* urged the Government of Pakistan to recognise the Communist government without waiting for a response from other states.[14]

Later, on 5 January 1950 (six days after India and a day before Britain decided to extend recognition to the PRC), Pakistan followed suit. In the absence of any diplomatic channel, the initial communication between China and Pakistan was conducted through their ambassadors in the Union of Soviet Socialist Republics (USSR). Through this correspondence, Pakistan informed China that it had cut-off diplomatic ties with the Nationalists (a pre-condition for the establishment of diplomatic ties with the PRC), and had recognised it as the legitimate representative of the Chinese people.[15] China replied in a week, expressing willingness to establish diplomatic relations with Pakistan.[16] On 6 January 1950, Pakistan recognised China as a nation. It became the first Muslim state, the second Commonwealth, and the third non-Communist country to do so.[17]

FACTORS LEADING TO RECOGNITION

Essentially, Pakistan's and China's decision to recognise each others' government was based on 'realpolitik calculations'.[18] Both the countries had emerged on the world map in a precarious environment and wanted allies, especially in the neighbourhood. For example, Pakistan was born as a truncated state comprising two parts, East and West Pakistan, separated by a thousand miles of 'hostile' Indian territory. The bloody partition of the Indian subcontinent, Hindu-Muslim animosity, territorial disputes (particularly Kashmir), the division of assets, water disputes, and the first India-Pakistan war in 1948, cumulatively put Pakistan's relations with India permanently on a hostile footing.[19] On top of that, the Pakistani elite interpreted Indian leaders' occasional statements about the tragedy of Partition as indicative of their annexationist designs. After independence, Pakistan approached the UN, the Commonwealth, and the Islamic countries; seeking their good offices for the settlement of their disputes with India, but failed to obtain any significant relief.[20]

In addition to India, Pakistan also had troubled relations with

Afghanistan. The nature of Pakistan-Afghanistan ties could be measured from the fact that Kabul was the only UN member to vote against Pakistan's application for membership of the world body. The Afghan government disputed the Durand Line which separated the two countries and expressed sympathies for the Pashtuns living on the Pakistani side.[21] Thus, by the time the Communist victory in mainland China took place, Pakistan had developed palpable security issues with two of its neighbours, Afghanistan and India. Pakistan, therefore, sought to develop a good rapport with its other neighbours, including China.

The Kashmir factor also played a role in Pakistan switching recognition to the Communists. As Garver points out, 'If, as then seemed likely, the PRC was going to assume China's seat on the Security Council, Pakistan did not want that to happen with Beijing more favourably inclined toward India than toward Pakistan. Thus, once India decided to recognise the PRC, Pakistan quickly followed suit.'[22] Similarly, Burke argued that New Delhi's early recognition also pushed Pakistan to establish ties with the Communists.[23]

Trade was another factor behind Pakistan's move to extend recognition, hence, the country had already started trade with the Nationalists. In the backdrop of the India-Pakistan trade deadlock, which was at its peak at the time of the Communist victory, China appeared to be a suitable alternative and Pakistan found it appropriate to switch its recognition to the new regime. As Burke notes, 'Only a few weeks before Mao's party replaced the Nationalist government in China, Pakistan's trade with India had come to a virtual halt in the wake of the devaluation of the Indian rupee, and Pakistan was anxiously looking for customers for her raw jute and cotton and for suppliers of coal.'[24] During his visit to the US in May 1950, Pakistani Prime Minister Liaquat Ali Khan explained to Washington that his country recognised the PRC, 'accepting an established fact and in order to ease the flow of trade'.[25]

This decision benefited Pakistan's trade sector, at least for a few years. Meanwhile, the Korean War (1950–53) broke out. China's direct involvement in the war badly damaged its trade with other countries. It, nonetheless, opened the door for Pakistan to export its goods to China. Pakistan exported its surplus jute and cotton to China in exchange for well-needed coal. In 1952, Pakistani exports to China reached US$83.8 million—15 per cent of its total exports that year—whereas the imports from China were a mere US$2.2 million. This boom, however, was confined to the Korean War period. In the following years, Pakistan's trade with China fell substantially.[26]

Similarly, China emerged on the world map, in 1949, faced with a variety of internal and external challenges. Internally, it was devastated by a long civil war and needed resources for national reconstruction. Externally, China's outright Communist outlook and Mao's decision to 'lean' towards the Soviet-led Communist bloc imposed limitations on expanding relations with many non-Communist countries. The Chinese leadership realised that it was too weak to guarantee its protection and thus aligned itself with the Soviet Union by signing a security pact with Moscow in 1950.[27] Since China did not have many allies back then, it immediately accepted Pakistan's extended recognition. Vertzberger writes about China's policy to develop relations with Pakistan:

> Geopolitical considerations, the desire to cultivate relations with the Muslim countries of the Middle East through Pakistan, uncertainty about the future of Chinese relations with India, the hope of preventing Pakistan from becoming an antagonistic satellite of the West, and Pakistan's cautious policy toward China—all these elements motivated China to establish a correct relationship.[28]

After having established diplomatic ties, Pakistan adopted a pro-PRC stance on Taiwan, Tibet, and the Korean War. In early 1950, it opposed the Nationalists' resolution demanding an embargo on aid to the PRC. Instead, Pakistan supported a motion which stipulated an end to outside interference in China's internal affairs.[29] In September 1950, when the issue of representation (whether the Nationalists or the Communists should represent China) was brought to the UN for debate, the US and its allies adopted a stance which was not supportive of the Communists. They insisted that since the Communists had gained power through the use of force, they could not be considered as a legitimate party.[30] Pakistan, on the other hand, supported an Indian resolution which demanded the replacement of the Nationalists by the Communists in the UN.[31] Pakistan's chief delegate, Sir Muhammad Zafrullah Khan, argued that the Nationalists had ceased to exercise jurisdiction over any part of mainland China for months, and could no longer claim to be the representative of the Chinese people. It was these grounds on which he urged that the Nationalists should be replaced by the Communists.[32]

During the Korean War (1950–53), Pakistan adopted a neutral ground; it neither antagonised the West nor China. A sudden increase in Pakistan's exports to China during this period could be one of the reasons Pakistan abstained from criticising China's role in the Korean War. Although Pakistan condemned the North Korean aggression and supported the unification of the Korean Peninsula, it refrained from voting in the General Assembly that branded the PRC an aggressor and imposed sanctions on China and North Korea.[33] Pakistan also refused to contribute to the US-led UN 'Police action', pleading that it had no spare troops given the tense state of Indo-Pakistan relations.[34] According to an analyst, 'Pakistan resisted very strong pressure and blandishments from the US by refusing to send even a token force to participate in the Korean War and was careful not to condemn China.'[35]

The Tibet issue emerged simultaneously with the Korean War when, in October 1950, China moved about 40,000 troops to 'liberate' the Himalayan state. This was the first time Chinese and Indian policies conflicted with each other.[36] Nehru sent a protest note deploring the Chinese action. In a speech, Nehru stated, 'Violence might perhaps be justified in the modern world… but one should not resort to it unless there is no other way. There was another way in Tibet as we pointed out. That is why the action of China came to us as a surprise.'[37] China termed Tibet an 'integral part' and declared that the current crisis was a 'domestic problem'. It deplored the Indian reaction, calling it 'inspired by foreign influence'.[38] There was an exchange of protest notes between China and India while China was consolidating its hold over Tibet. Nehru eventually acquiesced to the Chinese control of Tibet.[39]

Unlike India, Pakistan had neither any important historical links nor a security threat emanating from Tibet. Chinese control therefore did not cause any 'stir in the Pakistani capital'.[40] *Dawn* reported that Pakistan had no direct interest in Tibetan affairs which, according to the daily, had always been under the suzerainty of China.[41] A Pakistani official claimed that it would not make any difference to his country if the Communists took control over Tibet. On these grounds, Pakistan decided to remain neutral in the UN proceedings concerning Tibet.[42]

LIMITED RELATIONSHIP

In the initial years of their diplomatic history—despite early recognition of each other's governments—the beginning of trade and Pakistan's somewhat pro-China stance on Taiwan, Tibet, and the

Korean War, Sino-Pakistan relations remained limited. A survey of *People's China*—the official mouthpiece of the Chinese government and one of the few English publications in the country—shows that there was hardly any news on Pakistan while the weekly covered a number of stories on India.[43] The first story on Pakistan was published in 1953. Coverage of Pakistan only began after the summit-level visits between the two countries which took place in 1956.

Furthermore, low enthusiasm on both sides was obvious from the fact that even after extending recognition to one another, it took over a year to exchange ambassadors. Moreover, in November 1951, when the first Pakistani Ambassador to China, Major General Nawabzada Agha Mohammad Raza, presented his credentials, Mao's response was lukewarm. According to Choudhury, this was in sharp contrast to his warm reception of the Indian Ambassador, Panikkar, the previous year. While receiving the Pakistani Ambassador's papers, Mao mentioned the historical contacts between the peoples on the two sides and expressed his hope for good relations in the future[44] but he also referred to Pakistan's dominion status. 'I have great pleasure,' Mao stated, 'in receiving the letters of credentials of the King of Great Britain, Ireland, and the British dominions beyond the seas, presented by you.'[45] As an Indian diplomat 'gleefully' pointed out, 'There was no mention of the fact that the Ambassador was representing Pakistan.'[46]

Some factors explain Mao's unenthusiastic attitude while meeting Pakistan's Ambassador and the limited relationship in the initial years. First, Pakistan remained a dominion until 1956 when it adopted its first constitution. Secondly, at the time of Ambassador Raza's meeting with Mao, Pakistan's ruling elite was working to build closer ties with the US.[47] This was reflected in Liaquat Ali Khan's preference for the US over the Soviet Union. In 1949, Moscow had extended an invitation to Liaquat which he accepted. However, sometime later, when he received a similar invitation from Washington, Liaquat set aside the first and went to the US in May 1950. Some analysts argue that this set the direction of Pakistan's foreign policy, giving it a Western orientation.[48] Pakistan and China were clearly drifting towards opposite security blocs. Given the nature of its own relations with the US, China was apprehensive of Pakistan's policies. Thirdly, Pakistan and China held different views on how to resolve the Kashmir conflict. After its first war with India over Kashmir in 1948, Pakistan had realised its constraints and inability to settle the dispute with New Delhi on a bilateral level. It had also approached the UN, the US, the Commonwealth, and Muslim countries to get support. China regarded most of these sources as imperialists or their tools. Instead, China emphasised that any issue between Afro-Asian nations, including Kashmir, should be resolved through negotiations, and no imperialist power should be given a chance to interfere in those nations' affairs. Thus, from China's view, Pakistan's policy could open the door for imperialistic intervention in South Asian affairs.

IN OPPOSITE SECURITY BLOCS

By the mid-1950s, China and Pakistan had sided with opposing security camps created by the Cold War. The PRC entered the Soviet-led Communist bloc while Pakistan joined the US-led capitalist alliance by signing defence pacts. In May 1954, Pakistan and the US concluded the United States-Pakistan Mutual Defence Assistance Agreement under which the US agreed to provide US$430 million of military assistance to Pakistan from 1955–58. In September 1954, Pakistan became one of the founding members of the Southeast Asia Treaty Organisation (SEATO), and in 1955 signed the Baghdad Pact, which later became the Central Treaty Organisation (CENTO).[49] By

1959, the US and Pakistan had signed four defence pacts—some of which were anti-China as well as anti-Communist. More importantly, it must be noted that China did not lodge any protest with Pakistan at an official level. This attitude was in sharp contrast to that of the USSR which reacted strongly against Pakistan's decision to join Western defence pacts. Pakistan's relations with the USSR began to deteriorate almost parallel to the US-Pakistan negotiations for a defence pact and the arrival of US aid in Pakistan by 1953. From the mid-1950s onwards, the USSR started openly supporting India and Afghanistan in their disputes against Pakistan. Moscow, which had abstained in the UN debate on the Kashmir issue, started backing India. It also began advocating Kabul for the creation of a state, 'Pakhtoonistan'.[50] The government-controlled Chinese media did, however, express a mild rebuke warning Pakistan of the harmful effects of these pacts. For instance, the *People's Daily* in a commentary stated, 'Pakistan's decision to join the Turco-Iraq pact is dangerous. This pact is an important step taken by the United States to establish aggressive military blocs in the Middle East and prepare for another war…' The paper added that it was inconsistent with Pakistan's stance taken during the Bandung Conference.[51] In another commentary, the paper claimed that the defence pacts had increased Pakistan's military expenditures which put a great burden on its economy, and various circles in the country, especially business and industry, had questioned their necessity.

Most of China's criticism of the defence pacts was focused on US intentions rather than on the motives of Asian members. The PRC stated that through these agreements the US was attempting to 'sow discord among Asians and to prevent them from cooperating with one another in mutually beneficial ways, undermine the spirit of Bandung, turn Asia into her sphere of influence, seize Asia's strategic raw materials, and make its nations into satellites'.[52] Some of the concerns of the Chinese were not out of context. Many circles in Pakistan were also worried about the country's deep alignment with the West. Their apprehension increased, particularly after Soviet premier Khrushchev's warnings to Pakistan during his visit to India. They felt a 'sense of isolation and of being surrounded by powerful enemies and supported by uncertain allies, who are too far away or unwilling to render immediate assistance'.[53]

The contrast in the reactions of China and the USSR did not go unnoticed; some quarters in Pakistan applauded it. A Pakistani scholar termed China's tolerance as a part of Beijing's policy of promoting Afro-Asian solidarity[54] while another explained it in the following words:

> First of all, being shrewd observers of the Asian scene, the Chinese no doubt knew that Pakistan felt insecure about India, and they probably interpreted Pakistan's alignment with the United States as prompted largely by this feeling and not by hostile intentions toward themselves. Secondly, the Chinese were probably aware that Pakistan was not too deeply involved in the defence arrangements contemplated under SEATO. With the exception of the modest role of the Pakistan navy, no Pakistani troops had participated in SEATO military exercises although Pakistan maintained a larger defence establishment than either the Philippines or Thailand. There was no indication that any groundwork had been laid for SEATO military aid to Pakistan. US military aid to Pakistan seemed to be directed against Moscow and not Beijing.[55]

There are some other aspects that also explain the rationale of China's 'benign' attitude. Firstly, China was confronted with internal challenges at that time and was not in a position to react to Pakistan's 'anti-China' policies. Secondly, Beijing had realised that Pakistan's chief concern was India, not China. Thirdly, according to the Chinese side, premier Zhou En-lai genuinely wanted close relations with neighbouring countries since, according to him, that was China's policy.[56] Whatever the reasons may be, China's patience prevented any major disruption in future relations with Pakistan.

THE BANDUNG CONFERENCE

Simultaneous to Pakistan having signed two defence agreements with the US and having made arrangements for a third, the Afro-Asian Conference was held at Bandung from 18–25 April 1955. Pakistan was one of the sponsors of the conference and its Prime Minister, Mohammad Ali Bogra, attended it with an 'open mind'. He was accompanied by diplomats, Nawabzada A. M. Raza and Agha Shahi, who were both known for their friendly views towards China.[57] During the Bandung Conference, Raza arranged at least two meetings between Bogra and Zhou En-lai. This was the first time, since the establishment of diplomatic relations, that the top leadership of China and Pakistan met each other. In one of these meetings, Bogra explained that the security threat it faced from India was the raison d'etre behind Pakistan joining the Western alliance, adding that his country harboured no hostility towards China. Zhou En-lai was apparently satisfied by this explanation, which he stated before the Political Committee of the conference:

> He [Bogra] told me that although Pakistan was a party to a military treaty, Pakistan was not against China. Pakistan had no fear China would commit aggression against her. As a result of that, we achieved a mutual understanding although we are still against military treaties.

> The Prime Minister of Pakistan further assured [me] that if the United States should take aggressive action under the military treaty or if the United States launched a global war, Pakistan would not be involved in it just as it was not involved in the Korean War. I am grateful to him for this explanation. Because through these explanations we achieved a mutual understanding. This creates agreement and harmony among us in understanding each other on collective peace and cooperation.[58]

During the conference, in the midst of a debate regarding colonialism, a delegate referred to Soviet colonialism. Bogra supported this point by adding that it was unrealistic to ignore Soviet imperialism, which had turned many countries into its satellites and had suppressed many people. However, he made a clear distinction between China and the USSR by specifying that China did not fall in that category since it had no satellite state in any part of the world. He further clarified to Zhou En-lai that his criticism only focused on the USSR.[59] It was reported that Bogra convinced Zhou En-lai to issue a conciliatory statement on Taiwan. Most importantly, the 'Pakistani premier was stated to have wrung a promise from Zhou En-lai that, if the Americans responded favourably to his offer of negotiations, Zhou would announce the release of American fliers then in Chinese custody.' Upon his return, Bogra stated, 'I am anti-Communist but I do realise that China has its own problems, some of which may have been solved by Communism.'[60] During the conference, Zhou En-lai invited Bogra to visit China. Generally, the Bandung Conference is regarded as the start of the Sino-Pakistan entente cordiale. Two years later, however, their relations took a nosedive. This study argues that the Sino-Pakistan entente emerged in the early 1960s in the wake of the Sino-Indian border war in 1962 and the Sino-Pakistan border agreement signed in March 1963.

The Bandung Conference seemed to remove the growing misunderstanding between China and Pakistan over the latter's joining of Western pacts. After Bandung, a number of visits by politicians, parliamentarians, lawyers, industrialists, writers, artists, public officials, and even religious scholars took place.[61] Important among them was the ten-day visit of Madame Soong Ching Ling (Madame Sun Yat Sen), Vice-Chairman of the PRC, to Karachi, Lahore, and Dhaka. She was accompanied by members of the Standing Committee of the National People's Congress, among other women. This visit's importance could be measured from the fact that Pakistan's Prime Minister, Foreign Minister, and other dignitaries came to receive and see off the delegates at the airport. According to declassified British documents, the treatment she received was warmer and more lavish than that accorded to dignitaries from the United States with whom Pakistan had far more cordial relations.[62]

In her speeches, Madame Soong included references to the iniquities of colonialism, appreciated the contribution China and Pakistan had made in the success of the Bandung Conference, and emphasised the policy of co-existence. Additionally, Dhaka University awarded her an honorary degree. The British High Commission, Karachi, reported back to London: 'It seems from the tone of Madame Soong's public statements that Chinese policy at present is to try to woo Pakistan with words of sweet reasonableness. In this she was pursuing the path set down by Chou En-lai [sic] at the Bandung Conference.'[63]

During another visit, Liu Shaoqi told Mujibur Rahman, then Minister in East Pakistan, 'Although we speak different languages and have different political systems, these are no impediments to the establishment of friendly and cooperative relations between our two countries.'[64] Pakistani dignitaries returned with the impression that Chinese Muslims enjoyed religious freedom; the Chinese as hard working people; and the country investing in the development of its economic, agricultural, and technological sectors. These visits helped 'improve the general tone of Sino-Pakistan relations' but not beyond a certain level.[65]

As a result of this increased interaction and the prospects of future ties, the Chinese media began to give Pakistan wider coverage. According to an article on trade relations published in New China News Agency (NCNA), trade between the two sides averaged US$30 million since 1950. During this period, China bought 200,000 metric tonnes of cotton worth US$181.19 million while Chinese companies established contacts with over 400 Pakistani industrialists. According to the article, the unscrupulous dumping of US cotton in the world market had affected Pakistan's cotton export, which along with jute constituted of nearly 80 per cent of the country's total export. China's purchase of cotton helped Pakistan achieve its export targets. Moreover, in the post-Bandung period, Pakistani authorities encouraged its business community to buy from China. This policy benefited both countries. Under different contracts, China supplied 425,000 tons of coal and 60,000 tons of rice. In addition, it gifted 4,000 tons of rice to overcome food shortages in East Pakistan. Both countries were rich in resources and were engaged in large scale economic construction. This provided favourable conditions for the expansion of two-way trade between the countries. The article concluded that a steady growth of trade between China and Pakistan, in accordance with the Bandung Conference commitments, would expand cooperation between the two peoples, and contribute to the prosperity of Asian-African regions and to bringing peace in the world.[66]

SUMMIT MEETINGS[67]

During the Bandung Conference, Pakistan's Prime Minister received an invitation to visit China. All arrangements were made but Muhammad Ali Bogra postponed it, at first for a few weeks and then indefinitely due to health issues. Bogra relinquished power to Chaudhri Muhammad Ali who was soon replaced by Huseyn Shaheed Suhrawardy. The postponement episode embarrassed the Chinese side. It was Suhrawardy who finally went to China in October 1956. The US reportedly pressured Pakistan to cancel the trip. According to Suhrawardy's granddaughter, as cited by a Chinese scholar, 'It was really not easy for grandfather to decide to visit China in those days due to huge pressure and strong opposition.' However, 'he was very pleased that the visit was successful. After returning home, he told us he believed he had done the right thing.'[68]

The Chinese government had invited eighteen Pakistani journalists—including some from the vernacular press—led by the eminent poet and writer, Faiz Ahmed Faiz, to visit China when the Prime Minister was to be visiting. They were to be guests of the Chinese government which would bear their expenses. A British diplomat termed China's move as a 'shrewd and generous offer' incomparable to any gesture by the Western countries.[69] Even though the official visit was postponed twice, the press delegates went to China as scheduled, and on their return projected a positive image of China in Pakistan. Following the visit, China increased the circulation of attractively illustrated pictorial magazines.[70]

Suhrawardy was a staunch pro-American ruler and his visit to China took place at the peak of the US-Pakistan friendship.[71] Regardless, it was a success. China gave Pakistan's Prime Minister a red-carpet welcome and extensive media coverage.[72] Suhrawardy held several rounds of talks with Zhou En-lai and Mao Zedong which 'covered a wide range of subjects'.[73] Mao bestowed upon him a rare honour by attending a banquet arranged by Suhrawardy. According to British declassified papers, the degree of frankness and straight talking in Suhrawardy's public and private talks was quite new compared to other Asian leaders who had visited China.[74]

However, during his stay in China, Suhrawardy spent considerable time discussing Sino-American relations and clarifying US intentions vis-à-vis China, claiming that China's perception of the US was 'mistaken'. He told Chinese leaders that his country shared the American policy of containment, limiting the further expansion of Communism. In discussions on colonialism, Suhrawardy defended it by saying that although Pakistan had suffered from colonialism, it had also 'conferred' certain benefits on the country. Regarding the issue of American prisoners, he stated it would add to China's prestige if it released them. Although Zhou En-lai appreciated any Pakistani role in improving Sino-American relations, China's opposition to US military pacts was obvious.[75] In a talk with Suhrawardy, Mao said, 'The only area of disagreement between us was on [Pakistan joining] the Western treaties and pacts.' Again, to defend the US stance, Pakistan's Prime Minister added, 'Americans are not enemies of China but are only afraid of China.' Mao replied, 'If because the USA is afraid of us, they must control the Philippines, Thailand, [and] Japan then we can say we are afraid of the USA. We must control Mexico, Nicaragua, and even Pakistan.'[76] Despite these differences, the two sides issued a joint statement which stressed the need for increased commercial and cultural ties. The statement did not touch upon Taiwan and Hong Kong which were crucial to China. Both sides pledged to carry forward the Bandung spirit, work for international peace, resolve their mutual differences, and enhance cultural and commercial contacts.[77]

Suhrawardy later stated before the Parliament, 'I feel perfectly certain that when the crucial time comes China will come to our assistance.'[78]

Regardless of his remarks, China did not fail to take note of Suhrawardy's strong pro-American orientation. Meanwhile, Pakistan changed its stance on the question of China's seat in the UN which gave weight to China's perception of Pakistan as pro-West. Even before Zhou En-lai's visit to Pakistan, the Chinese press hardened its position against the Pakistani government in general and Suhrawardy in particular. It went 'out of its way' to publish reports of Pakistani opposition parties that were critical of the government's policies. Beijing criticised Suhrawardy's preference to attend the Tehran meeting of allies instead of the session of Asian states, members of the Colombo Plan. Later, Pakistan voted against the Indian proposal, demanding the PRC's membership in the UN. The criticism was still mild when compared with the treatment meted out to other countries which had voted against China, such as Britain whose voting was termed intolerable, shameful, and unreasonable. This restraint was probably maintained to observe the outcome of Zhou En-lai's imminent visit.[79]

In December 1956, the Chinese premier reciprocated Suhrawardy's visit which reflected, according to a Pakistani analyst, China's seriousness in promoting two-way relations and warding off the US encirclement policy.[80] In a joint statement, both sides stated that there was no conflict of interest and that different political systems and outlooks on issues should not hamper their mutual cooperation.[81] Importantly, China continued its neutrality on Indo-Pakistan conflicts, especially regarding the Kashmir dispute. In Karachi, responding to a journalist's question about China's view on Kashmir, Zhou En-lai did not take any position and simply stated that his government was still studying the issue. He repeated China's traditional stance, saying that altercations among Afro-Asian nations, including the Kashmir dispute, should be settled amicably and the 'colonialists' who actually created this issue should be kept away from it.[82] The PRC had good relations with both India and Pakistan at that time. A pro-Pakistan stance on Kashmir could affect this balance; Zhou therefore avoided taking sides.

HIATUS IN RELATIONS

The mutual understanding between China and Pakistan, which developed after the Bandung Conference and was reinforced during summit meetings, began to fade away in early 1957, taking their relations to its lowest ebb in 1959. The period during which Suhrawardy and Ayub visited the US, in 1957 and 1961 respectively, Sino-Pakistan relations remained low, if not hostile. A pro-US leadership had established its hold on power in Pakistan. On the other hand, the US also put pressure on Pakistan to fulfil its obligations under the defence pacts. Naturally, Pakistan could not expect large-scale military and economic assistance without fulfilling its responsibilities.[83] In China, on the other hand, ultra-radical elements gained a greater influence over foreign policy. They were less tolerant towards 'reactionary regimes', such as in Pakistan.[84] Each of these factors contributed to the overall downward trend in their relationship.

The change in Pakistan's policy towards China became pronounced during Suhrawardy's visit to the US in July 1957. Earlier, Pakistan had justified its participation in Western pacts on security grounds by citing threats from India. It now changed its tone and claimed that it was a matter of pride to be part of the pacts created by the 'free world'. During his address to the House of Representatives and Senate, Prime Minister Suhrawardy praised American moral integrity, adding that the world was safe in American hands. He termed it a privilege to become a US ally and a partner in the 'great adventure of establishing in the world the rights of the individuals and opposing the measures that tend to trample that spirit', an explicit denunciation of Communism.[85] Later, in an interview, he described some of the Chinese gestures in the region as aggressive and expansionist acts, posing a threat to peace and freedom in Asia.[86]

In March 1957, Pakistan's delegation to the United Nations praised the moral support it had received from the Nationalists during the UN debate over Kashmir. At the UN session in October 1957, Pakistan cast its vote against the PRC.[87] As Syed noted, 'This might have impelled Suhrawardy to reciprocate the Nationalist Chinese favour by saying something nasty about their foes.' In 1958, amidst tense Sino-US relations over the Taiwan Strait, the PRC protested against Pakistan's support for US policies on important international issues, including Taiwan. In a note, China stated, 'She [China] would like to know the attitude of Pakistan as an Asian nation in the dispute over the status of Taiwan.'[88] Pakistan replied that it had not given de facto or de jure recognition to Taiwan, but added, 'The juridical position of sovereignty over Formosa is not clear.'[89] This was in sharp contrast to the position it had adopted in the early 1950s that was in favour of the PRC.

Some argued that Suhrawardy adopted pro-American policies since his coalition government was dependent upon US economic and military assistance, and he wanted to keep his donors pleased by supporting their policies. At the end, his overwhelming tilt towards, and unqualified support of Washington on issues concerning Hungary, the Middle East, and the Suez Canal crisis, lost him popularity and prestige inside the country, leading to his eventual fall. A year later, the country saw the advent of the first martial law.[90]

The downward trend in Sino-Pakistan relations continued during the initial years of General Ayub Khan's regime. In fact, Ayub's ascendency to power, in October 1958, was viewed with suspicion by China, which considered him to be the architect of the Pakistan-US military alliance.[91] Within months of his taking power, the Ayub government signed another defence agreement with the US in March 1959, which further strengthened China's concerns. The *People's Daily* termed the signing of the agreement a deviation from the Bandung spirit and harmful to socialist states and China's neighbours. The *Daily* claimed that Pakistan could not improve its defence through such pacts.[92]

On the other hand, Ayub left no ambiguity in his choice of a Western alliance over a Communist alliance. In an article published in *Foreign Affairs* in 1960, Ayub wrote, 'Pakistan has openly and unequivocally cast its lot with the West, and unlike several countries around us, we have shut ourselves off almost completely from the possibility of any major assistance from the Communist bloc. We wish to follow, and are following, a clear and unambiguous path.'[93] Pakistan also changed its stance on Indo-China. Foreign Minister, Malik Firoz Khan Noon, stated that SEATO had saved East Asian nations from Communist aggression, and had maintained peace and tranquillity in the region.[94] In December 1960, while commenting on the situation in Laos, Ayub stated, 'If Pakistan (as [a] SEATO member) is called upon to shoulder its burden and responsibility, we will never hesitate to do it.'[95] However, Pakistan's revived commitment to SEATO had come in the wake of China's assertive move on India's northeast border, which Pakistan perceived as a threat to East Pakistan because of its geographical proximity.[96]

In mid-1959, a group of Muslims from Taiwan, en route to Mecca for the Haj pilgrimage, stayed in Pakistan. The delegation met with Pakistan's foreign minister and religious leaders. Both sides made statements on Pakistan-Taiwan relations. China reacted severely and termed Pakistan's hospitality to the Taiwanese delegation an interference in its internal affairs. Beijing stated that the Pakistani authorities should not have entertained a group of Chiang Kai-shek's agents, self-styled as Chinese Muslim Hajis, on its territory.[97]

In the late 1950s, the CIA, in collaboration with the Republic of China (ROC), used Indian territory to launch an operation in support of the Tibetan uprising against the PRC. For China, Tibet has become a 'barometer' of friendship. 'Beijing would consider any support of the Tibetan cause, whether at the UN or elsewhere, an act of aggression.'[98] In such a situation, Pakistan's changed stance on Tibet angered China. In 1959, Pakistan supported a General Assembly resolution which criticised the PRC's action in Tibet.[99] It repeated the exercise the following year, which led China's Ministry of Foreign Affairs to summon the Pakistani Ambassador in Beijing. While scolding the diplomat, Vice Minister Geng said that Pakistan was toeing American policy, its act was unfriendly, and it was interfering in China's internal affairs. He also referred to Pakistan's changed stance on China's lawful seat in the UN.[100] Supposedly, in the wake of Chinese actions in Tibet, Foreign Minister, Manzur Qadir, expressed his fears regarding Communist expansion and urged Asian countries to form a joint regional defence against such a threat. Pakistan's President, Ayub, warned that Russian-Chinese expansion in the Indian Ocean was a major part of the Communist drive for global domination.[101]

PAKISTAN'S PROPOSAL FOR JOINT DEFENCE WITH INDIA

Some regional developments in the late 1950s led Pakistan's leadership to extend to India an unusual offer for a joint defence of the subcontinent. Pakistan had observed, with deep concern, Chinese actions in Tibet, and the Soviet Union's increased activities and road construction in Afghanistan. President Ayub stated that the activities of giant Communists could not be 'overlooked by wishful thinking'.[102] It was against this backdrop that he suggested to the Indian Prime Minster, Jawaharlal Nehru, that India and Pakistan should stop squabbling and make arrangements for a common defence of the subcontinent against the inexorable push from the north i.e. China and the Soviet Union.[103] Ayub stated that the subcontinent was 'one geographic unit' whose defence was indivisible. He explained his concept of joint defence in the following words:

> As a student of war and strategy, I can see quite clearly the inexorable push of the north in the direction of the warm waters of the Indian Ocean. This push is bound to increase if India and Pakistan go on squabbling with each other. If, on the other hand, we resolve our problems and disengage our armed forces from facing inwards as they do today, and face them outwards, I feel we shall have a good chance of preventing a recurrence of history of the past, which was that whenever this subcontinent was divided—and often it was divided—someone or other invited an outsider to step in.[104]

This was the first and, so far, the last proposal of its kind. Had it been given serious thought, it could have changed the trajectory of India-Pakistan relations. Nehru rejected Ayub's proposal saying 'Defence against whom?'[105] China too accused Ayub concerning his self-created obsession with China, and asked Pakistan whom this common defence was being proposed against since China did not harbour any expansionist policies.[106] Amidst this, the emergence of the boundary controversy further worsened Sino-Pakistan relations. In 1959, the daily *Dawn* reported an image of a Chinese map, which showed some Pakistani border territory as that of China. This further raised Pakistan's concern and its leadership issued rhetorical statements. Foreign Minister, Manzur Qadir, stated that Pakistan would defend its frontiers with all available means while President Ayub added, 'If any force was used and Pakistani territory was penetrated, Pakistan would have to defend it with every means at its disposal.'[107] However, the newly emerged border dispute proved to be a blessing in disguise as it led to Pakistan inviting China to border negotiations.

BEGINNING OF A NEW ERA

The Sino-Pakistan relationship, which later turned into an 'all-weather' alliance, began to evolve during this unfriendly phase. In the late 1950s and early 1960s, three sets of bilateral relationships were restructured, pushing Pakistan and China closer. They were the Sino-Indian, Sino-Soviet, and US-Pakistan ties.

SINO-INDIAN DIFFERENCES

The heyday of *Hindi-Chini Bhai Bhai* (Indians and Chinese are brothers) ended as substantial differences surfaced between the two giant neighbours in the late 1950s, leading to a short border war in 1962. Sino-Indian differences had surfaced once before, during China's occupation of Tibet in 1950, at the Bandung Conference in 1955, and during Zhou En-lai's visit to India in 1956. Fortunately, the two countries contained them and prevented a conflict from occurring both times. However, given the magnitude of the disputes, the rigidity in the viewpoints of the two sides, and the role of external factors, the Sino-Indian conflict became inevitable. In 1958, when the border conflict began to escalate, Zhou En-lai suggested to his Indian counterpart that they maintain a temporary status quo until a final settlement was reached.[108] Before the two sides could deliberate on their dispute, demonstrations in Tibet, against Chinese control, erupted. In March 1959, the Dalai Lama, along with his government and thousands of followers, fled to India where he received political asylum. India expressed sympathy with the Tibetans, which China deemed interference in its internal affairs.[109] Parallel to Tibet, the Sino-Indian boundary issue became explosive. Nehru termed the McMahon Line as the 'border' between the two sides, which China refused to accept.[110] The final attempt to normalise relations took place when Nehru and Zhou held talks in India in April 1960, which failed to produce any results. An exchange of notes followed during which the two sides accused each other of interfering in the other's territory.[111] These differences culminated in the Sino-Indian border war in October 1962; this was a short war but it left a deep impact on regional politics. It changed the pattern of alliances, ended the Sino-Indian entente, enhanced India's importance in American policy hence improving their bilateral ties leading to a massive inflow of US economic and military assistance into India, and estranged Pakistan from its Western allies. These developments paved the way for the establishment of the Sino-Pakistan entente cordiale.

CRACKS IN THE US-PAKISTAN ALLIANCE

Since the late 1950s, the US and Pakistan—who were allies by virtue of four defence pacts—began to develop differences over Washington's assistance of New Delhi. President Eisenhower's Secretary of State, John Foster Dulles, was a staunch advocate for the creation of an alliance system in Asia to counter Communist expansion. The policy lost its importance when John Kennedy was voted into the White

House. Kennedy was not only averse to the alliance system but also held strong views regarding building up India to counter China. Well before his presidential campaign was launched, he had outlined a strategy of making India the linchpin of US foreign policy. He attributed China's progress to generous Soviet assistance and believed that had India been offered similar support, it could have matched or even surpassed China. In his opinion, no struggle in the world deserved as much attention from the administration in Washington than the struggle for power between India and China.[112] According to an American scholar, 'Cultivation of Indian friendship had ranked high among the objectives of the new American Administration.'[113] In 1958, the World Bank and thirteen Western countries, led by the US, established an Aid-to-India Consortium, which provided meaningful economic assistance to India in various fields.[114] Kennedy's words best explain his desire to build India as a bulwark against China:

> Unless India can compete equally with China, unless she can show that her way works as well as or better than dictatorship, unless she can make the transition from economic stagnation to economic growth, so that it can get ahead of its exploding population, the entire Free World will suffer a serious reverse. India herself will be gripped by frustration and political instability, its role as counter to the Red Chinese in Asia will be lost, and Communism will have won its greatest bloodless victory.[115]

Kennedy emphasised that the US must join the Western countries to launch a serious long-term loan, and technical and agricultural support strategies to 'enable India to overtake the challenge of Communist China'.[116] The US concern for India could be measured from the fact that immediately after the Sino-Indian border skirmishes of November

1959 in Ladakh, the US President, Dwight D. Eisenhower, especially flew to India to discuss the security situation with Nehru.

Right from the start of Indian independence, Nehru's neutrality in regards to the East-West conflict and unwillingness to play a role against the Communist 'threat' was the major hurdle in any possible formal or informal Indo-US alliance. With the emergence of Sino-Indian differences in the late fifties, this obstacle began to disappear as Nehru sought Western assistance. This opened up the prospects of a new level of Indo-US cooperation.

As the possibilities of Indo-US engagement increased in the context of a growing Sino-Indian rivalry, the US changed its Kashmir policy from a slightly pro-Pakistan stance to a neutral one. Unlike in the past, the US was no longer willing to use its economic assistance to India to exert pressure on New Delhi to find a settlement with Pakistan. Later in 1963, a US official made it clear that US military assistance to India was not made conditional on the success of on-going Indo-Pakistan negotiations, which started in 1962 under US and British influence. The changed American position on Kashmir reduced Pakistan's interest in negotiating with India on this issue.

United States assistance to India, especially in the defence sector, had a potentially negative impact on US-Pakistan relations. Islamabad complained that the aid to non-allied India against an allied Pakistan was out of proportion to the Sino-Indian conflict.[117] According to Zulfikar Ali Bhutto—then minister in Ayub's cabinet—until 30 June 1959, the total US economic aid to India since independence was about US$1.7 billion, including US$931 million in agricultural commodities. In contrast, within a short period of less than four years, 1959–63, India received US$4 billion from the US, mostly in the defence sector.[118] With this aid, India increased its armed forces by 40 per cent. According to Bhutto, after receiving this aid, instead of resolving differences with its neighbours, India doubled the size of its armed forces.[119] President Ayub also raised similar concerns. He stated:

> The fact of the matter is that, taking advantage of the favourable Western response to her demands for arms, India is planning to raise two armies, one with which to face China and the other to use against Pakistan and her other smaller neighbours in pursuance of her expansionist objectives. Any army meant for China would by the nature of things be so positioned as to be able to wheel round swiftly to attack East Pakistan. Thus both the armies pose a grave threat to Pakistan.[120]

Besides the reaction from policymakers, US aid to India created a negative image in Pakistan. According to a Pakistani diplomat, 'As the US and the UK rushed arms to India, opinion in Pakistan was outraged. People felt betrayed, realising that the arms would enhance India's offensive capability to the detriment ultimately of Pakistan.'[121] The aid to India continued despite Pakistan's protest, which led the latter to explore alternative options. According to an analyst, 'The rush of Western arms to India caused Pakistan to move out of the Western orbit, making itself virtually a non-aligned country, although Pakistan maintained its membership of SEATO and CENTO.'[122]

In Pakistan, debate regarding the productivity of Western alliances had already started. Some quarters were of the view that the US and Britain, which brought India and Pakistan to the negotiating table on Kashmir, were not exerting the required degree of pressure on New Delhi to address the Kashmir dispute in all seriousness. By the start of the 1960s, Pakistan concluded that its relations with India and the Soviet Union were unlikely to improve in the near future; it should thus explore new options and cultivate closer ties with other countries such as China.

SINO-SOVIET DIFFERENCES

Another important development of consequence was the emergence of a split between China and the Soviet Union that developed almost parallel to the Sino-Indian conflict. The two giant neighbours fell apart over the leadership role that they should play in the Communist bloc and the Third World. China was disappointed at 'Soviet leader Nikita Khrushchev's cozying up to Washington through the "spirit of Camp David", as well as Moscow's failure to back the PRC's actions in the 1959 Sino-Indian border crisis'.[123]

The Sino-Soviet differences further intensified China's concerns in a number of ways. First, through this rift, Beijing lost its prime Communist ally that had provided considerable economic, technical, and military support. As those differences sharpened, Moscow called back thousands of technicians, abandoning China's development plan midway. Secondly, the Soviet Union was contiguous with China's, resource-rich but troubled, Xinjiang region and had a history of influencing the area through its aid policy. Even after the PRC took control of Xinjiang, Moscow continued to have a sway over the region. As Sino-Soviet differences intensified, Soviet leverage in Xinjiang added to China's worries. Pakistan's geographical proximity with Xinjiang increased Islamabad's importance for Beijing. As an observer noted, 'In fact, it was China's insecurity in the western border, particularly its uneasy relationship with the Soviet Union that prompted China to look toward Pakistan.'[124] Sino-Soviet differences escalated Moscow's support to New Delhi. As China's ties with the US were already antagonistic, the emergence of India and the Soviet Union as new rivals further increased its insecurity.[125] Garver noted, 'Following Nehru's rejection in April 1960 of Zhou En-lai's proposal for a comprehensive compromise settlement of the boundary issue, Chinese leaders concluded that India was colluding with US covert operations to support the Tibetan insurgents.' He added, 'Mao became convinced that the United States and India, along with (increasingly) China's erstwhile ally, the USSR, were all working together against China.'[126] In this environment, when China felt encircled, relations with Pakistan appeared to be a suitable option.[127]

The change in China's policy coincided with Pakistan distancing itself from American opposition to China's entry into the UN. In 1960, Bhutto led the Pakistani delegation to the UN where 'for the first time he broke ranks with the US position on the People's Republic of China, abstaining rather than voting against Beijing's membership in the world forum'.[128] Bhutto took this decision without approval from Foreign Minister, Manzur Qadir. Thereafter, Pakistan not only resumed its support for China's seat in the UN but vocally championed China's cause in this campaign. Bhutto, who assumed the portfolio of foreign minister a few years later, defended his stance: 'I feel that the time has come for Pakistan to adopt an attitude in the United Nations more consistent with its recognition of the Beijing regime than has been the case since 1954.'[129]

LEADING UP TO THE BORDER AGREEMENT

As discussed above, the genesis of the Sino-Pakistan entente emerged during the unfriendly phase of their relations in the late 1950s and the early 1960s. At that time, Cold War rivalry was at its peak, Sino-

Pakistan relations were at their lowest, and Pakistan's commitments to the US were at an all-time high. Moreover, Pakistan had made an offer to India for a joint defence of the subcontinent against a common threat from the North: China and the Soviet Union. Amidst this avid anti-China position, Pakistan feared a possible clash with China as well; similar to the one that had been developing between China and India over their undefined border. Pakistan also had an unmarked border with China that came into the limelight during that period.

In September 1959, Pakistan acquired a Chinese map showing a fairly large portion of Pakistan's Northern Areas (Gilgit-Baltistan) as Chinese territory. Although China had not officially claimed any territory, the map raised concerns in Pakistan. Meanwhile, there were reports of incursions of an unidentified jet aircraft in the Hunza and Iskoman areas of Pakistan. To avoid a confrontation with China due to an unmarked boundary, Pakistan sent the first formal proposal to China for border demarcation in October 1959.[130]

Upon not receiving any reply, it repeated the offer in December 1960. China did not respond to Pakistan's proposal to negotiate the Sino-Pakistan border until early 1962.[131] Until that time, China and India were trying to mend fences with each other. China feared that a positive response to Pakistan might antagonise India since Pakistan was suggesting border talks that involved an area India also had a claim to. As Kapur noted, 'Although Chinese leaders were eager to keep the door open for eventual negotiations with Pakistan, and even perhaps to use them to obtain a border concession from India, they did not wish to begin formal negotiations because such a step would aggravate tension between China and India.'[132] The PRC began formal border talks with Pakistan only after the doors of reconciliation with India were closed. Finally, in March 1962, China expressed its willingness to talk about the unmarked boundary. In May 1962, both sides agreed to negotiate a demarcation line between Xinjiang and the contiguous area on the Pakistani side.

Importantly, the appointment of some pro-China figures on some key posts in Pakistan's Foreign Office, in 1961–62, accelerated the negotiation process. In late 1961, S. K. Dehlavi was appointed as foreign secretary. He was regarded as the staunchest advocate in the Foreign Office of a disengagement policy from Western pacts. He was in favour of forging close bonds with China.[133] Dehlavi termed China's March 1962 response to the offer of holding border talks as a step forward, although the reply came after a long delay. He described the relationship between the two countries as cordial. In June 1962, Mohammad Ali Bogra returned from the US, where he was serving as the ambassador, and assumed the portfolio of foreign minister. Bogra had been the prime minister of Pakistan when he met Chinese premier Zhou En-lai at Bandung in 1955. The third important appointment was of General Raza as Pakistan's ambassador to China for the second term. During his first term, Raza had established close personal contacts with Zhou En-lai and was held in high esteem in China. He had been instrumental in arranging meetings between Bogra and Zhou En-lai at the Bandung Conference. These individuals managed to push forward the Sino-Pakistan border talks.

Upon Ambassador Raza's arrival in Beijing, in July, both the sides exchanged border maps. On 13 October 1962, about a week before the outbreak of the Sino-Indian border war, Beijing began negotiations with Pakistan which, given the environment, progressed rapidly. By December 1962, both sides agreed on 'the location and the alignment of the boundary actually existing between the two countries', and in March 1963, signed the Border Agreement which ushered in a new era in their relations.[134]

The China-Pakistan border agreement followed the Karakoram

watershed. According to details, out of 3,400 square miles of territory to which both sides laid claim, Pakistan received 1,350 and China the rest. China kept control at the Shaksgam Mustagh drainage area, about 1,050 square miles, which Pakistan also claimed. Out of Pakistan's share of 1,350 square miles, 750 square miles of territory was under China's actual control.[135] Thus, it was Pakistan that gained more territory; including rights to the water drainage into the Indus River, six of the seven mountain passes, and three quarters of the K-2 (the second highest mountain peak in the world). Syed states that possession of water drainage into the Indus River had an 'advantage in view of Pakistani apprehensions about the future of streams falling into West Pakistan from the Indian-occupied part of Kashmir'.[136] In return, Pakistan made a 'symbolic gesture by giving up [its] claim over 2,050 square miles of territory' which was already under China's control.[137] The acquired territory was rich in natural resources, particularly the salt mines of Oprange Valley, which the people of Hunza and the surrounding areas considered necessary for their needs and well-being.

Importantly, the border agreement was a provisional document and valid until the final settlement of the Kashmir dispute. Article VI of the Agreement states, 'After the settlement of the Kashmir dispute between Pakistan and India, the sovereign authority concerned will reopen negotiations with the Government of the People's Republic of China... so as to sign a formal Boundary Treaty to replace the present agreement.'[138] After the final settlement, if Pakistan gains control of the concerned territory, the border agreement will be considered final. However, if India gains control of the disputed territory, China will start fresh talks with them.[139]

The Agreement had far-reaching implications. First, it removed the possibility of future conflict between Pakistan and China.[140] Secondly, as Syed puts it, 'It placed China formally and firmly on record as maintaining that Kashmir did not, as yet, belong to India.'[141] Thirdly, Pakistan withstanding the US pressure, especially for not 'ceding' the territory upon which India had laid claim to, 'proved to Beijing that Pakistan could act independently of its fellow SEATO and CENTO member[s]'.[142] China's concerns regarding Pakistan's participation in Western defence pacts were eased and Beijing started to ponder the advantage of Pakistan's role in those pacts.[143] Afterwards, Pakistan and China also propagated that if they could resolve territorial issues amicably, India was the one at fault if it could not settle border disputes.

Not surprisingly, India opposed Sino-Pakistan border negotiations right from the beginning. New Delhi stated that Pakistan and China could not negotiate that part of Kashmir which, though presently in Pakistan's 'occupation', was a part of Indian Jammu and Kashmir. Only New Delhi had the right to negotiate on its behalf.[144] New Delhi also accused Islamabad of surrendering 1,600 square miles of its territory to China,[145] and claimed that the agreement contained a secret clause against India. Pakistan denied these accusations, and stated that the agreement was not targeted against any third country and was solely aimed at maintaining a peaceful coexistence.[146]

Keeping in view the nature of India's relations with China and Pakistan, New Delhi's reaction was quite understandable. However, it appears that it was the timing and not the border agreement alone that seemed to be a concern. The pact was signed at a time when anti-China sentiments in India were at an all-time high. India's defeat at Chinese hands shocked its leaders and the public. In November 1962, within a month of the Sino-Indian war, the Indian Parliament passed a 'historic' resolution. This 'bound' successive Indian leaders from making any move towards improving China-India ties until they had obtained every inch of India's sacred territory that had been claimed or occupied by Beijing.[147] This resolution also referred to the territory which China and Pakistan were negotiating over. Following the border agreement, any development in China-Pakistan relations was seen by India with deep suspicion.

Consequently, the Sino-Pakistan entente emerged in the wake of the Sino-Indian war, leading to the Sino-Pakistan border agreement.[148] The entente was the product of an amalgamation of interrelated developments, during the late 1950s and early 1960s, but was not intentionally planned, at least, in its genesis. In fact, during the late 1950s, Pakistan's policy towards China was hardly conducive to the development of confidence and amity between the two. At the start of the Sino-Indian conflict, Pakistan had tried to exploit it to curry favour with the US and India. President Ayub's offer of joint defence of the subcontinent, against the threat from the 'North' (China and Soviet Union), was in no way a friendly gesture vis-à-vis China. In Kapur's words, 'Obviously, this was an important proposal and would have rendered the Chinese position more difficult had India accepted it.'[149] Pakistan at that time also supported US policies against China on issues dealing with Taiwan, Tibet, and Indo-China. On the other hand, China was more serious in its relations with India than with Pakistan. That is why Beijing delayed, for a considerable period, Islamabad's proposal for border talks. Sino-Pakistan border negotiations only began after the prospects of Sino-Indian negotiations were doomed. Lastly, had the Zhou-Nehru talks succeeded, or had Nehru given a thought to Ayub's proposal for the joint defence of the subcontinent, regional politics would have been different and perhaps the Sino-Pakistan entente would not have emerged. As Bhutto stated, 'It [Sino-Indian conflict] is not as a result of some inaccurate or faulty decision or action of the people and the Government of Pakistan. It is outside the ambit and scope of our own effort to reduce it or to eliminate it.'[150]

CONCLUSION

A lack of historical animosity and conflict of interests led China and Pakistan to establish and maintain relations in the initial years. In the late 1950s, the relationship, which was neither strong nor weak, began to change as a result of Pakistan's participation in the Western defence pacts and pro-US policies. It was during this unfriendly phase of the late 1950s and early 1960s that some interrelated developments reshaped the regional pattern of alliances bringing Pakistan and China closer to each other. Once the relationship emerged, it soon expanded, bringing about a wide range of cooperation within its ambit.

NOTES

1. Wei Weikang, 'My Cultural Tour of Pakistan' in Lu Shulin (comp), *You and Us: Stories of China and Pakistan* (Beijing: China International Press, 2015), 133.
2. Talat A. Wizarat, 'Reviving Historical Trade Routes: A Case Study of the Silk Route - Gateway to China', *Strategic Studies*, vols. 34 & 35, nos. 4 & 1 (Winter 2014 and Spring 2015),19.
3. Henry Kissinger, *On China* (London: Penguin, 2011), 8.
4. Hafeez-ur-Rahman Khan, 'Pakistan's Relations with the People's Republic of China', *Pakistani Horizon*, no. 3 (1961), 214.
5. 'Note from Qureshi, Ambassador of Pakistan in the Soviet Union, to Chinese Ambassador in the USSR, Wang Chia-chiang, 29 January 1950', in R. K. Jain, *China South Asian Relations: 1947–1980,* vol. 2 (New Delhi: Radiant Publishers, 1981), 4.
6. Yaacov Vertzberger, *The Enduring Entente: Sino-Pakistani Relations 1960–1980*, The Washington Papers/95 (New York: Praeger, 1982), 1.
7. Qin Shi (comp), *China: 1998* (Beijing: New Star Publisher, 1998), 62–4.
8. *Keesing's Contemporary Archives* (1950), 10575.
9. For the list of countries see A. H. Halpern (ed.), *Policies Towards China: Views*

from Six Continents (New York, Toronto, London: The Council on Foreign Relations, 1965), Appendix A, Table A-1, Table A-2, and Table A-3, 496–502.

10. According to the press communiqué issued by the Indian government, the Communists had approached India on October 1949 to establish diplomatic relations. 'Press communiqué on India's decision to establish diplomatic relations with China, 30 December 1949', R. K. Jain, *China-South Asia Relations: 1947–1980,* vol. 1 (New Delhi: Radiant Publishers, 1981), 17.
11. Earlier, Panikkar had served as the Indian Ambassador to the Nationalists. 'Annual Report of India's Ministry of External Affairs and Commonwealth Relations for the year 1948–49, 24 February 1949' in ibid. 4.
12. Vertzberger, *The Enduring Entente: Sino-Pakistani Relations 1960–1980*, 2.
13. By this time, the capitalist world had already started projecting Communism as a threat to world peace.
14. *Dawn* (3 and 17 October 1949).
15. 'Note from Qureshi, Ambassador of Pakistan in the Soviet Union, to premier and Foreign Minister, Chou En-lai, 5 January 1950', in Jain, *China South Asia Relations: 1947–1980,* vol. 2, 3.
16. 'Chinese Vice Foreign Minister Le Ke-lung's reply to Pakistani note of 29 January 1950 delivered by Chinese Ambassador in the Soviet Union to Pakistan's Ambassador in USSR, 4 February 1950', in *China South Asian Relations: 1947–1980,* vol. 2, 5.
17. 'Note from Qureshi, Ambassador of Pakistan in the Soviet Union, to Chinese Ambassador in USSR, Wang Chia-chiang, 29 January 1950', ibid. 3–4.
18. Vertzberger, *The Enduring Entente*, 2.
19. For instance, according to an analyst, 'After the crisis with India in the summer of 1951, Pakistan's expenditure on defence inevitably escalated.' See S. M. Burke, *Pakistan's Foreign Policy: An Historical Analysis* (Oxford: Oxford University Press, 1973), 149.
20. Paul J. Smith, 'The China-Pakistan-United States Strategic Triangle: From Cold War to the War on Terrorism', *Asian Affairs: An American Review*, vol. 38 (2011), 200.
21. The Durand Line was drawn by Sir Mortimer Durand in 1893. After independence from the British in 1919, successive Afghan leaders rejected the demarcation which, in their opinion, had unfairly divided Pashtuns on the two sides. See Marvin G. Weinbaum, *Pakistan and Afghanistan: Resistance and Reconstruction* (Boulder: Westview Press, 1994), 1–2.
22. John W. Garver, *Protracted Contest: Sino-Indian Rivalry in the Twentieth Century* (Seattle and London: University of Washington Press, 2001), 190.
23. Burke, *Pakistan's Foreign Policy*, 102.
24. Ibid.

25. Mushtaq Ahmad, *The United Nations and Pakistan* (Karachi: Pakistan Institute of International Affairs, 1955), 85, cited in ibid.
26. For trade during the initial years, see Hafeez-ur-Rahman Khan, 'Pakistan's Relations with the People's Republic of China', *Pakistani Horizon*, no. 3 (1961), 217–18.
27. Devin T. Hagerty, 'China and Pakistan: Strains in the Relationship', *Current History*, vol. 101, no. 656 (September 2002), 284–5.
28. Vertzberger, *The Enduring Entente*, 2.
29. Mushtaq Ahmed, *The United Nations and Pakistan* (Karachi: The Times Press for the Pakistan Institute of International Affairs, 1955), 88–94.
30. Ghulam Ali, 'China's Seat in the United Nations: An Analysis of Pakistan's Role', *IPRI Journal*, vol. IV, no. 2 (Summer 2004), <http://ipripak.org/journal/summer2004/china.shtml#_ftnref17>.
31. K. Arif, *China Pakistan Relations, Documents*, 36–8.
32. Speech of Sir Mohammed Zafrullah Khan at the fifth session of the UN General Assembly held on 25 September 1950, ibid. 36–8.
33. Hafeez-ur-Rahman, 'Pakistan's Relations with the People's Republic of China', *Pakistani Horizon*, no. 3 (1961), 217.
34. Pakistani Prime Minister's address to the National Assembly, *Pakistan News* (Karachi, 29 October 1950), in Mohammed Ahsen Chaudhri, *Pakistan and the Great Powers* (Karachi: Council for Pakistan Studies, 1970), 80.
35. Gurnam Singh, 'Pakistan's China Policy: Casual Considerations 1960s', in K. Arif (ed.), *Pakistan's Foreign Policy: Indian Perspective* (Lahore: Vanguard, 1984), 274.
36. G. W. Choudhury, *India, Pakistan, Bangladesh, and the Major Powers: Politics of a Divided Subcontinent* (New York: Macmillan, 1975), 153.
37. *Nehru's Speeches—vol. II: 1949–1953*, 174, in Choudhury, *India, Pakistan, Bangladesh, and the Major Powers*, 154.
38. *People's Daily* (31 October 1950), ibid. 154.
39. Burke, *Pakistan's Foreign Policy*, 105–6.
40. *Dawn* (28 October 1950), cited in Burke, *Pakistan's Foreign Policy*, 106.
41. Ibid.
42. Burke, *Pakistan's Foreign Policy*, 106–7.
43. *People's China* was twice renamed as *Review* and *Beijing Review*.
44. Arif, *China Pakistan Relations: Document*, 7.
45. Choudhury, *India, Pakistan, Bangladesh, and the Major Powers*, 152.
46. Purnendu Kumar Banerjee, 'China in India and Pakistan', speech to the United States Congress, Congressional Record (Washington DC, 13 June 1966), 12961–4, as cited in Andrew Small, *The China-Pakistan Axis: Asia's New Geopolitics* (London: C. Hurst & Co., 2015), 20.

47. Chaudhury wrote, 'Pakistan was hungering for U.S. economic and military help', ibid. 152.
48. Werner Levi, 'Pakistan, the Soviet Union and China', *Pacific Affairs*, vol. 35, no. 3 (Fall 1962), 214.
49. Ibid.
50. John W. Garver, *Protracted Contest: Sino-Indian Rivalry in the Twentieth Century* (Seattle and London: University of Washington Press, 2001), 190. Also see Werner Levi, 'Pakistan, the Soviet Union and China', *Pacific Affairs*, vol. 35, no. 3 (Fall 1962), 214–16; 'Moscow came down squarely on India's side on the Kashmir issue in 1955, China on Pakistan's side in 1964', in John W. Garver; 'Sino-Indian Rapprochement and the Sino-Pakistan Entente', *Political Science Quarterly*, vol. III, no. 2 (Summer 1996), 327; and Mohammed Ahsen Chaudhri, 'Pakistan's Relations with the Soviet Union', *Asian Survey*, vol. 6, no. 9 (September 1966), 494.
51. Jain, *China South Asia Relations,* vol. 2, 10.
52. For a detailed account of the Chinese response to these pacts, see Syed, *China & Pakistan*, 53–66.
53. United Kingdom High Commission (Karachi, 10 February 1956). *The National Archives*, FO371/120909.
54. Khalid Mahmud, 'Sino-Pakistan Relations: An "All-Weather" Friendship', *Regional Studies,* vol. XIX, no. 3 (2001), 4.
55. Sayeed, 'Pakistan and China', *Policies Towards China*, 234–5.
56. Interview with a Chinese scholar, November 2014, Beijing, China.
57. Later in the early 1960s when Pakistan reviewed its foreign policy, both proved instrumental in establishing connection with China. Raza had served as Pakistan's Ambassador to China and earned Zhou En-lai's respect.
58. Jain, *China South Asia Relations,* vol. 2, 8–9.
59. *Dawn* (23 April 1955). Also see Burke, *Pakistan's Foreign Policy*, 178.
60. Burke, *Pakistan's Foreign Policy*, 180.
61. To see the names of the prominent figures from Pakistan and China who visited each other's country during this period, see Syed, *China & Pakistan*, 63–4.
62. The United Kingdom High Commission (Karachi, 10 February 1956). *The National Archives*, FO371/120909.
63. Ibid.
64. Mahmud, 'Sino-Pakistan Relations', 5.
65. Syed, *China & Pakistan*, 64.
66. *People's Daily* in NCNA (English), FBIS (31 July 1956).
67. This heading has been adopted from G. W. Choudhury, 'Reflections on Sino-Pakistan Relations', *Pacific Community*, vol. 7, no. 2 (January 1976), 254.

68. Cited in An Qiguang, 'Touching Stories about the Friendship between China and Pakistan' in Shulin (comp), *You and Us*, 67.
69. United Kingdom High Commission (Karachi, 17 April 1956). *The National Archives*, FO 371/120909.
70. British Information Services (Karachi, 30 August 1956). *The National Archives*, FO371/120909.
71. Ibid.
72. Syed, *China & Pakistan,* 66–7.
73. Jain, *China South Asia Relations,* vol. 2, 12.
74. British Embassy (Beijing, 8 November 1956). *The National Archives*, FO 371/120909.
75. Ibid.
76. Choudhury, 'Reflections on Sino-Pakistan Relations', 254.
77. Syed, *China & Pakistan,* 67–8. Also in Khalid Mahmud 'Sino-Pakistan Relations: An "All-Weather" Friendship', *Regional Studies*, vol. XIX, no. 3 (Summer 2001), 7.
78. Burke, *Pakistan's Foreign Policy*, 215.
79. British Embassy (Beijing, 22 November 1956). *The National Archives,* FO 371/120909.
80. NCNA (24 June 1957).
81. Jain, *China South Asia Relations,* vol. 2, 12–13.
82. Syed, *China & Pakistan,* 69.
83. Mahmud, 'Sino-Pakistan Relations', 5.
84. Vertzberger, *The Enduring Entente*, 6.
85. Mahmud, 'Sino-Pakistan Relations', 68.
86. Syed, *China & Pakistan*, 72–3.
87. An editorial in an English daily criticised Pakistan's stance. *Pakistan Times* (1 October 1957), in Syed, *China & Pakistan,* 73.
88. 'Chinese note to Pakistan, 22 September 1958', in Jain, *China South Asia Relations,* vol. 2, 17.
89. 'Pakistani reply to Chinese note of 22 September 1958, 1 October 1958', ibid. 17
90. Syed, *China & Pakistan*, 73 and 240.
91. Earlier as a defence minister and commander-in-chief of the Army, Ayub Khan had played a leading role in concluding defence agreements with the US. See Syed, *China & Pakistan,* 74–5.
92. Arif, *China Pakistan Documents: Documents*, 17.
93. Mohammad Ayub Khan, 'Pakistan Perspective', *Foreign Affairs*, vol. 38 (July 1960), 555.

94. Statement by Pakistan Foreign Minister Malik Firoz Khan Noon on 8 September 1958, Jain, *China South Asia Relations,* vol. 2, 16–17.
95. *Dawn* (15 December 1960), in Sayeed, 'Pakistan and China', *Policies Towards China*, 233.
96. Ibid.
97. *Peking Review*, no. 30 (28 July 1958), 18–19.
98. Sulmaan Wasif Khan, *Muslim, Trader, Nomad, Spy: China's Cold War and the People of the Tibetan Borderlands* (University of North Caroline Press, 2015), 48.
99. 'Statement by the representative of Pakistan in the UN General Assembly on the question of Tibet, 20 October 1959', Jain, *China South Asia Relations: 1947–1980,* vol. 2, 22–3.
100. Khan, *Muslim, Trader, Nomad, Spy*, 49.
101. Chaudhri, *Pakistan and Great Powers*, 84–5.
102. 'Ayub Khan's press interview with the correspondent of Kayhan International in Karachi, 9 November 1959' in Jain, *China South Asia Relations: 1947–1980,* vol. 2, 23.
103. Chaudhri, *Pakistan and Great Powers*, 85.
104. Khan, 'Pakistan Perspective', 556.
105. Singh, 'Pakistan's China Policy', *Pakistan's Foreign Policy*, 274.
106. Arif, *China Pakistan Relation: Document*, 17–18.
107. *Dawn* (1 October 1959).
108. Amardeep Athwal, *China-India Relations: Contemporary Dynamics* (New York: Routledge, 2008), 21.
109. Choudhury, *India, Pakistan, Bangladesh, and the Major Powers*, 168.
110. Ibid. 169.
111. William J. Barnds, *India, Pakistan, and the Great Powers* (London: Pall Mall Press, 1972), 170–3.
112. John F. Kennedy, *The Strategy For Peace* (New York: Harper and Row, 1960), 142.
113. Richard P. Stebbins, *The United States in World Affairs 1961* (New York, 1962), 209, in Sherwani, *India, China and Pakistan*, 64.
114. Ibid. 65.
115. Kennedy, *The Strategy For Peace*, 142.
116. Ibid.
117. To understand the difference of opinions over the purpose of Pakistan-US alliance, see W. Howard Wriggins, 'The Balancing Process in Pakistan's Foreign Policy', in Lawrence Ziring, et al. (eds.) *Pakistan: The Long View* (Durham: N.C. Duke University Press, 1977), 301–39.

118. Zulfikar Ali Bhutto, *Myth of Independence* (Karachi: Oxford University Press, 1969), 48–50.
119. Zulfikar Ali Bhutto, *Foreign Policy of Pakistan: A Compendium of Speeches made in the National Assembly of Pakistan 1962–64* (Karachi: Pakistan Institute of International Affairs, 1964), 55.
120. Muhammad Ayub Khan, *Friends, Not Masters: A Political Autobiography* (Islamabad: Mr Books, 2001), 136.
121. Abdul Sattar, *Pakistan's Foreign Policy 1947–2009: A Concise History*, Second Edition (Karachi: Oxford University Press, 2006), 86.
122. Fazal-ur-Rehman, 'Pakistan's Relations with China', *Strategic Studies*, vols. XIX & XX, nos. 4 & 1 (Winter and Spring 1998), 65–6.
123. Christopher Tang, 'Beyond India: The Utility of Sino-Pakistani Relations in Chinese Foreign Policy, 1962–1965', Cold War International History Project, Working Paper no. 64 (November 2012), 3.
124. Abanti Bhattacharya, 'The Xinjiang Factor' in Swaran Singh (ed.), *Sino-Pakistan Strategic Relations: Indian Perspective,* 352.
125. Mohammad Yunus, *Reflections on China: An Ambassador's View from Beijing* (Lahore: Services Book Club, 1987), 133.
126. John W. Garver, *Protracted Contest: Sino-Indian Rivalry in the Twentieth Century* (Seattle and London: University of Washington Press, 2001), 57.
127. Yunus, *Reflections on China*, 133.
128. Stanley Wolpert, *Zulfi Bhutto of Pakistan: His Life and Time* (Oxford: Oxford University Press, 2007), 65.
129. The US expressed its dissatisfaction over Pakistan's decision but Bhutto disregarded this as well as the Foreign Minister's order to avoid discretionary power on UN voting. Ibid.
130. George L. Montagno, 'Peaceful Coexistence: Pakistan and Red China', *Western Political Quarterly*, vol. 18, no. 2, part 1 (June 1965), 312. Also see Syed, *China & Pakistan,* 84.
131. The Sino-Indian border clashes also set off alarm bells in Pakistan which had an undefined boundary with China as well. Although Pakistan was proposing to India for a joint defence of the subcontinent at the same time, it wanted to prevent any confrontation with China.
132. Haris Kapur, 'China's Relations with India and Pakistan', *Current History*, vol. 57, no. 337 (September 1969), 160.
133. Syed, *China & Pakistan*, 198.
134. For the same argument also see Mohan Ram, 'Karakoram Highway', *Economic and Political Weekly*, vol. 13, no. 26 (1 July 1978), 1058.
135. According to a former Pakistani foreign minister, Pakistan gained this territory

as a special gesture of premier Zhou En-lai. After the demarcation of the border was agreed upon, Pakistan realised that the grazing lands along the Murtagh River, on the other side of the Karakoram waterlands, were essential for the inhabitants of Hunza. Pakistan 'appealed for an exception to the watershed principle' to which Zhou En-lai generously agreed. Sattar, *Pakistan's Foreign Policy 1947–2009*, 80.

136. Syed, *China & Pakistan*, 88.
137. Samina Yasmeen, 'Sino-Pakistan Relations and the Middle East', *China Report*, vol. 34, nos. 3 & 4 (1998), 330.
138. Full text of the agreement is available at <http://www.tpprc.org/documents/agreements/1963-A.pdf>.
139. Interview with Akram Zaki, former Pakistani Ambassador to China, Islamabad, April 2011.
140. Bhutto, *Foreign Policy of Pakistan*, 10.
141. Syed, *China & Pakistan*, 88.
142. Khan, *Muslim, Trader, Nomad, Spy*, 130.
143. Chinese premier Zhou began to project it more publicly. He argued that Pakistan's participation in those pacts could be a 'voice of reason' and beneficial to Afro-Asian countries. The author, however, termed it as an 'astonishing development' that Communist China was praising an ally of anti-Communist military pacts. Ibid. 132.
144. Bhutto, *Pakistan's Foreign Policy*, 79.
145. Chaudhri, *Pakistan and the Great Powers*, 88.
146. Bhutto, *Pakistan's Foreign Policy*, 23. Also see Syed, *China & Pakistan*, 87.
147. The resolution became a 'legal hurdle' in resuming Indian talks with China. Twenty-six years later in November 1988, the All-India Congress Committee passed another resolution which changed the contents of the previous resolution to find a peaceful settlement with China based on the mutual interests of the two countries. Swaran Singh, *China-South Asia: Issues, Equations, Policies* (New Delhi: Lancers Books, 2003), 129.
148. In tracing the roots of the Sino-Pakistan entente cordiale, most of the credit is given to the Sino-Indian rivalry. The significance of the Sino-Pakistan border agreement, regardless of whether it was influenced by the Sino-Indian conflict or not, is no less important. The mutually agreed border settlement resolved all territorial issues, and paved the way for a stable relationship in the future. Despite all other developments, an unresolved border between China and Pakistan could have remained a potential source of conflict between them.
149. Kapur, 'China's Relations with India and Pakistan', 159.
150. Bhutto, 'Pakistan—and China?', 222.

2

Strengthening and Deepening of Relations (1963–77)

Once the China-Pakistan entente was established, both the countries adopted mutually supportive policies. China found that Pakistan was an important ally to help break its self-imposed isolation, put a check on India's role in South Asia, and neutralise Soviet and US encirclement policies. To please its new South Asian ally, China changed its policy on Kashmir from a neutral to a pro-Pakistan one. It also started backing Pakistan in Indo-Pakistan conflicts, and began extending economic and diplomatic support. Most importantly, military relations, which were almost non-existent earlier, were not only established but also acquired a central place in the relationship. China began to term Pakistan a progressive country that resisted foreign pressure and pursued an independent foreign policy. On many occasions, it issued statements guaranteeing Pakistan's independence, state sovereignty, and territorial integrity. However, most of these statements only held symbolic value.

For Pakistan, its new relations with China emerged as a suitable alternative to uncertain relations with the US. In July 1963, within months of the border agreement, then Foreign Minister, Zulfikar Ali Bhutto, stated rather recklessly, in the National Assembly of Pakistan, that any future Indian attack on Pakistan would not be confined to the security and territorial integrity of Pakistan alone; it would involve 'the territorial integrity and security of the largest state in

Asia', alluding to China.[1] Three days later, President Ayub remarked that his country would seek Chinese protection if the Western world continued to assist to India.[2] Bhutto's statement created a stir affecting Pakistan's relations with India, the US, and even placed China in an awkward situation.

As a result of its entente, Pakistan resumed its support for the PRC in the UN, helped in breaking China's isolation, worked as a bridge between China and the Muslim world, and played the role of a broker in Sino-US rapprochement. Moreover, Pakistan maintained silence over China's internal policies, including its suppression of Muslims in Xinjiang.[3]

Following the border agreement, the two sides signed a series of accords in various areas. Both sides granted each other Most Favoured Nation (MFN) treatment.[4] China agreed to provide long-term credit to Pakistan for small industries; this was the beginning of China's economic assistance to Pakistan. In August 1963, they signed an air agreement for the Dhaka-Canton-Shanghai air service of Pakistan International Airlines (PIA), a commercial deal with substantial political significance that helped break China's isolation.[5] In April 1964, PIA made its maiden flight to Shanghai, becoming the first airline from a non-Communist country to operate on Chinese territory.[6] Under a cultural agreement for the exchange of students in September 1964, China sent some students to Karachi to learn Urdu. One of those students, Lu Shulin, later became China's Ambassador to Pakistan while Wei Weikang became director of Pakistan Affairs in the Ministry of Foreign Affairs, China.[7] In 1965–66, China and Pakistan signed agreements to establish direct radio and telecommunication links,[8] to facilitate visas to promote exchanges,[9] and establish sea lines of communication, allowing their vessels to anchor in each other's harbours.[10] This wide-ranging interaction in a short period indicated the potential of this relationship, highlighted Pakistan's role in the international environment, and broke China's isolation.

As their friendship began to deepen, China offered loans to Pakistan,[11] most of which were long-term and interest-free. On occasions, especially when Pakistan faced economic hardship, the loans were converted into grants. This gesture was particularly meaningful because China itself was a poor country at the time. The first Chinese loan worth US$60 million (to import coal, cement, iron, steel, and electrical and other equipment from China) was granted in 1965. China also provided 100,000 tons of wheat and 50,000 tons of rice to Pakistan, assisted two industrial projects, and contributed over US$300 million towards Pakistan's second, third, and fourth five-year plans.[12]

Another feature of the new relationship between China and Pakistan was the start of two-way visits by the top leadership which became a regular element of their future ties. In February 1964, after a seven-year hiatus, Zhou En-lai came to Pakistan.[13] On that occasion, both sides expressed 'identical views' on their mutual relations, spoke of their desire to hold a second Afro-Asian Conference on the lines of the Bandung Conference, and condemned colonialism and the hegemonic attitudes of states. Pakistan supported China's case for a permanent seat on the UN Security Council.[14] Zhou En-lai stated that Sino-Pakistan relations were 'an important contribution' to peace in the region and beyond. As stated by Choudhury, it is possible that New Delhi, Washington, and Moscow did not agree.[15] In the context of its rapidly growing ties with Pakistan, China also moved away from its earlier concerns regarding Pakistan's participation in the Western pacts. In response to a question on Islamabad joining SEATO and CENTO, Zhou stated that China was satisfied with Pakistan's reasoning that joining these agreements was for defence purposes, not aggression against others.[16] In the 1950s, China had accepted Pakistan's explanations at the Bandung Conference in April 1955, and during Suhrawardy's China visit in October 1956. However, it was not 'deeply convinced' about Pakistan's motives. It was after the new relationship was launched in the early 1960s that China completely shed its concerns about Pakistan's role in the Western defence pacts.[17] Not only this, China decided to take advantage of Pakistan's membership of said pacts.

An important outcome of Zhou En-lai's visit, from Pakistan's point of view, was China moving closer to accepting Islamabad's stance on the Kashmir issue. China indicated a change in its Kashmir policy from a neutral stance, which the PRC had adopted during the 1950s, to pro-Pakistan leanings.[18] While showing its tilt towards Pakistan, in the joint communiqué, China appreciated Islamabad's attitude in seeking a peaceful settlement of the Kashmir dispute. It added that an early solution of the dispute would be conducive to peace in Asia and globally.[19] This appeared as a thinly veiled warning to India; Kashmir was a disputed territory whose early resolution was essential for regional peace. The Pakistani side considered Zhou's visit a 'striking success for President Ayub Khan'.[20]

In return, Islamabad began to support China's policy on different international issues including Beijing's stance on the Nuclear Test Ban Treaty and its nuclear test in 1964. These developments took place during the 1960s when Sino-Soviet relations had already started deteriorating. Moscow withdrew its help and declined to assist China in acquiring nuclear technology. China regarded this move as a Soviet strategy to maintain monopoly over nuclear technology. In mid-1963, the US, the USSR, and the UK initiated talks on the partial test ban treaty which restricted further nuclear tests but allowed underground experiments. In Beijing's view, underground testing facilities were privileges reserved for developed countries. China labelled those talks as American 'imperialism' which was supported by Soviet revisionists. It accused Moscow of readily allowing the US to develop nuclear weapons; and abandoning the socialist countries, including China. In response to the proposal for a partial test ban treaty, Zhou En-lai called for a world conference to negotiate a total and resolute prohibition of nuclear weapons. In August 1963, he wrote a letter to all heads of states demanding the convening of such a conference. Pakistan was among those countries that supported this proposal.

In October 1964, China conducted its first nuclear test. Unlike India, which expressed its deep concerns, Pakistan termed it a positive move, arguing to the international community that China's acquisition of nuclear capability had further strengthened its case for a UN seat. As an observer noted, 'By helping to define the Chinese nuclear capability as peaceful and defensive, Pakistani leaders assisted the PRC in forging an identity as a protector of peace that was clearly distinct from the two superpowers.' At the request of Zhou En-lai, President Ayub Khan worked hard at the Commonwealth Conference, in July 1964, to dispel the myth of the 'China threat' that was intensified in the wake of the nuclear test. At the conference, Pakistan emphasised PRC's 'fondness for peace' while criticising India for collaborating with the Soviets to isolate China. Ayub denounced the Soviet-American détente that unfairly isolated China, and urged the immediate entry of the PRC in the UN.[21] Islamabad also supported China's no-first-use policy with regards to nuclear weapons. It demanded a summit-level conference to discuss the total prohibition and thorough destruction of nuclear weapons.[22]

In response to Pakistan's pro-China attitude, Zhou En-lai reported to the first session of the third National People's Congress, held in December 1964, that Pakistan had pursued an independent foreign policy. China appreciated that Pakistan withstood various pressures, mainly from the US, and consistently maintained friendly relations with China and other Asian and African countries.[23]

In the context of growing friendly relations with Pakistan, when Ayub visited China in March 1965, China gathered nearly a million people in Beijing to welcome him. It was the 'most colourful reception ever accorded to an Asian Head of State'.[24] Both sides expressed their satisfaction at the progress on boundary demarcation, stressed the unity of Afro-Asian nations, and finalised an agreement on cultural cooperation. Islamabad reiterated its support for China's seat in the UN and its nuclear policy. In response, China came closer to Pakistan's stance on the Kashmir issue, and started demanding a settlement in accordance with the aspiration of the Kashmiri people as agreed by Pakistan and India.[25] Importantly, despite China's favourable stance on the Kashmir dispute, in the joint communiqué, Pakistan remained silent on the issue of the Vietnam War in which China was directly involved. Presumably, Pakistan avoided antagonising the US which remained an important source of economic and military assistance. China showed its understanding of Pakistan's position.[26] To address Ayub's concerns over Soviet and US military aid to India, Chinese leaders assured him, 'If India commits aggression against Pakistan's territory, China would definitely support Pakistan.'[27] This appeared to be Beijing's first categorical assurance against New Delhi. According to Choudhury, China-Pakistan relations were 'dramatized' by Ayub's meeting with Mao who told Ayub that 'China and Pakistan could trust each other'. Mao added, 'China does not look upon India as an enemy; China had very few troops on the Indian border, yet Nehru went back and published a document as a white paper containing all sorts of untrue things.' Both the leaders also discussed China's road connections with Pakistan and Nepal. These roads later 'unsettled'

New Delhi, raising concerns about Beijing's growing activities in India's neighbourhood. Mao concluded his meeting with Ayub by saying, 'We agree with you and we are not with Shastri.' In return, as Choudhury wrote, Pakistan for the first time spoke relatively loudly against colonialism and imperialism, opposed the US presence in the Indian Ocean, and supported China's seat in the UN.[28] Again, in April 1965, premier Zhou En-lai and Foreign Minister Chen Yi visited Pakistan.[29] Thus a series of frequent visits of the top leaders of the two countries started and became a regular feature of their relationship.

US CONCERNS REGARDING SINO-PAKISTAN TIES

Pakistan's growing ties with China did not correspond to the policy of containment pursued by the US. According to Nur Khan, the Air Commodore and Managing Director of PIA during Pakistan's air agreement with China, the border and the air agreements 'put additional strain on Pakistan's relations with the United States'. The US regarded these agreements as a breach of its containment policy as they could allow Communist China to reach out to Africa and Latin America. Washington warned that 'Pakistan was playing with fire in inviting a militant Communist nation to the doorstep in this part of Asia.'[30] Nur Khan recalled that US pressure over Pakistan initiating the air service to China was so intense that 'many Pakistani top leaders and senior generals got cold feet'.[31]

In November 1963, when Bhutto attended the funeral of John F. Kennedy, US President Lyndon Johnson warned him about Pakistan's growing ties with China. Johnson told Bhutto, 'Look here, I have a teenage daughter and she goes out with her boyfriend. I don't care what she does with him behind my back, but I'll be damned if she does anything in front of me.'[32] Reportedly, in the mid-1960s, Johnson wrote a letter to Ayub urging him to expel Bhutto from his cabinet due to his socialist views and for wanting closer ties with China. In a Commonwealth Conference in London, Johnson sent a message to Ayub warning him that if Pakistan continued its ties with China, the US would stop its aid which at the time amounted to about US$500 million annually and a huge supply of military weapons.[33] The US postponed US$4 million of aid for the construction of an airport in East Pakistan on the grounds that such an airport would be used by Communist China.[34] In April 1965, President Johnson cancelled Ayub Khan's scheduled visit to the US and the annual meeting of the Aid-to-Pakistan Consortium, due in the summer of 1965, which was to determine the funds for Pakistan's third Five Year Plan.[35]

Thus, the US-Pakistan relations came under stress. Washington's sanctions against Pakistan, imposed on the eve of the 1965 Indo-Pakistan war, further complicated matters. Although sanctions were imposed on both India and Pakistan, they severely affected Pakistan which then had 'near-total dependence' on the US for arms procurement.[36] India, on the other hand, continued to receive the bulk of its arms from the Soviet Union during and after the war. According to a Pakistani diplomat, the US-Pakistan relations had reached a point where Washington had virtually lost its influence on Pakistan. The US thus surrendered the subcontinent to the USSR which brokered the Tashkent Declaration between India and Pakistan in 1966.[37]

The most severe reaction to the growing China-Pakistan relations came from New Delhi. The Indian Ministry of External Affairs in a statement expressed its concerns in the following words:

> The Chinese and Pakistan governments entertain a common hatred and a common hostility against India. Both have committed aggression

> against India in Kashmir; both have laid claims against Indian territory and grabbed a portion of it illegally; and both have constantly applied military, political and propaganda pressure against India in order to make India submit to their aggressive demand.[38]

THE BIRTH OF MILITARY RELATIONS

The most important outcome of the Sino-Pakistan entente was the birth of defence and strategic ties, which had hardly existed in the past and could become the bedrock of their overall relationship. In July 1966, China and Pakistan signed their first military agreement worth US$120 million. When China started providing arms to Pakistan, it became one of its largest arms suppliers. As mentioned earlier, the US sanctions against Pakistan, before the outbreak of the 1965 war, pushed Pakistan closer to the Chinese side. According to Faruqui:

> After the [1965] war, Pakistan sought to diversify its arms supplies by going to France and China. French equipment was very expensive, and had to be confined to a few squadrons of Mirage III and V fighter-bombers and three Daphne-class submarines. Beijing became Pakistan's arms supplier of first resort, with its bulk supplies.[39]

CHINA AND THE INDO-PAKISTAN WAR OF 1965

Soon, China's commitment of friendship with Pakistan was tested during the Indo-Pakistan war, in September 1965, sparked off by the Kashmir dispute. Although war clouds had been hovering over the subcontinent for quite some time, the immediate reason was unrest and agitation in the Indian-held Kashmir over the theft of a holy relic in 1964. This resulted in escalated tensions between the arch-rivals, leading to clashes in the Rann of Kutch in April 1965. At that time, a segment of Pakistan's ruling elite, especially the military establishment, decided to adopt a confrontational policy towards India. Pakistan's involvement in Indian-held Kashmir, in an attempt to provoke an uprising (Operation Gibraltar), caused India to launch a full-scale attack against Pakistan on 6 September 1965.

This was the first Indo-Pakistan military clash since the Sino-Pakistan entente was created. It appears, from certain accounts, that China's public and private positions were different. Publicly, Beijing supported Pakistan in its confrontation with India, including on the Rann of Kutch. Some Pakistani officials who were involved in decision making, however, stated that privately China disapproved of Pakistan's adventurist policies. For example, two days before the outbreak of war, on 4 September 1965, Chinese Foreign Minister, Chen Yi, stopped over in Karachi on his way to Mali and held a five-hour conversation with his Pakistani counterpart, Z. A. Bhutto. Choudhury, who claimed to have read all of the minutes regarding discussions between the two foreign ministers, stated that Chen Yi's public assurance of help in case of 'Indian aggression' had 'no conclusive' evidence in the minutes. According to Choudhury, China did not encourage Pakistan in its military confrontation with India. Instead, China stressed 'restraint' and 'caution'. Choudhury added that Bhutto probably 'reacted too enthusiastically' to China's 'assurances' and made a 'grand miscalculation' about Chinese help.[40]

However, once war broke out, China sided with Pakistan and extended political, economic, and military support. In a statement issued on 7 September 1965, China denounced the Indian attack on Lahore as an act of 'naked aggression' which had enlarged a local conflict into a general war. A commentary published in *Peking Review* stated:

> [The Indian attack on Pakistan] not only is a crude violation of all principles guiding international relations, but also constitutes a grave threat to peace in this part of Asia. The Chinese government sternly expresses firm support for Pakistan in its just struggle against aggression and solemnly warns the Indian government that it must bear responsibility for all consequences of its criminal and extended aggression.[41]

China denounced the Indian claim that Pakistan was fanning an insurgency in Indian-held Kashmir. Instead, it called the uprising an indigenous movement which erupted in reaction to Indian military atrocities. China called out Indian Prime Minister, Lal Bahadur Shastri's, rationale of attacking Lahore as a defensive move. Instead, China termed it 'gangster logic'; it believed the Indians had learned it from the US.[42] On 7 September, Zhou En-lai held a long meeting with the Pakistani Ambassador and assured him that 'China would await further developments and would consider further steps as and when necessary'. In the meeting, Zhou sought assurances that Pakistan would not succumb to the US, USSR, or UN's pressure to accept any solution with regards to Kashmir that would be favourable to India. Ayub reassured them through a cable message. In a letter to Ayub on 8 September, President Liu Shaoqi reaffirmed that China would respond if India attacked East Pakistan. On 12 September, the Pakistani leadership appointed Air Marshal Asghar Khan to prepare a strategy to examine the nature of China's help that could be required.[43]

The war took a new turn when, on 17 September, the Chinese Ministry of Foreign Affairs summoned the Indian chargé d'affaires and handed him a warning note demanding India immediately dismantle all aggressive military works built on the Chinese side, return kidnapped men and sheep, and pledge to refrain from harassing raids across the Sino-Indian border within three days. Otherwise, the note warned, New Delhi would be solely responsible for dire consequences.[44] China then further extended its deadline for another three days. The note, which became popularly known as an 'ultimatum', was intended, according to Hussain, to 'strengthen a newly found friend which was slowly but surely distancing itself from the US'.[45] After having received China's note, India consulted the British, the US, and the Soviets. The latter two assured New Delhi of military help in case of Chinese involvement.[46]

China's involvement in the war could have escalated the tension with the possibility of embroiling it, or either or both the US and the USSR, into the war. To preempt such a scenario, the big powers accelerated the peace process and, with their accumulated pressure on both India and Pakistan, induced them to accept a ceasefire on 22 September.[47]

It was when China issued its note-cum-ultimatum that, in an act of 'courage and statesmanship', Ayub secretly flew to Beijing for consultations. Although some circles in Pakistan, especially the military establishment, intended to prolong the war, Ayub wanted an early ceasefire. Before making any decision, he wished to take China into confidence, especially because Beijing had committed its support. According to Choudhury, China knew that the cost of its involvement in the war on behalf of Pakistan would be very high, yet it was ready to intervene if Pakistan so desired. 'Mr President', Mao told Ayub, 'if there is a nuclear war, it is Peking and not Rawalpindi that will be the target.'[48] According to an aide who accompanied Ayub, there was no pressure; China gave Pakistan a free hand to make the decision about the ceasefire. Ayub was 'fully satisfied' with his meetings with Chinese leaders and, on his return to Rawalpindi, Pakistan accepted the ceasefire.[49]

Various observers interpret China's role in the 1965 war, the so-called 'ultimatum' in particular, differently. Some argue that the Chinese were bluffing and the 'ultimatum' was a pressure tactic designed to divert Indian attention from the India-Pakistan border. China had no serious intention of involving itself in a war when it was weak and faced many challenges internally.[50] By issuing warning notes, whose deadline was twice extended, China did not specifically indicate that it was ready to intervene on Pakistan's behalf. Instead, this only created false hopes which were badly shattered six years later, in a similar conflict, and on many other occasions in the following years.[51] Another school of thought argues that the Chinese were serious in their intentions and were ready to intervene should Pakistan require any assistance. A former Pakistani Ambassador to China stated that the Chinese had, in fact, made all preparations before issuing a statement. According to Tahir Amin, given the nature of Sino-Indian relations at that time, the threat of China's involvement was 'real'. He further states, 'Even if it was rhetoric, it helped Pakistan a lot.'[52]

Nevertheless, China's overall support in general and the 'ultimatum' in particular won immense popularity among the people of Pakistan. According to Mahmud, 'the foundation of an "all-weather" friendship was laid in September 1965, and change of regimes or shift in policies since then has been inconsequential in defining the parameters of Sino-Pakistan relationship'.[53]

PAKISTAN, THE USSR, AND THE ASIAN SECURITY PLAN

As mentioned previously, a review of Pakistan's foreign policy, in the early 1960s, led Islamabad to develop closer ties with China. Pakistan also decided to improve relations with the USSR, India's traditional ally. Islamabad had assumed that such a move would help reduce

Moscow's support for New Delhi. The Soviets, however, had their own reasons to respond positively to Islamabad's overtures. A relatively balanced approach, the USSR calculated, could decrease Pakistan's dependence on China and the US. While retaining some hold on New Delhi, Moscow felt it could expand its influence in South Asia by gaining some leverage in Pakistan as well. Moscow de-escalated its propaganda against Pakistan, moderated its policy on the Kashmir dispute, and offered economic and military assistance to Islamabad. These moves led to an improvement in their bilateral ties. In 1964, President Ayub visited Moscow—the first Pakistani head of state to do so. During the Indo-Pakistan war of 1965, Moscow continued to supply arms to India, however, its attitude towards Pakistan was not as antagonistic as before. Soviet Prime Minister, Alexei Kosygin, used his good offices to bring Indian Prime Minister, Lal Bahadur Shastri, and Pakistani President, Ayub Khan, to the negotiating table to sign the Tashkent Declaration in 1966.

This improvement corresponded to mounting Sino-Soviet tension. China's unstated displeasure was obvious. Beijing regarded the signing of the Tashkent Declaration as a Soviet triumph.[54] While the Tashkent talks were in session, Beijing issued a warning to New Delhi to stop the incursions into Chinese territory or face the consequences. This was meant to pressure India or express Chinese unhappiness over Pakistan's closer ties with Moscow. [55] According to Bhutto, 'when the terms of the Tashkent accord became known, the Chinese were deeply disappointed'.[56] They termed the talk a product of a Soviet-US plot to back up the Indian reactionaries.[57] In March 1966, Liu Shaoqi warned Ayub against Russia's so-called friendship. According to Choudhury, '[Beijing] resented Pakistani acquiescence to the Tashkent declaration'.[58] In spite of these concerns, the Chinese refrained from direct criticism of Pakistan: 'Even if they were not comfortable with the post-Tashkent disposition of the Ayub government, it did not inhibit the Chinese pursuing, with the same vigour and determination as before, the task of cementing ties and expanding areas of cooperation with Pakistan.'[59]

By the late 1960s, regional developments provided additional space for the USSR to manoeuvre in international politics. The Cultural Revolution and the Vietnam War had weakened China and the US respectively. Their reputation in the region was also damaged. During this period, Britain also decided to withdraw its forces from the Indian Ocean. The situation led the Soviet leadership to draw up a strategy to expand its area of influence among Asian countries through military and economic assistance. In May 1968, Kosygin suggested economic and trade cooperation among India, Pakistan, Afghanistan, and Iran.[60] In June 1969, three months after the Sino-Soviet border clashes, Brezhnev outlined the Asian Security Plan, which a Pakistani official titled 'the Russian version of SEATO'.[61] Through these proposals, the Soviet leaders intended to curtail the influence of China and the US by promoting economic and strategic cooperation among major Asian states and linking them to a pro-Soviet cooperative framework. Moscow had good relations with India while ties with Pakistan had developed considerably.[62] An improved relationship with Pakistan, a close ally of China and the US, was particularly significant to this Soviet strategy.

Against this backdrop, the Asian Security Plan became an important agenda of discussion during President Yahya's visit to the USSR in June 1969. Undoubtedly, Islamabad wanted to improve ties with Moscow, but not at the expense of good relations with China. Hence, Yahya politely but firmly declined the Soviet offer. An unhappy Kosygin warned him, 'You cannot expect Soviet arms while you are unwilling to endorse our Asian Security System.'[63] Islamabad also refused Moscow's request to establish a radio relay communication centre near its provincial capital, Peshawar. Upon his return from Moscow, Yahya sent his top security advisor, Air Marshal Nur Khan, to China to assure its leaders that Pakistan would not become a part of any scheme against China. Khan termed China a peaceful nation and a source of stability in the region.[64] Islamabad's refusal angered Moscow which put a halt to its economic and military assistance to Pakistan in 1970, and resumed its backing of India with renewed vigour. Pakistan accepted the Soviet vitriolic response as it did not went to forego its relations with China.

The Cultural Revolution (1966–69) in China also slowed down the pace of Pakistan-China relations.[65] During this period, China adopted a rigorously isolationist policy by cutting itself off from global affairs and limiting overseas travels of its leaders. It adopted an introverted policy and kept a low profile in its relations with the outside world. The frequency of visits and bilateral interaction between Islamabad and Beijing also decreased. A small number of Pakistani officials who visited China were received by low-ranking officials and given less media coverage.[66] Regardless, China's relations with Pakistan, as compared to other countries, remained stable.[67] As Garver noted, 'Pakistan was the only non-Communist friend of China to escape criticism during the Cultural Revolution; even extreme Maoist leaders put Pakistan in a class by itself as a friend of China.'[68]

Furthermore, the flow of Chinese economic aid to Pakistan continued uninterrupted. In October 1967, both sides signed an agreement to facilitate overland trade between Gilgit and Xinjiang. In December 1968 and November 1970, China extended a credit of PKR200 million and assistance of US$200 million. By the end of 1971, China had pledged a total of US$307 million to Pakistan.[69] In the late 1960s, China assisted in building three roads across their border with Pakistan. The most important among them was the legendary Karakoram Highway, which was completed in 1978.[70] The other two roads connected Azad Kashmir and the Northern Areas with China's Xinjiang via the Mintaka Pass and the Karakoram Pass respectively. The construction of these roads reduced travel time and opened new trade opportunities for businessmen on the two sides.[71]

During the 1960s, China also agreed to establish the Heavy Mechanical Complex (HMC) at Taxila to meet Pakistan's industrial needs. The HMC consisted of two industrial units: the Mechanical Works that was completed in the late 1960s, and the Foundry and Forge Works completed in the late 1970s.[72] It became a major source of capital goods and played an important role in the industrial development of the country. By the 1970s, the HMC had started the production of rollers, vibrating rollers, sugar and cement plants, Pakistani-designed industrialist boilers, and cranes, amongst other products.[73]

The exchange of visits of top-level leadership between China and Pakistan continued. In November 1970, General Yahya Khan visited China where he received an elaborate and colourful reception, equivalent to the one given to Ayub during the mid-sixties. Yahya held long and 'cordial' conversations with Zhou En-lai.[74] Although it was a goodwill visit, it came in the wake of important developments and had particular objectives. Yahya wanted to procure Chinese arms in the face of deteriorating Indo-Pakistan relations as the USSR continued to supply arms to India, and US arms to Pakistan had been hit by sanctions. Pakistan also wished to 'prevent any possible thaw in Sino-Indian relations'.[75] During Yahya's visit, China wrote off economic loans, provided assistance for Pakistan's fourth five-year economic plan, and signed agreements for military equipment. China supported Pakistan's position vis-à-vis India on the Kashmir dispute and on the distribution of the Ganges water, and assured Islamabad of its support for the territorial integrity and national sovereignty of Pakistan. In return, Pakistan supported China's case for the UN seat as well as its Indo-China and nuclear policies. Both sides extended solidarity towards the Afro-Asian nations and the Palestinian people.[76] More importantly, it was during this visit that Yahya personally passed on Nixon's secret message to the top Chinese leadership to start diplomatic discussions between the US and China.[77] Afterwards, relations between China and Pakistan seemed to return to their pre-Cultural Revolution phase.

THE 'GRAND ASSIGNMENT': PAKISTAN'S ROLE IN SINO-US RAPPROCHEMENT

Pakistan played an important role in facilitating initial contacts between China and the US. After the establishment of its entente with China, Pakistan asked Beijing to allow it to play a mediatory role between the two estranged powers. Since Pakistan had good relations with the US, it believed it could facilitate the normalisation process. However, at that time, China showed a lukewarm response to this idea. A few years later, the US invaded Vietnam in 1965, which raised China's concern as hostilities could expand up to its territory. To prevent a direct conflict with the US, China approached Pakistan. In a meeting with Ayub in April 1965, Chinese premier, Zhou En-lai, asked him to convey his message to the US. The message could not be sent on time as Ayub Khan's planned visit to the US was postponed at the behest of the American President. China's choice of Pakistan as a mediator showed Beijing's confidence in Islamabad. As an observer noted, 'Beijing's decision to entrust Pakistan with "signalling" the PRC's deterrence bespeaks the degree to which Pakistan served to benefit the PRC's larger goal of avoiding unnecessary hostilities and defending the Third World from imperialism.'[78]

Later in the late 1960s, the US approached Pakistan for a similar role. This successful mediation paved the way for the secret visit of National Security Adviser Henry Kissinger to China in 1971, the first by any US official since the establishment of the PRC. In February 1972, the US president, Richard Nixon, visited China and in January 1979, China and the US established full diplomatic relations.[79] The normalisation of Sino-US ties changed the dynamics of the Cold War. During the 1980s, both the sides cooperated closely with each other to defeat the Soviets in Afghanistan. Pakistan could work as a broker because it enjoyed the confidence of both China and the US. According to Barnds, 'China's approval of Pakistan's foreign policy was a key factor in the US decision to approach Peking via Islamabad.'[80] Earlier, the US had used other channels to initiate a dialogue with China without much success.[81]

During his visit to Pakistan in August 1969, President Richard Nixon held a ninety-minute, one-on-one meeting with Yahya and asked him to act as a broker. It was reported that Yahya looked nervous before the meeting but he emerged beaming.[82] Pakistani officials waiting outside the meeting room assumed that Nixon might have 'agreed to Pakistan's frantic plea for military supplies'. Nobody could imagine that Yahya was given the 'grand assignment' to act as 'courier' to normalise relations between China and the US. According to Choudhury, 'Pakistan was greatly delighted to have this opportunity as the Sino-Pakistan relationship was not only approved by the United States but the US President sought to utilise it for improving ties with Beijing.' At that time, Pakistan was the main non-Communist country which had cordial and intimate relations with both China and the US.[83]

The modus operandi adopted was secretive. The Chinese leadership sent sealed messages to Pakistan via its ambassador in Islamabad, Zhang Tong, who directly handed them over to Yahya. Yahya prepared hand-written notes, doubled-sealed them, and sent them directly to Henry Kissinger via Pakistan's ambassador to the US. Both the ambassadors involved were not authorised to open the messages.[84] Yahya personally conveyed messages to top leaders during his visits to the US and China in October and November 1970 respectively. He did the job 'most conscientiously and with the utmost secrecy'. The level of secrecy could be measured from the fact that neither Pakistan's Ministry of Foreign Affairs nor the US State Department were informed.[85] Once all preliminary work was done, Henry Kissinger undertook a tour of Asian countries in July 1971. During his stay in Pakistan, Kissinger made a classified visit to China on a PIA plane, while the media reported that he was ill and resting at a Pakistani hill resort. In China, Kissinger held talks with Zhou En-lai and made arrangements for Nixon's visit which took place in February 1972.[86]

Pakistan's role in the rapprochement helped strengthen its own relations with both China and the US, but irked the Soviets considerably. The Sino-US normalisation was perceived in New Delhi and Moscow as a Pakistan-China-US nexus against them, and led Moscow and New Delhi to upgrade their ties to a strategic level. In August 1971, both signed the Indo-Soviet Treaty of Friendship and Cooperation containing a defence clause. Article IX of the Treaty stated, 'In the event of either being subjected to an attack or a threat thereof, the High Contracting Parties shall immediately enter into mutual consultations in order to remove such threat and to take appropriate effective measures to ensure peace and the security of their countries.'[87] This Treaty was later adapted to form the text of the Indo-Bangladeshi Treaty of Friendship, Cooperation, and Peace signed in March 1972. The Indo-Soviet Treaty might have influenced India's decision to intervene in the East Pakistan crisis in December 1971.

PAKISTAN'S ROLE IN SINO-IRAN TIES

Almost parallel to Sino-US rapprochement, Pakistan played a role in establishing diplomatic ties between China and Iran in the early 1970s. Initially, general contacts between the two sides were quite limited. Pakistan's friendly ties with both Iran and China put it in the position to act as a mediator. During the 1960s, Pakistan had tried to establish contacts between the two sides. Then Pakistan's Foreign Minister, Zulfikar Ali Bhutto, tried to arrange a stopover of Zhou En-lai in Tehran but was unsuccessful. In January 1971, Bhutto made another attempt. He informed Beijing that the younger sister of the Shah of Iran, Princess Ashraf Pahlavi, wanted to visit China. With Mao's approval, Zhou En-lai issued an official invitation to Pahlavi who visited China in April 1971. On her way there, she made a two-day stopover in Pakistan and was accompanied by the wife of the head of Pakistan's Air Force for the rest of her journey. Within two weeks, Princess Fatema (another sibling of the Shah) also embarked on a visit to China. Although Pahlavi called it a personal tour, it achieved many political objectives. During her next visit to China in 1973, she made a stopover in Pakistan again where she was received and seen off by Bhutto.

Pakistan's good offices paved the way for the establishment of full Sino-Iranian diplomatic relations. On 16 August 1971, the Chinese and Iranian Ambassadors to Pakistan signed an agreement to institute diplomatic ties between the two sides. Iran recognised the PRC as the legitimate representative of the Chinese people. In return, China supported Iran in its struggle to protect its national interests. Later, Iran used the Chinese channel to convey its concerns to Pakistan over Islamabad's support for the Sunni sect of Islamic militants in Afghanistan.[88]

CHINA AND THE INDO-PAKISTAN WAR OF 1971

From 1970–71, the political situation in Pakistan deteriorated. During the 1970 general elections, the Awami League led by Sheikh Mujibur Rahman won a sweeping majority in East Pakistan but could not win a single seat in West Pakistan. On the other hand, the Pakistan People's Party (PPP), led by Zulfikar Ali Bhutto, won a majority in West Pakistan but could not get a single seat in the east wing. Election results further polarised the political parties which failed to agree on a power sharing formula. This pushed the country towards civil war.[89] In March 1971, Mujibur Rahman declared East Pakistan independent, calling it Bangladesh.[90] Yahya called in the military to control the situation. The excessive use of force by the armed forces, however, closed the door of political reconciliation, leading to the dismemberment of Pakistan.

Yahya's military operation in East Pakistan put the Chinese in an awkward situation.[91] Ideologically, China was in favour of revolutionary movements in Afro-Asian nations. Nevertheless, in the case of East Pakistan, this policy could harm China's relations with its ally, Pakistan, hence giving a free hand to its rivals, India and the Soviet Union.[92] China was faced with the dilemma of how to handle the crisis. On account of this contradiction, Beijing's public views differed from its private ones. Publicly, China condemned Indian actions and assured Pakistan of its support, yet not as categorically as it had done so in 1965.

Privately, however, it urged Yahya to find a political settlement with the Bengalis.[93]

China's cautious policy towards Pakistan was obvious from the fact that it took over two weeks for Zhou En-lai to respond to Yahya's March 1971 military action.[94] Zhou termed the situation in East Pakistan as Pakistan's internal matter and assured Islamabad that 'should Indian expansionists dare to launch aggression against Pakistan, the Chinese government and people would, as always, firmly support the government and people of Pakistan in their struggle to safeguard their sovereignty and independence'.[95] China continued providing diplomatic support, economic assistance, and the supply of arms to Pakistan. However, it did not make any promise for active military involvement. In May 1971, China provided a US$20 million interest-free loan, not tied to the purchase of Chinese goods, to provide economic relief to Pakistan.[96]

In November 1971, shortly before the outbreak of the war, Bhutto visited Beijing as Yahya's special emissary. Again, China's public and private gestures were different. Publicly, it assured Pakistan of 'resolute' support but privately it pressured Pakistan to find a 'rational solution', and disapproved of military action and atrocities. China reportedly presented to Bhutto a list of pro-Beijing, Bengali leaders who were killed during the military operations. Bhutto could not get Chinese assurance of intervention in case of an Indian attack. There were reports that Pakistan sought a defence pact with the PRC similar to the Indo-Soviet Treaty but China did not show any willingness to enter into an agreement of this nature. In addition, China indicated its inability to meet Pakistan's extraordinary arms needs to repel an expected Indian attack, though routine arms supplies to Pakistan continued. 'In substance', according to Mehrotra, 'China appears to have urged Pakistan to avoid war with India, and if that was not possible to confine it to as small an area as possible.'[97] Contrary to this, the Pakistani elite portrayed a different outcome of the visit. Bhutto termed it a complete success with tangible results while Yahya announced that the Chinese would come to help Pakistan as much as possible if there was war with India.[98]

On 3 December 1971, a full-fledged war between India and Pakistan broke out which was fought in both East and West Pakistan. Verbally, China strongly favoured Pakistan. For instance, on 4 December, China's representative in the UN, Huang Hua, termed the Indian attack on Pakistan as 'naked aggression' and deplored the Indian stand that the attack on East Pakistan was in self-defence as 'sheer gangster logic'. He also reassured Pakistan of China's support.[99] The UN became a battleground for the Chinese and Soviet diplomats in support of their allies. On 5 December, China presented a resolution in the Security Council (SC)—the first since its membership—urging an immediate ceasefire.[100] China also blocked a move intended to invite a representative from East Pakistan to attend the SC proceedings. Moscow vetoed all resolutions until India had consolidated its victory over Pakistan.[101]

Pakistan faced a humiliating defeat in which its eastern wing separated from West Pakistan and became an independent country, Bangladesh. India held about 93,000 Pakistanis as Prisoners-of-War (PoW), and threatened many of them with war crime trials. India also captured 5,000 square miles of territory in West Pakistan. The war severely hit Pakistan's economy, weakened its military, and degraded the country's morale.

During the 1971 war, China's support of Pakistan was largely confined to a diplomatic stance, void of any posturing of physical involvement as was seen during the 1965 war. A number of factors explained China's limited and cautious role in this war. Firstly, it was hard to approve of Pakistani authorities' gross mishandling of the East Pakistan crisis. Civilian casualties caused by the use of force were so high that it was difficult to defend them. Secondly, endorsing Pakistan against a 'Bangladeshi freedom movement' was in sharp contrast to China's revolutionary ideology under which the PRC had been supporting oppressed people against authoritarian regimes. Thirdly, 'The Chinese military was in a state of turmoil' since the Lin Biao incident in which his plane crashed in the Mongolian desert in ostensibly a 'coup attempt'. Mao had removed 'virtually the entire high command'. 'Over a thousand senior Chinese military officials were purged, the air force was grounded, the PLA itself was in disgrace…' yet China had to provide military support to North Vietnam.[102] On top of that, the Soviet Union became a direct party to the conflict. Article IX of the Indo-Soviet Treaty of Peace, Friendship, and Cooperation, signed on 9 August 1971, provided India with direct Soviet backing. The Article stipulated, 'In the event of either being subjected to an attack or a threat thereof, the High Contracting Parties shall immediately enter into mutual consultations in order to remove such threat and to take appropriate effective measures to ensure peace and the security of their countries.'[103] The Treaty came amidst tense Sino-Soviet relations since the Ussuri River crisis (1969). Forty-four Soviet divisions faced China along its border. Beijing's fear of retaliation from Moscow, possibly a nuclear one, seemed real. During his visit to China, Bhutto had realised that China was making grand preparations against such an attack.[104] Although China had gained the permanent seat of the UNSC by replacing Taiwan a few months earlier, it had no experience in regards to using this platform to support its ally. Under these constraints, China's role was confined to rhetoric.

POST-1971 SINO-PAKISTANI RELATIONS

During and after the 1971 crisis, the Pakistani leadership complained about the unreliability of the US-led defence pacts which deepened the schism in Islamabad-Washington ties. Bhutto, who assumed power as President of a truncated Pakistan, stated that the US had repeated its 1965 policy. Instead of helping Pakistan, it imposed sanctions before the outbreak of the 1971 war.[105] He termed the US policy as 'pressure and interference' and subject to the whims of various US administrations.[106] He rejected the claim that there was a US 'tilt' towards Pakistan during the course of war and referred to Secretary of State William Rogers' statement that the US would not interfere in the subcontinent's affairs. In Bhutto's opinion, Rogers' statement gave India the necessary assurance to carry out aggression against Pakistan.[107] The early recognition of Bangladesh by the US further disappointed Pakistan.[108] As soon as the members of the Commonwealth and SEATO began accepting Bangladesh as a separate state, Pakistan withdrew from these organisations.[109]

Bhutto felt betrayed, and thought that US intervention could have prevented India from dismembering Pakistan. After assuming power, he further revised Pakistan's foreign policy to reduce dependence on the US and the West. He introduced a new concept of 'bilateralism' under which Pakistan tried to maintain relative neutrality in the Cold War. Pakistan emphasised the unity of the Third World, and attempted to maintain close relations with Islamic countries. Overall, Pakistan's relations with the US and the Western world declined during the Bhutto period and the initial years of the Zia regime. Consequently, it pushed Pakistan closer to the Chinese side.

Pakistan's defeat during the 1971 war had tilted the regional balance of power decisively in favour of India, which suited neither

China nor Pakistan. As a result of its loss, Pakistan was reduced in size and its former eastern wing, after becoming an independent country, Bangladesh, adopted pro-Indian and pro-Soviet policies. 'The remainder of the small states in the region', as Sutter wrote, 'were cowed by India's demonstration of power during the war against Pakistan, and were unwilling to help Beijing challenge India and its Soviet backers in the region'.[110] Pakistan was the only country left which could still resist Soviet or Indian influence in the region.[111] Against this backdrop, China continued its support of Pakistan in the post-1971 crisis. It extended moral, political, and economic assistance, and provided reasonably large quantity of military weapons to replenish Pakistan's war losses. On a diplomatic front, it supported Pakistan's position on the issue of Bangladesh's entry into the UN, the return of Pakistani PoWs, and the territory captured by India during the war.[112]

In a message of felicitation to the new President of Pakistan, Zulfikar Ali Bhutto, Zhou En-lai appreciated Pakistan's 'heroic' struggle against 'naked Indian aggression' and reaffirmed China's support. It was reported that Beijing was the major driving force behind Bhutto's decision to release Mujibur Rahman.[113] In January 1972, Bhutto congratulated Qi Pengfei on becoming Foreign Minister of the PRC, and thanked China for its help in the recent crisis.

From 31 January to 2 February 1972, Bhutto visited China which was his second visit abroad since assumption of power. He was accompanied by the heads of the three armed forces.[114] To support Pakistan's moribund economy, China converted four loans worth US$110 million into grants and deferred the payment of another loan of US$200 million from ten to twenty years.[115] China stated that relations between the two erstwhile wings—East Pakistan, now

Bangladesh, and West Pakistan—should be established through negotiations between the elected leaders, without foreign intervention. The PRC demanded the implementation of the UN resolutions, withdrawal of Indian forces from Pakistani territory, and repatriation of the PoWs stranded in India. It warned India and Bangladesh that without resolving disputes with Pakistan, Bangladesh could not enter the UN.[116] Bhutto's visit was followed by a series of exchanges on both sides.

After the 1971 war, Pakistan's defence capabilities, which were substantially weakened, were restored with China's help. According to Vertzberger, 'China took responsibility for rehabilitating the Pakistan army and equipping it with the most modern weapon systems it had available—all at no cost to Pakistan.'[117] In the post-1971 war period, China became 'Pakistan's main military aid supplier, re-equipping all three branches of the Pakistani armed forces'.[118] According to an Indian source, China in particular helped Pakistan strengthen the army division based along the Line of Control in Kashmir.[119] The US Embassy in Islamabad noted China's increased military assistance to Pakistan. In a report sent to Washington, it maintained that Pakistan's military capability was not only fully restored to the pre-war level but also improved in some areas, notably air defence and ground forces.[120] By 1971–72, China delivered to Pakistan an 175 F-6 aircraft,[121] four bomber aircraft (I1-28/Beagle), four trainer aircraft, and twelve patrol crafts. For Pakistan's ground forces, China provided 750 T-59 tanks, 100 light tanks (50 T-63 and 50 T-60), 650 towed guns (400 M-30 122mm, 50 ML-20 152mm, and 200 D-74 122mm), and various fire control radars. By the start of the 1970s, China had supplied 25 per cent of Pakistan's entire tank force, 33 per cent of Pakistan Air Force's 270 planes, 65 per cent of all interceptor-bombers, and 90 per cent of its first-line modern fighters.[122]

In 1972, China signed a protocol to build a repair centre for the Chinese-origin F-6 aircraft in Pakistan. After the 1971 war with India, the Pakistan Air Force needed an aircraft repair facility. According to a report, when Pakistan approached the PRC with this need in mind, 'the Chinese not only agreed in principle but also offered a more advanced facility than had been requested, including full overhaul and rebuild capabilities.' China provided complete economic, technical, and technological facility to establish the centre.[123] This centre became the centrepiece of Pakistan Aeronautical Complex (PAC), Kamra, which in the following decades not only repaired and overhauled but also started manufacturing aircraft such as JF-17.

Generally, there was an increase in high-profile military visits between the two countries. In January 1973, Pakistan's Chief of Army Staff visited China and a senior PLA delegation came to Pakistan in January 1974. Defence relations were also discussed during Bhutto's three visits to China from 1972–76.

CHINA'S ROLE IN BANGLADESH'S ENTRY INTO THE UN

China's help was particularly helpful during Bangladesh's request for UN membership, which it applied for in August 1972. Pakistan approached China to stall the move until the return of their PoWs and Pakistani territory that had been captured by India during the war. Beijing 'obliged' Islamabad and blocked Bangladesh's entry into the UN by using its first-ever veto.[124] The Chinese representative to the UN, Huang Hua, stated in the UN that Bangladesh's UN membership was 'inseparably' linked to the implementation of UN General Assembly Resolution 2793 (XXVI) and Security Council

Resolution 307 (1971). He added that Indian threats to try Pakistani PoWs for war crimes were a gross violation of those resolutions.[125] The PRC also blocked Bangladesh's admission to other UN bodies.[126]

However, it must be noted that China was not totally opposed to Bangladesh's UN membership. Beijing stated that its decision was based on 'existing circumstances'; the implementation of UN resolutions and normalisation of relations between Pakistan, India, and Bangladesh.[127] China's actual policy towards Bangladesh's entry into the UN was clear from the statement made by a Chinese official in the United Nations General Assembly (UNGA):

> China's stand for postponing the consideration of this question does not mean that we are fundamentally opposed to the admission of 'Bangladesh' into the United Nations. China cherishes friendly sentiments for the people of East Bengal and has no prejudice against Mr Mujibur Rahman. We stand for postponing the consideration of this question, in order to promote reconciliation among the parties concerned and the implementation of the United Nations resolutions, which are the very immediate concern.[128]

China's stance not only supported its ally but also helped resolve issues between three countries. In fact, a stable subcontinent was higher in China's interests than any other big power. The PRC welcomed the India-Pakistan Simla Agreement of July 1972 and the Delhi Pact of August 1973. Similarly, China supported Pakistan's decision to recognise Bangladesh at the Organisation of Islamic Cooperation (OIC) summit held in Lahore in February 1974. China allowed Bangladesh's entry into the UN after Pakistan had established diplomatic relations with it.[129]

BHUTTO'S SECOND VISIT TO CHINA

The main objectives of Bhutto's second visit to China in May 1974 were to: inform China about the outcome of the OIC summit held in Lahore in which Pakistan had recognised Bangladesh, talk about Indo-Pakistan relations, and discuss matters of mutual concern. By this time, major post-war issues, such as the withdrawal of Indian troops from Pakistan's territory and the repatriation of Pakistani PoWs, had been settled. China expressed its satisfaction at the normalisation of the situation in the subcontinent.[130] In a joint communiqué, Pakistan supported China on Taiwan, and China reiterated its support to Pakistan in its 'just struggle in defence of national independence, state sovereignty'. Notably, there was no reference to 'territorial integrity', which in the past was part of the Chinese rhetoric. Beijing also extended support to the Kashmiri people for their right to self-determination.[131] An analyst stated that China's satisfaction at the positive developments in South Asia indicated its intentions to normalise its own relations with India and Bangladesh.[132] However, this process was affected by India's nuclear test and the accession of Sikkim in 1974.

NUCLEARISATION OF SOUTH ASIA

On 18 May 1974, shortly after Bhutto's visit to China, India successfully conducted an underground 'peaceful nuclear test' that added a new dimension to South Asian security. Pakistan already lacked a parity in conventional weapons with India; the nuclear test changed the balance of power decisively in favour of India. With fresh memories of Indian 'aggression' in 1971, Islamabad termed the Indian test a first step towards acquiring nuclear weapons. In an address to the nation the next day, Bhutto assured his people that Pakistan was determined not to be intimidated by the Indian threat. His country would not compromise on national security, the right to self-determination for the people of Kashmir, or accept Indian hegemony. He added that from the day he assumed office, he was conscious of the 'dire necessity' to have a coherent nuclear programme.[133] He dispatched his envoy, Agha Shahi, to consult with Beijing. Upon his return, Agha Shahi stated that China had offered 'full and absolute support to Pakistan against foreign aggression and interference including nuclear blackmail'.[134]

China also reacted negatively to the Indian test, though in a far milder way. A commentary published in *Peking Review* condemned Indian nuclear ambitions, demanded the universal elimination of nuclear weapons, and reaffirmed China's support for Pakistan.[135] To counter the Indian threat, Bhutto devised a two-pronged strategy. First, he put forth the proposal that South Asia be declared a Nuclear Free Zone. Second, he clandestinely initiated Pakistan's own nuclear programme. Although Pakistan received Chinese support on both initiatives, it was not as forthcoming as the Pakistani government and media had expected. Furthermore, some quarters in Pakistan sought China's nuclear umbrella against the Indian nuclear threat but Beijing did not make any commitment to this end.

Pakistan also raised the issue of the Indian nuclear test at the Foreign Ministers' conference of the OIC held in Kuala Lumpur in June 1974. The participants supported Islamabad's proposal that the international community should provide guarantees and security to all non-nuclear states.[136] A commentary in the *People's Daily* endorsed the outcome of the OIC session in the following words:

> The Chinese government and people firmly support Pakistan and other countries in their just struggle to safeguard national independence and

> state sovereignty and oppose aggression and intervention from outside, including nuclear blackmail and threat... We hold that no policy of nuclear blackmail and threat by any country can cow the people of various countries. Countries which try to carry out expansion and aggression by resorting to a nuclear blackmail policy will be lifting a rock only to drop it on their own feet and will suffer ignominious defeat.[137]

China's more unambiguous support was directed towards Pakistan's proposal for the creation of a South Asia Nuclear Free Zone, which was first tabled at the IAEA forum in September 1972. After India's nuclear test, in October 1974, Pakistan presented the proposal at the UN forum where it received China's support. Qiao Guanhua, Chinese representative to the UN, termed the Indian nuclear test and the 'occupation' of Sikkim another overt act of expansionism, perpetrated by the Indian government after dismembering Pakistan through armed aggression. He stated that Pakistan's proposal was 'entirely reasonable' and gave his government's 'firm support'.[138] In April 1975, the visiting Chinese vice-premier, Li Xiannian, reiterated China's support of: South Asian peoples against hegemonism and expansionism, Pakistan's proposal for a Nuclear-Weapon-Free Zone (NWFZ) in South Asia, the right to self-determination for the people living in Kashmir, Sikh resistance against naked annexation by India, the King of Nepal declaring his country a zone of peace, and the Sri Lankan government making the Indian Ocean a zone of peace.[139]

BHUTTO'S THIRD VISIT

In May 1976, Bhutto went to China for the third time. By then, Pakistan had clandestinely started its nuclear programme, which troubled Islamabad's ties with Washington. Pakistan's nuclear programme was labelled an 'Islamic bomb', and Henry Kissinger reportedly warned Bhutto that the US would make a 'horrible example of him' if he continued with it. The US had already started legislation against nuclear proliferation in the form of the Symington Amendment adopted in June 1976. Against this backdrop, Bhutto's discussions with the Chinese leaders were focused on Pakistan's development of its nuclear programme, requesting China's help with it, and the unity of the Third World. As reported, the two sides signed a nuclear agreement, apparently for peaceful purposes but, which most probably contributed to Pakistan's weapons programme. Bhutto later referred to the agreement as 'one of the most important achievements of his presidency'.[140]

The visit was particularly significant from the defence point of view. Top military leadership—including General Mohammad Sharif, the Chairman of the Joint Chief of Army Staff Committee, and Air Chief Marshal Zulfiqar Ali Khan, Chief of Air Staff—also accompanied Bhutto. It was reported that Bhutto convinced Chairman Hua Guofeng to consider Pakistan's long-term military requirements in China's national strategy. China's arms transfer to Pakistan, from 1966–80, exceeded US$630 million. This was over one-third of the total arms transfers to Pakistan in that period.[141]

During the visit, Bhutto adopted a hard stance against the US and its threat of sanctions. He criticised neo-colonist designs, demanded an equitable international economic order, and urged the unity of Third World countries.[142] The joint communiqué supported: Nepal's proposal for making the country a zone of peace, Sri Lanka's proposal to make the Indian Ocean a zone of peace, and Pakistan's proposal to declare South Asia a NWFZ. China appreciated the Pakistan-Bangladesh rapprochement while Pakistan welcomed the establishment of diplomatic relations between China and Bangladesh. Islamabad extended its 'full support' for Chinese efforts to 'liberate' Taiwan. However, Pakistan failed to get traditional Chinese support on the Kashmir issue.[143] For the first time since the mid-1960s, China did not express its support for the right to self-determination for the Kashmiri people. This indicated a change in China's Kashmir policy and its veiled desire to normalise relations with India.

1976: END OF AN ERA IN CHINA

In 1976, two founding leaders of the PRC, Chairman Mao Zedong and Zhou En-lai, passed away. Pakistan announced a week-long mourning period on both occasions while its parliament passed condolence resolutions.[144] Following the deaths of Zhou and Mao, many in Pakistan expressed concern that the Sino-Pakistan relations, which were particularly guided by these leaders, might cool down in future. However, Prime Minister Bhutto ruled out such speculations. In an interview with a foreign journalist, Bhutto stated:

> My assessment of Pakistan-China relations derives from the fact that these relations are not, and never have been, based on changing expediencies. It was not a fortuitous set of circumstances but a natural recognition of geostrategic realities that helped their establishment. The sentiments of mutual support and sympathy, following from certain shared principles, infused warmth and cordiality into the relationship. The policy of bilateralism that we follow insulates this friendship from any warping pressures.[145]

PAKISTAN'S NEW MILITARY RULER AND RELATIONS WITH CHINA

Bhutto's assessment that Pakistan's ties with China would remain stable regardless of internal and external changes proved to be correct. The relations remained unaffected, despite the change of leadership in both countries. In July 1977, the Pakistani Chief of Army Staff General, Mohammad Zia ul-Haq, toppled Bhutto's government and imposed martial law. The Sino-Pakistan relationship had already matured by this time; its continuity was not affected by the far-reaching changes of leadership in the two countries which serves as a testament to its deep roots.

Zia's choice of Agha Shahi as his adviser on foreign affairs further consolidated the relationship with China. Shahi had a long association with China and had already contributed to enhancing two-way ties in different capacities. After taking up his portfolio, until his resignation from Zia's cabinet in 1982, he made further contributions in this field. His rapport with Chinese officials helped him in his job.[146] Zia too had had opportunities to interact with Chinese officials prior to his coup.[147] After assuming power, he further expanded his contacts. At the start of his regime, Zia sent a number of messages of felicitation to Chinese leaders conveying to them his regime's desire to develop good relations as had existed under his predecessor. Within days of his military coup, Zia sent a message of felicitation to Deng Xiaoping welcoming his restoration to the post of vice-premier and head of the People's Liberation Army (PLA). A few months later, Zia sent another message congratulating Chinese leaders on their national day.[148] Zia's first formal contact with the Chinese officials in Pakistan took place in November 1977 when he inaugurated the new building which would house the Chinese embassy in Islamabad.[149]

After building sufficient rapport, it was in December 1977 when Zia embarked on his first visit to China, which was also his first foreign visit outside the Islamic world. According to an Indian analyst, this clearly showed the military regime's desire to continue the policy of maintaining close ties with China.[150] Deng Xiaoping personally went to the airport to receive Zia. This hospitality signalled that China, unlike many Western countries (which were perturbed at the imposition of martial law), regarded the change of government in Pakistan as an internal affair.

In a meeting with Zia, Deng admired Pakistan's spirit of defying brute force and 'standing like a rock' against those who wanted to establish hegemony in South Asia.[151] This was a thinly veiled reference to the Soviet Union and India, whose collaborative strategy facilitated the dismemberment of Pakistan in the Indo-Pakistan war of 1971. Zia reassured the continuation of Sino-Pakistan relations and thanked China for its invaluable support, which according to him enabled Pakistan to overcome 'insurmountable difficulties in the way of an honourable settlement'.[152] The visit provided relief to Zia's regime, which had been facing Western pressure due to his military coup, and helped in developing understanding between the new leadership of the two countries.[153] While commenting on the continuity of China's relations with a new military ruler in Pakistan, a Pakistani scholar observed:

> The Chinese response to developments in Pakistan provided yet another proof that Sino-Pakistan relations had matured into an 'all-weather friendships' [*sic*] not affected by shift in policies or change of personalities. Regardless of Bhutto's contribution in giving an ideological content to a political relationship and going beyond identity of perceptions on security in South Asia in sharing a worldview with

China, his removal from power did not inhibit the Chinese from doing business as usual with Zia ul-Haq's military regime in Pakistan.[154]

CONCLUSION

During the period in question, the Sino-Pakistan entente cordial developed and strengthened, partially due to the common hostility towards India. Both sides signed a number of agreements which expanded their cooperation, and readjusted their respective policies to accommodate each other's interests. Pakistan resumed its support for China's seat in the UN and ignored China's harsh policies towards its minorities, especially towards the Muslims in Xinjiang. China, on the other hand, backed Pakistan on the Kashmir and other Indo-Pakistan issues, and started providing considerable economic assistance. Importantly, military relations, which were almost non-existent until the early 1960s, began to take a central role in the relationship. China showed its commitment to Pakistan during the Indo-Pakistan wars of 1965 and 1971. The US arms embargo and the tenuous nature of US-Pakistan relations generally increased Pakistan's dependence on China. During the Cultural Revolution (1966–69), China went into self-imposed isolation while Pakistan made overtures towards the USSR. In the course of this period, the relationship witnessed neither any high nor any downturn. Pakistan's refusal to join the Soviet Asian Security Plan, and its role in Sino-US rapprochement, affected its ties with the USSR but considerably improved its alliance with China and the US. Moscow and New Delhi perceived the emerging relationship between the US, Pakistan, and China as a nexus against them. This led them to sign the Indo-Soviet treaty of friendship containing a military clause. Due to various factors, China provided limited and cautious help to Pakistan during the 1971 war. Most of China's help came after the war in terms of replenishing Pakistan's defence losses. The PRC started building economic and strategic infrastructures in Pakistan, such as roads, highways, the HMC, and the PAC. This indicated China's long-term interests in Pakistan. In their bilateral relations, there were frequent references to the unity of Third World countries and support for the revolutionary movements of Afro-Asian nations. However, such references only held symbolic importance. Parallel to growing ties with Pakistan, in the late 1960s, China showed its intention to improve ties with India. However, Sino-Indian normalisation was halted due to India's 'naked aggression' against Pakistan during the 1971 war, and then in 1974 through India's 'peaceful nuclear test' and the accession of Sikkim. These developments did not completely destroy Sino-Indian desires for the normalisation of their relations. In 1975, the PRC indicated that it would expand the nature of its relationship with South Asian countries, adopt a balanced policy towards Indo-Pakistan disputes, and restore relations with India. China and India finally resumed full ambassadorial-level relations in 1976. The Sino-Indian rapprochement further progressed with the advent of reformists in China. Meanwhile, China and Pakistan started cooperating in the nuclear sector, which entered a crucial stage in the following decade. China's management of its contradictory policies; rapprochement with India amidst continued support to Pakistan's nuclear and missile programme, and other aspects of the relationship have been discussed in the next chapter.

Notes

1. Z. A. Bhutto, 'Pakistan—and China?', *Survival*, vol. 5, no. 5 (September–October 1963), 222.
2. *Pakistan Times*, 18 and 21 July 1963.
3. Sujit Dutta, 'China and Pakistan: End of a "Special Relationship"', *China Report*, vol. 30, no. 125 (1994), 128.
4. Fazal-ur-Rehman, 'Pakistan's Relations with China', *Strategic Studies*, vol. XIX & XX, nos. 4 & 1 (Winter and Spring 1998), 66.
5. Mohammed Ahsen Chaudhri, *Pakistan and the Great Powers* (Karachi: Council for Pakistan Studies, 1970), 91–2.
6. Shaheen Akhtar, 'Pak-China Economic Relations: Forging Strategic Partnership in the 21st Century', *Regional Studies*, vol. XIX, no. 3 (Summer 2001), 47–8.
7. Wei Weikang, 'My Cultural Tour of Pakistan' in Lu Shulin (comp), *You and Us: Stories of China and Pakistan* (Beijing: China International Press, 2015), 130.
8. Chaudhri, *Pakistan and the Great Powers*, 91.
9. Akhtar, 'Pak-China Economic Relations', 47–8.
10. *Keesing's Contemporary Archives* (1965–66), 20811 & 21706 in Yaacov Vertzberger, 'The Political Economy of Sino-Pakistani Relations: Trade and Aid 1963–82', *Asian Survey*, vol. XXIII, no. 5 (May 1983), 643.
11. Chaudhri, *Pakistan and the Great Powers*, 91–2.
12. Akhtar, 'Pak-China Economic Relations', 45.
13. Chaudhri, *Pakistan and the Great Powers*, 92–3.
14. 'China-Pakistan joint communiqué on premier Zhou En-lai's visit to Pakistan, 23 February 1964', R. K. Jain, *China South Asian Relations: 1947–1980*, vol. 2 (New Delhi: Radiant Publishers, 1981), 46–7.
15. G. W. Choudhury, 'Reflections on Sino-Pakistan Relations', *Pacific Community*, vol. 7, issue 2 (January 1976), 255.
16. 'Zhou En-lai's press conference in Dhaka, 25 February 1964', in Jain, *China South Asian Relations*, vol. 2, 49.
17. Liu Shaoqi candidly disclosed this to Bhutto in 1963. See Choudhury, 'Reflections on Sino-Pakistan Relations', 251.
18. 'China-Pakistan joint communiqué, 4 March 1963', in Jain, *China South Asian Relations*, vol. 2, 39.
19. For details, see 'China-Pakistan joint communiqué on premier Zhou En-lai's visit to Pakistan, 23 February 1964', 46–7 in ibid.
20. Choudhury, 'Reflections on Sino-Pakistan Relations', 254–5.
21. Christopher Tang, 'Beyond India: The Utility of Sino-Pakistani Relations in Chinese Foreign Policy, 1962–1965', *Cold War International History Project*, Working Paper no. 64 (November 2012), 21–2.

22. 'Ayub's reply to Zhou En-lai's letter of 17 October 1964, 2 December 1964', in Jain, *China South Asian Relations*, vol. 2, 51.
23. 'Premier Zhou En-lai's Report on the Work of the Government at the First Session of the Third National People's Congress, 21–22 December 1964', in Ibid. 51–2.
24. Chaudhri, *Pakistan and the Great Powers*, 92–3.
25. 'China-Pakistan joint communiqué, 7 March 1965', ibid. 52–4.
26. O. N. Mehrotra, 'Sino-Pak Relations: A Review', *China Report* (September–December 1976), 59.
27. Choudhury, 'Reflections on Sino-Pakistan Relations', 255.
28. Ibid. 256.
29. Mehrotra, 'Sino-Pak Relations: A Review', 59.
30. Anwar Hussain Syed, *China & Pakistan: Diplomacy of an Entente Cordiale* (Amherst: University of Massachusetts Press, 1974), 94–5.
31. Interview of Air Marshal (retired) Nur Khan published in the daily *Dawn* (10 May 1989).
32. Mushahid Hussain, *Pakistan's Politics: The Zia Years* (Lahore: Progressive Publishers, 1990), 9.
33. National Assembly Debates, vol. III, no. 4 (21 December 1973), 204.
34. Yaacov Vertzberger, *The Enduring Entente: Sino-Pakistan Relations, 1960–1980* (New York: Praeger, 1983), 83.
35. Mohammed Ahsen Chaudhri, 'Pakistan's Relations with the Soviet Union', *Asian Survey*, vol. 6, no. 9 (September 1966), 496–7.
36. Devin T. Hagerty, 'China and Pakistan: Strains in the Relationship', *Current History*, vol. 101, no. 656 (September 2002), 285.
37. Interview with Akram Zaki (former Pakistani Ambassador to China), Islamabad, April 2011.
38. 'Statement by the spokesman of the Ministry of External Affairs of India on 7 May 1965', K. Arif (ed.), Pakistan's Foreign Policy: Indian Perspective (Lahore: Vanguard, 1984), 65.
39. Ahmad Faruqui, 'China card could yet trump Musharraf', *Asia Times* (25 May 2002), <http://www.atimes.com/ind-pak/DE25Df02.html>.
40. Choudhury, 'Reflections on Sino-Pakistan Relations', 258.
41. *Peking Review* (10 September 1965), 6.
42. Syed, *China & Pakistan*, 111.
43. Choudhury, 'Reflections on Sino-Pakistan Relations', 258–9.
44. *Peking Review* (24 September 1965), 10.
45. Mushahid Hussain, 'Pakistan-China Defence Cooperation: An Enduring Relationship', *International Defense Review*, vol. 26, no. 2 (February 1993), 108.
46. Choudhury, 'Reflections on Sino-Pakistan Relations', 259.

47. Samina Yasmin, *Pakistan's Relations with China 1947–1979* (Islamabad: Institute of Strategic Studies, 1980), 22.
48. Choudhury, 'Reflections on Sino-Pakistan Relations', 260.
49. Ibid. 260.
50. Interview with Akram Zaki and a Chinese scholar, April 2011 and January 2014.
51. Andrew Small, *The China-Pakistan Axis: Asia's New Geopolitics* (London: C. Hurst & Co., 2015), 17.
52. Interview with Professor Tahir Amin, Quaid-i-Azam University, Islamabad, November 2013.
53. Khalid Mahmud, 'Sino-Pakistan Relations: An "All-Weather" Friendship', *Regional Studies*, vol. XIX, no. 3 (Summer 2001), 10.
54. Mehrotra, 'Sino-Pak Relations: A Review', 60.
55. *Peking Review*, No. 3 (14 January 1966), 3–4 in Mehrotra, 'Sino-Pak Relations: A Review', 60.
56. Mahmud, 'Sino-Pakistan Relations', 11.
57. *Peking Review*, no. 6 (4 February 1966), 10–12.
58. Choudhury, 'Reflections on Sino-Pakistan Relations', 261.
59. Mahmud, 'Sino-Pakistan Relations', 11.
60. Mehrotra, 'Sino-Pak Relations: A Review', 63. Also Rizvi, *Pakistan and the Geostrategic Environment*, 119.
61. Choudhury, *India, Pakistan, Bangladesh and the Major Powers*, 65.
62. Hasan-Askari Rizvi, *Pakistan and the Geostrategic Environment: A Study of Foreign Policy* (London: Macmillan, 1993), 119.
63. Ibid. 67–8.
64. *Peking Review*, no. 30 (25 July 1969), 8–9 in Mehrotra, 'Sino-Pak Relations: A Review', 63.
65. According to Mehrotra, during the Cultural Revolution, Sino-Pakistan relations were 'only preserved and not strengthened' while 'trade continued but did not expand'. Mehrotra, 'Sino-Pak Relations: A Review', 62.
66. Vertzberger, *The Enduring Entente*, 46.
67. The absence of a substantial overseas Chinese community and a Communist Party in Pakistan was a major reason for the Sino-Pakistan ties not being affected during the Cultural Revolution.
68. John W. Garver, 'China's Kashmir Policies', *Indian Review*, vol. 3, no. 1 (January 2004), 7.
69. Mehrotra, 'Sino-Pak Relations: A Review', 62–3.
70. 'Karakoram Highway', *Beijing Review*, vol. 21, no. 23 (9 June 1978), 42–3.
71. Vertzberger, 'The Political Economy of Sino-Pakistan Relations', *Asian Survey*, vol. XXIII, no. 5 (May 1983), 643.

72. Hussain Ahmad Siddiqui, 'Need to Restructure Heavy Mechanical Complex', *Business Recorder* (17 January 2007).
73. *Peking Review*, vol. 20, no. 12 (18 March 1977), 27.
74. G. W. Choudhury, *India, Pakistan, Bangladesh and the Major Powers: Politics of a Divided Subcontinent* (London: Collier Macmillan Publishers, 1975), 195.
75. Mehrotra, 'Sino-Pakistan Relations: A Review', 64–5.
76. For the text of joint communiqué see *Peking Review*, no. 47 (20 November 1970), 8–9.
77. F. S. Aijazuddin, *From a Head, Through a Head, to a Head: The Secret Channel between the US and China through Pakistan* (Karachi: Oxford University Press, 2000), 40.
78. Christopher Tang, 'Beyond India: The Utility of Sino-Pakistani Relations in Chinese Foreign Policy, 1962–1965', *Cold War International History Project*, Working Paper no. 64 (November 2012), W. J. Barnds, *India, Pakistan, and the Great Powers*, 24–5.
79. S. M. Hali, 'Pak-US vs Pak-China Relations' (14 July 2010), <http://www.pkcolumns.com/2010/07/14/pak-us-vs-pak-china-relations-by-s-m-hali/>. Accessed on 22 March 2016.
80. William J. Barnds, 'China's Relations with Pakistan: Durability Amidst Discontinuity', *The China Quarterly*, no. 63 (September 1975), 482.
81. Sultan Muhammed Khan, 'Pakistani Geopolitics: The Diplomatic Perspective', *International Security*, vol. 5, no. 1 (Summer 1980), 28.
82. Yahya was reported to have said before the meeting, 'I should have an aide; after all, I am a General. I need an expert'. Choudhury, 'Reflections on Sino-Pakistan Relations', 264.
83. Ibid. 264.
84. Ibid. 265–6.
85. Barnds, 'China's Relations with Pakistan', 482.
86. Mehrotra, 'Sino-Pak Relations: A Review', 13.
87. See full text of 'Indo-Soviet Treaty of Friendship and Cooperation' at *Mainstream Weekly*, <http://www.mainstreamweekly.net/article2950.html>.
88. For instance, during Pakistan's Prime Minister Benazir Bhutto's visit to China in February 1989, Iranian Ambassador to China, Alaeddin Broujerdi, met her to discuss the issue of Pakistan-based Afghan guerrillas' support to those in Iran.
89. For a detailed account of the results of the 1970 elections, see G. W. Choudhury, *The Last Days of United Pakistan* (London: C. Hurst & Co., 1974), 106–36.
90. *Pakistan Times* (Lahore, 27 March 1971).
91. Mahmud, 'Sino-Pakistan Relations', 13.
92. Mehrotra, 'Sino-Pakistan Relations: A Review', 65.
93. Mahmud, 'Sino-Pakistan Relations', 13–14.

94. Mehrotra, 'Sino-Pak Relations: A Review', 65.
95. *Keesing's Contemporary Archives* (1971–72), 24629.
96. Mehrotra, 'Sino-Pak Relations: A Review', 65.
97. Ibid. 66. Also see Choudhury, 'Reflections on Sino-Pakistan Relations', 267.
98. Mehrotra, 'Sino-Pak Relations: A Review', 66.
99. Jain, *China South Asia Relations*, vol. 2, 220–1.
100. 'Draft resolution submitted by China in the UN Security Council, 5 December 1971', in ibid. 221–2.
101. Vertzberger, *The Enduring Entente*, 48.
102. Small, *The China-Pakistan Axis*, 14.
103. For the full text of the treaty, see *Mainstream Weekly*, <http://www.mainstreamweekly.net/article2950.html>. Accessed on 22 March 2016.
104. Small, *The China-Pakistan Axis*, 14–15.
105. *National Assembly of Pakistan Debates: Official Record*, vol. 11, no. 4 (21 December 1973), 148.
106. Devin T. Hagerty, 'Pakistan's Foreign Policy under Bhutto', *Journal of South Asia and Middle Eastern Studies*, vol. XIV, no. 4 (1991), 60.
107. Bhutto's interview with the *Time* magazine on 5 March 1973.
108. William Rogers in his statement on the occasion said that the principal US officer in Dhaka, Herbert D. Spivack, was on his way back to Bangladesh following consultation in Washington and was carrying a message from President Nixon to Sheikh Mujibur Rahman, informing him of recognition and avowed 'desire to establish diplomatic relations at the embassy level'. In *Keesing's Contemporary Archives* (1971–72), 25196.
109. *Newsweek* (14 February 1972), 17.
110. Robert G. Sutter, *Chinese Foreign Policy after the Cultural Revolution, 1966–1977* (Boulder, CO: Westview Press, 1978), 132, as cited in Naveed Ahmad, 'Sino-Pakistan Relations (1971–1981)', *Pakistan Horizon*, vol. 34, no. 3 (1981), 60.
111. Ibid.
112. Hasan-Askari Rizvi, *Pakistan and its Geostrategic Environment: A Study of Foreign Policy* (New York: St. Martin's Press, 1993), 142.
113. *Keesing's Contemporary Archives* (1971–72), 25109.
114. Government of Pakistan, Joint Communiqués: January 1968–December 1973 (Islamabad: Ministry of Foreign Affairs, 1973), 129.
115. Ahmad, 'Sino-Pakistan Relations (1971–1981)', 61.
116. *Pakistan Horizon*, vol. XXV, no. 3 (1972), 129–30.
117. Vertzberger, 'The Political Economy of Sino-Pakistani Relations', 647.
118. *Military Balance, 1972–73* (London: IISS, 1972), 78, cited in Vertzberger, 'The Political Economy of Sino-Pakistani Relations', 647.
119. B. L. Bhola, 'Developments in Pakistan's Foreign Policy: 1972–76', in Verinderr

Grover and Ranjana Arora (eds.), *Political System in Pakistan*, vol. 6 (New Delhi: Deep and Deep Publications, 1995), 184.

120. Roedad Khan (comp), *American Papers: Secret and Confidential India, Pakistan and Bangladesh Documents 1965–1973* (Oxford: Oxford University Press, 1999), 967.
121. Out of this figure, 103 were provided after the 1971 war in which Pakistan had lost more than what it had in previous wars. Secondly, the deal included establishing an overhauling factory in Pakistan.
122. *Military Balance, 1970–71* (London: IISS, 1972), 67–8, cited in Vertzberger, 'The Political Economy of Sino-Pakistan Relations', 647.
123. *Aviation Week & Space Technology* (30 March 1981).
124. Rizvi, *Pakistan and its Geostrategic Environment*, 144.
125. For details of China's point of view, see statements by the Chinese representative Huang Hua in the UN Security Council on 24–25 August 1972, in Jain, *China South Asia Relations*, 243–7.
126. *Morning News* (Karachi, 24 April 1973).
127. Huang Hua's speech in the UN on 24–25 August 1972, ibid. 243–4. Also see Murad Rind, 'China and Bangladesh's U.N. Entry', *Pakistan Forum*, vol. 3, no. 4 (January 1973), 12–13.
128. 'Statement by Chinese Foreign Minister Chiao Kuan-hua in the UN General Assembly, 3 October 1972', in Jain, *China South Asia Relations*, 247–8.
129. Ahmad, 'Sino-Pakistan Relations (1971–1981)', 63.
130. *News Bulletin*, 'Cultural Information Office, Embassy of the People's Republic of China in Pakistan' (13 May 1974), 3.
131. 'China-Pakistan joint communiqué on Bhutto's visit to China, 14 May 1974', in Jain, *China South Asia Relations*, 152–4.
132. Ahmad, 'Sino-Pakistan Relations (1971–1981)', 64.
133. For a full statement of Z. A. Bhutto on India's nuclear explosion, 19 May 1974, *Pakistan Horizon*, vol. 27, no. 2 (1974), 131–4.
134. Choudhury, *India, Pakistan, Bangladesh, and the Major Powers*, 240.
135. A commentary published in *Peking Review*, cited in Arif, *China Pakistan Documents*, 157.
136. Choudhury, *India, Pakistan, Bangladesh, and the Major Powers*, 240.
137. Jain, *China South Asia Relations*, vol. 2, 156.
138. *Peking Review*, no. 41 (11 October 1974), 12.
139. Vice-premier Li Hsien Nien's speech on 20 April 1975, in *Foreign Affairs Pakistan*, vol. II, no. 4 (1975), 26.
140. Fitzpatrick, *Nuclear Black Markets*, 25–6.
141. *Military Balance, 1970–71* (London: IISS, 1972), 67–8, cited in Vertzberger, 'The Political Economy of Sino-Pakistan Relations', 647–8.

142. Mahmud, 'Sino-Pakistan Relations', 15–16.
143. 'China-Pakistan joint communiqué on premier Bhutto's visit to China, 30 May 1976', in Jain, *China South Asia Relations*, 167.
144. The Resolution was passed on 26 February 1976. For the text of the resolution see *Pakistan Horizon*, XXIX, no. 1 (1976), 175. Also see Rizvi, *Pakistan and its Geostrategic Environment*, 146.
145. Extract of Bhutto's interview to George Hutchinson, Deputy Editor of Spectator on 11 September 1976 in Arif, *China Pakistan Documents*, 169.
146. Agha Shahi was a career diplomat and younger brother of Agha Hilaly, Pakistan's Ambassador to the US at the time of Sino-US rapprochement. Shahi's association with China started during the 1950s. He was part of Pakistan's delegation to the Bandung Conference, and thus had the opportunity to interact with premier Zhou En-lai and vice-premier, Chen Yi. He also participated in China-Pakistan border talks in the early 1960s. During his appointment as Pakistan's permanent representative to the UN, in 1967–72, he played a positive role for China's seat in the UN. At the UN platform, Shahi developed close links with Huang Hua who later became China's Deputy Premier and Foreign Minister. In 1972, Bhutto appointed Shahi as Pakistan's ambassador to China and, in 1973, as Foreign Secretary. Lu Shulin, 'Precious Memories' in Lu Shulin (comp), *You and Us: Stories of China and Pakistan* (Beijing: China International Press, 2015), 61–2.
147. For instance, in March 1977, Zia had hosted a dinner in honour of a visiting Chinese military delegation led by Yang Chengwu, Deputy Chief of General Staff of the People's Liberation Army, also attended by the Chinese Ambassador to Pakistan and other Chinese officials. See *Xinhua General News Service* (24 March 1977), accessed via LexisNexis Academic.
148. See *Xinhua General News Service*.
149. Rizvi, *Pakistan and the Geostrategic Environment*, 146.
150. Keshav Mishra, *Rapprochement Across the Himalaya: Emerging India-China Relations* (New Delhi: Kalpaz Publications, 2004), 93.
151. 'Peking banquet welcomes head of government of Pakistani General Mohammad Zia ul-Haq and begum Zia ul-Haq', *Xinhua General News Service* (17 December 1977), accessed via LexisNexis Academic.
152. Rafique Afzal, *Pakistan Year Book 1978* (Karachi, Lahore: East West Publishing Company, 1978), 190.
153. Ahmad, 'Sino-PakistanRelations (1971–1981)', 67.
154. Mahmud, 'Sino-Pakistan Relations', 16.

3

China's Reforms and Modernisation, and Relations with Pakistan (1978–89)

After the deaths of Zhou En-lai and Mao Zedong in 1976, China witnessed a tense power-struggle between the reformists led by Deng Xiaoping and ultra-radicals led by the 'Gang of Four'. By 1978, the reformists had defeated the radical faction and consolidated their hold on power. After taking control, they introduced structural changes internally and externally. They abandoned their ideological fervour and adopted a more pragmatic approach. China's economic development became their foremost priority. Externally, this deradicalised the country's foreign policy, opened up China to the outside world, and began to normalise relations with other countries, especially around the periphery as peaceful borders were important for domestic economic growth. India as one of its important neighbours got priority. However, to improve its ties with New Delhi, Beijing needed adjustments in its 'special' ties with Islamabad. As a result, China gradually separated its relations with Pakistan from those with India and started dealing with the two neighbours independently. Beijing began to distance itself from Indo-Pakistan conflicts by taking a relatively neutral position. For instance, on the Kashmir issue, China's position shifted from total support for the right to self-determination of the people of Kashmir to a neutral position labelling the dispute a bilateral matter between India and Pakistan that should be resolved through peaceful means. Moreover, China expanded the scope of its South Asian policy by showing greater interest in maintaining good relations with all member South Asian countries. In the past, China had mainly focused on Pakistan.

Another important shift in the wake of reforms and opening up was a change in China's economic and military assistance policy towards other countries. Pakistan was particularly affected by this policy. During the late 1970s, China stopped its grants and started giving concessional loans which Pakistan had to repay. A Chinese official reportedly stated that Pakistan should understand the modern economic realities that had forced Chinese authorities to pursue a different policy.[1] This policy applied equally on China's arms transfers to Pakistan. Until this period, almost all Chinese weapons to Pakistan were free of cost. Since then, this commercial aspect has been moderating Sino-Pakistan relations.

China had first indicated a shift away from its pro-Pakistan position to a balanced stance on the Kashmir issue in the mid-1970s. It took almost one and a half decades for Beijing to adopt a completely neutral stance on the dispute. This slow change enabled Islamabad to adjust to changing realities. In this new period, while simultaneously trying to improve relations with India, China continued economic and military aid to Pakistan, partly in order to achieve a balance between Pakistan and India. Besides its support in the nuclear and missile programme, China helped Islamabad develop defence infrastructure, and licensed and joint production.

At the start of this period, the Soviet Union invaded Afghanistan. This new development affected the security dynamics of the entire region. The US launched an international campaign against the Soviets, and Pakistan and China joined that coalition which initiated a new era of trilateral cooperation between them.[2] These three states, along with the international community, coordinated their policies and formed a common front to force the Soviets to pull out of Afghanistan—a task which was finally accomplished in 1989. For this purpose, the US, Pakistan, and Saudi Arabia, with the support of other Islamic countries, recruited thousands of Muslim guerrillas, known as mujahideen, to fight a proxy war against the Soviets in Afghanistan. China also contributed in terms of economic assistance including reportedly sending some Uighur Muslims to fight with other mujahideen. In the ensuing decades, these mujahideen turned into Islamic militants, posing a new challenge for peace. Repercussions of the policy that involved training militants had started during the 1980s itself, though its most unwanted consequences manifested themselves at the start of the new century. On the other hand, under the guise of the Afghan war, Pakistan accelerated its nuclear weapons programme during which the PRC provided useful assistance. By the time of the Soviet's withdrawal from Afghanistan in 1989, Pakistan had reportedly reached or even crossed the nuclear threshold.[3]

BILATERAL RELATIONS DURING THE ZIA REGIME

As mentioned in the previous chapter, it did not take long for General Zia ul-Haq to develop a rapport with the Chinese leadership. During his December 1977 visit to China, Zia received a warm welcome which showed the continuity of friendly relations between the two sides. The regime sent messages of felicitation to Chinese leaders on a number of occasions to gain Beijing's attention. For instance, in August 1978, at the fifty-first anniversary of the People's Liberation Army (PLA), it congratulated the PRC's Ambassador in Pakistan. It also sent separate messages of congratulations to Washington and Beijing on the occasion of the establishment of Sino-US relations in December 1978. Zia termed the occasion a historic event, which according to him would benefit the peoples of the two countries and contribute to peace not just in Asia, but also the rest of the world.[4] The normalisation of Sino-US relations was particularly significant to Pakistan, which had played an important role in establishing the initial contacts between the two sides.

China reciprocated Zia's December 1977 visit by sending vice-premier, Geng Biao, in June 1978 and the vice-premier, Li Xiannian, in January 1979 to Pakistan. Geng came to Pakistan for the inauguration ceremony of the Karakoram Highway (KKH). The building of this 1,300 kilometre road connecting Islamabad with Kashgar added new economic and strategic dimensions to Sino-Pakistan relations. The road was opened for general traffic eight years later in 1986. During its construction, members of the People's Liberation Army (PLA) worked along with the Engineering Corps of the Pakistan Army. Because of the highway's potential strategic and economic importance, and its location in the disputed territory between India and Pakistan, India lodged a formal protest 'for the record'.[5] The KKH later became the backbone of the China-Pakistan Economic Corridor (CPEC) which is discussed in Chapter 6.

On the other hand, China continued its new South Asian policy to expand relations with all member countries, which was obvious during Geng's visit as well. While reiterating Beijing's traditional support to Islamabad, he hoped for inter-state cooperation in the region. He stated that, 'as South Asia's neighbour, China already wishes that the countries in South Asia may continue to improve their mutual relations free from outside interference and that they treat one another as equals and live in amity...'[6]—an implied reference to India and Pakistan. He added, '[China will] resolutely support the South Asian countries in their just struggle to defend national independence and sovereignty against foreign aggression and interference'.[7] It was indicative of China's changing position that a top Chinese official, while in Pakistan, guaranteed the 'independence' and 'sovereignty' of all South Asian countries. In the past, such rhetoric was usually reserved for Pakistan.

The change of leadership in India further helped thaw ties with Beijing. The Janata Party led by Morarji Desai defeated the ruling Indian National Congress in the 1977 general elections. Beijing welcomed this change. In a congratulatory message to Desai, premier Hua Guofeng expressed his desire for a traditional relationship between the two peoples.[8] The Desai government showed its resolve, not only to improve relations with its neighbours, including China and Pakistan, but also to reduce India's dependence on the Soviets. In October 1978, Desai announced that the Indian Parliament's resolution passed in 1966, barring relations with China until all 'occupied' territories were vacated, would not stand in the way of normalisation of Sino-Indian ties.[9] New Delhi also rescinded its December 1962 notification that had prohibited trade with the 'Tibet Region of China'.[10] Despite warnings from Soviet premier, Alexei Kosygin, the Desai government sent Foreign Minister, Atal Bihari Vajpayee, to China in February 1979.[11] During the visit, Vajpayee complained about China's pro-Pakistan attitude in regards to Kashmir that had created 'additional and unnecessary complication to the prospects of Sino-Indian relations'.[12] In a meeting with Vajpayee, Deng Xiaoping stated that 'we should seek common ground while reserving our differences'. He added that the boundary issue could be resolved through peaceful means but should not prevent improving relations in other areas.[13] Chinese Foreign Minister, Huang Hua, told Vajpayee that China's support of the Naga and Mizo insurgencies in India was a thing of the past.[14] Although Vajpayee cut his visit short in protest against China's attack on Vietnam, the relations began to normalise.[15]

In the late 1970s, Beijing once again sought Islamabad's help to improve ties with the Islamic regime in Iran. After the establishment of Sino-Iranian ties in 1971, Beijing began to support the Shah of Iran. Although China did not take any position over conflict in Iran between the Shah's forces and the revolutionary Islamists, led by Imam Khomeini, at an official level, Chinese media portrayed a negative image of the Islamists. Furthermore, Chinese President, Hua Guofeng's, visit to Iran, in 1978, clearly put China on the Shah's side. As an observer noted, 'Hua Guofeng's visit to Iran coincided with the Shah's brutality against his own people, and was interpreted by Imam Khomeini and his associates as China's explicit support of the Shah's anti-national, anti-people despotic regime.' Imam Khomeini stated that the visit was made 'over the corpses of [their] martyrs'. The Islamists also viewed China's pro-US foreign policy with great disdain. Iran-China relations deteriorated rapidly after the Shah's regime fell in January 1979. Beijing realised its policy had badly damaged two-way ties. In order to prevent further deterioration, it sent an apology to Tehran through Pakistan. Agha Shahi, the adviser to the President of Pakistan on foreign affairs, conveyed this apology to Imam Khomeini in which Beijing admitted that Hua's visit to Iran was a mistake. According to an analyst, 'Pakistan mediated between Iran and China, and saved the relationship from collapse. Agha Shahi's successful mediation yielded results for Pakistan as well in the form of securing the trust of China.'[16] Not only were contacts between Beijing and Tehran restored, during the Iran-Iraq war (1980–88), Beijing supplied a large quantity of arms to Tehran.[17] Pakistan's diplomatic role once again highlighted its importance in China's calculations.

CHINA'S CONCERN AT BHUTTO'S EXECUTION

Former Pakistani Prime Minister, Zulfikar Ali Bhutto, was sentenced to death by the apex court in Pakistan, as an accomplice in the murder of a political rival. Bhutto had played an important role in developing Sino-Pakistan ties in different capacities; he had personal contacts with top Chinese leaders such as Chairman Mao Zedong and Zhou En-lai, and was held in high esteem in China. Beijing's concern at his execution orders could be measured from the fact that premier Guofeng made a rare, public intervention to save Bhutto's life. While terming Bhutto's trial an internal affair, Hua appealed in a message sent to Zia, 'China is a good neighbour and friend of Pakistan. I sincerely express to Your Excellency my concern about this matter and appeal to you to use your supreme power and influence as the President so that he [Bhutto] may be granted clemency.'[18] Zia had received similar requests from several other countries. After the Supreme Court of Pakistan's rejection of Bhutto's appeal, only Zia as the head of state had the constitutional power to grant clemency. Nevertheless, he resisted all such requests, arguing that justice must be applied equally. Bhutto was hanged on 4 April 1979. A spokesperson of China's Ministry of Foreign Affairs, while responding to Bhutto's execution, described him as an old friend of the Chinese people who made significant contributions in promoting Sino-Pakistan relations. He said, 'Chinese leaders made several appeals to grant him clemency. We deeply regret his execution.'[19] Although Beijing appeared to be disappointed at Zia's refusal of its request, relations continued much as they had been before. As Rizvi noted, 'China, which highlighted non-interference in internal affairs of other states as a cardinal feature of its foreign policy, could not jeopardise its permanent interests in Pakistan for the sake of an individual, no matter what were his contributions.'[20]

THE SOVIET INVASION OF AFGHANISTAN

In response to the Soviet invasion of Afghanistan in December 1979, the US launched a global anti-Soviet front which Pakistan, Saudi Arabia, China, and many other countries joined. China became a part of the anti-Soviet coalition because of its 'vitriolic' opposition to Moscow.[21] For General Zia ul-Haq, the Soviet invasion proved a godsend opportunity to address both domestic and international audiences. Embracing the US anti-Soviet policy not only neutralised Western criticism over the military coup and human rights abuses, but also allowed considerable military and economic assistance to arrive in Pakistan. Domestically, the regime propagated that the Soviets had invaded a brother Islamic country with which Pakistan had deep religious and cultural ties; Pakistan could not abandon the Afghans at this crucial time.[22] Most importantly, the Soviet invasion brought together the interests of the US, Pakistan, and China on an anti-Soviet agenda, taking their cooperation to new heights.[23] As an observer noted, 'During this period, the US Central Intelligence Agency, Pakistan's ISI, and Chinese Intelligence Services developed a close, collaborative relationship based on convergent perceptions of the Soviet Union and the exchange of information.'[24]

As a result of the Soviet invasion, Sino-US, US-Pakistan, and their triangular relationship improved quickly indeed. In less than a month after the Soviets marched into Afghanistan, President Carter's Defence Secretary, Harold Brown, visited China. The two sides, which had recently established diplomatic relations, 'found growing convergence of views' and 'parallel interests'. A series of high-profile visits ensued in the following years.[25] Washington agreed to provide a wide variety of non-lethal weapons to China. In 1981, Sino-US trade reached US$5 billion; an approximately thousand fold increase as compared to the previous decade. Importantly, China and the US entered an unprecedented agreement under which China allowed the US to establish two strategically important electronic intelligence posts in Xinjiang to monitor Soviet activities. The US also obtained an agreement for over-flights above Chinese territory for planes carrying assistance for the mujahideen.[26]

The Soviet invasion only succeeded in further deepening Sino-Pakistan relations—Beijing expanded its diplomatic, economic, and military assistance to Pakistan. According to reports, China covertly provided military supplies worth US$200 million annually to support Afghan guerrillas. China also gave considerable diplomatic, economic, and military aid to anti-Soviet resistance groups. Chinese weapons included approximately 2,000 heavy machine guns; 1,000 anti-tank rockets; the Chinese version of the Kalashnikov AK-47; recoilless rifles such as the Chinese 82 mm, B-10, and 75 mm Type 56; and nearly half a million rounds of ammunition. The weapons travelled from northwest China, using the Wakhan corridor (Chitral), and reached Peshawar where they were distributed among the mujahideen.[27] Some Chinese experts not only provided training to mujahideen inside Pakistan but also established some training camps in Xinjiang.[28]

China also played the Islamic card against the Soviets. Beijing portrayed its sizeable Muslim population as a qualification for special relations with Islamic countries.[29] In its statements, Beijing repeatedly referred to Afghanistan as an 'Islamic country' which had been facing Soviet aggression. On 5 January 1980, the Chinese Islamic Association, with the full backing of the Chinese government, stated that it would not tolerate the Soviet hegemonist invasion because of its close ties with the Afghan people.[30] During the Islamic Foreign Ministers' Conference in Islamabad in January 1980, China lobbied to gain support against the Soviet Union. Beijing emphasised to the

Islamic countries that if they did not oppose the Soviet Union, another Islamic state could be the next victim.[31]

There was a cooling down of US-Pakistan relations due to Islamabad's nuclear weapons programme, Zia's imposition of martial law in July 1977, and the November 1979 mob attack on the US embassy in Islamabad. The Soviet invasion of Afghanistan changed them overnight. The Zia regime, which was viewed in the US very negatively, suddenly began to receive remarkable attention from the US administration.[32] Pakistan became so important that Carter, in his State of the Union Address, reassured it that Washington would provide assistance to Islamabad. Zia quickly understood that Pakistan had acquired a critical place in the US policy to confront the Soviet occupier in Afghanistan.[33] Ronald Reagan's ascendency as the US president further boosted Islamabad-Washington ties; Reagan was even keener than his predecessor to defeat the Soviets in Afghanistan. Pakistan soon started receiving some of the most advanced weapons systems in the US arsenal.[34] Above all, the Reagan Administration turned a blind eye to Pakistan's nuclear programme, which had been the principal dispute in Pak-US relations during the 1970s. Under the cover provided by the Afghan war, Pakistan sped up its nuclear activities.

The new US attitude towards both China and Pakistan provided space for Sino-Pakistani relations to expand even further. According to an analyst, the Soviet invasion 'opened a new chapter of collaboration and cooperation between China and Pakistan'.[35] Beijing believed that the Soviet move threatened Pakistan, China's key ally in the region. In January 1980, China's Foreign Minister, Huang Hua, flew to Pakistan for consultations. He committed China's economic and military help, and urged other nations to stand by Pakistan. For the first 18 months of the Soviet invasion, Zia rejected the Carter Administration's aid package as 'peanuts', and so Pakistan depended on Chinese assistance.

The flow of arms and ammunition from China to Pakistan as well as to the mujahideen continued during the war.[36]

Within six months of the Soviet invasion, in May 1980, Zia made his second visit to China where he received a grand welcome. Premier, Hua Guofeng; Vice-Premier, Geng Biao; Vice Chairman of the Standing Committee of the National People's Congress, Tan Zhenlin; and Foreign Minister, Huang Hua, all came to the airport to receive him.[37] Both sides condemned the Soviet invasion and demanded an immediate and unconditional withdrawal.[38] Chinese leaders stated that Afghanistan and Cambodia were part of the USSR's strategy to encircle and isolate the PRC.[39] In a meeting with Zia, Deng Xiaoping stated that if the USSR was not stopped, it would continue its expansion in other countries. He urged the international community to give a 'tit for tat' response. 'Our objective is to win peace, but peace can only be won through struggle', Deng added. While endorsing Deng's views, Zia explained the difficulties Pakistan faced as a result of the invasion.[40] Pakistan, which had no direct security concerns in Southeast Asia, condemned Vietnam's occupation of Cambodia. The statement was probably issued to please Beijing—a practice which Pakistani rulers continued in the coming years as well.[41] As reported in the *Beijing Review*, Zia's visit 'further promoted the friendly relations and cooperation between the two countries'.[42] The Chinese authorities arranged an impressive farewell ceremony at the airport to see off Zia's delegation.[43] China's hospitality demonstrated that relations with the Zia regime were as cordial as they were with his predecessor.

In June 1981, Chinese premier, Zhao Ziyang, visited Pakistan, Nepal, and Bangladesh. This was the first visit by a Chinese Prime Minister to Pakistan in 15 years. This show of commitment did not prevent China from softening its tone towards the Afghan issue as a result of a thaw in its relations with the USSR. Zhao stated, 'We do not mean that this is not the time to pursue a political settlement.' He also briefed Zia about China's desire to further normalise relations with India. Zia accompanied Zhao throughout his stay in Pakistan. Zhao paid tributes to Pakistan's courage against the Soviet occupation and stated that China would support Pakistan in meeting its defence requirements. While Zhao was visiting Pakistan, Beijing sent its Foreign Minister to New Delhi, perhaps in an attempt to balance the visits.[44]

CHINA MOVES TOWARDS NEUTRALITY ON INDIA-PAKISTAN DISPUTES

In January 1980, Indira Gandhi resumed power as prime minister. She expressed her intentions to continue the process of normalisation with China as was started by her predecessor. During the funeral ceremony of Yugoslav leader, Marshal Tito, in Belgrade, Mrs Gandhi met China's Chairman, Hua Guofeng. This was the first contact at prime ministerial level since Zhou En-lai's visit to India in 1960. On that occasion, both sides decided to continue the rapprochement they had started. As a follow up, China's Foreign Minister, Huang Hua, visited India in June 1981. Both sides took the important decision of resuming border talks, which were later initiated in December 1981.

On the other hand, China had already started moving towards relative neutrality on Indo-Pakistan disputes. This was designed to help address some of India's concerns. For instance, during his visit to Pakistan in January 1979, China's vice-premier, Li Xiannian, had indicated a shift away from a pro-Pakistan stance on Kashmir.[45] In June 1980, Deng Xiaoping took a clearer position and stated that Kashmir was a bilateral issue between India and Pakistan, which should be resolved peacefully.[46] It was the first time since the mid-1960s that a top Chinese leader had suggested bilateral settlement of the Kashmir dispute.[47] During the 1980s, China's statements on Kashmir shifted from 'in accordance with the UN resolutions' to a 'bilateral settlement'. Generally, China would call for a bilateral solution of the dispute but would add a reference to the UN resolutions and the Simla Agreement at Pakistan's request. It was, however, clear that Beijing had made up its mind to distance itself from the Kashmir imbroglio.

STRONG DEFENCE TIES

By the time Zia made his third visit to China, in October 1982, China had completed two rounds of border negotiations with India, and had also started talks with Moscow for a boundary settlement. These developments caused anxiety in Pakistan as they continued to regard China as a partner in countering Indian influence in the region. China had designed its rapprochement with India in a way that it should not affect its traditional friendship with Pakistan. During Zia's visit (as well as on other occasions when China found Pakistan concerned), Chinese leaders would assure Islamabad that improvement in Sino-Indian relations, or changes in regional and international equations, would not affect Sino-Pakistan ties. This rhetoric was complemented by substantial measures of help in economic and strategic areas. Zhao Ziyang assured Zia that 'no matter how the international situation develops in the coming years, China's policy towards developing friendly relations with Pakistan will not change'.[48] Beijing continued to supply Islamabad with significant levels of military hardware. Moreover, there was an unprecedented degree of military exchanges between the two sides in the initial years of the 1980s.[49]

From the early 1980s, two pertinent trends in China's defence ties began to emerge. First, Pakistan started licensed production of Chinese weapons and military equipment such as tanks, armoured vehicles, guns, and aircraft. This cooperation further expanded in the following decades. Second, in 1980, China reorganised its arms industry along Western lines, bringing a greater focus on commercial aspects. China, which had initially supplied arms to Pakistan free of charge, began to charge for each arms deal.[50] As Wirsing states, 'In the 1980s, the relationship shifted to arms production cooperation; Pakistan was asked to pay for the hardware, and the loans carried interest.'[51] This policy also applied to nuclear and missile transfers.[52] However, Beijing remained a suitable option for Islamabad because of its availability and flexible conditions compared to other powers. Moreover, while the arms deals had become more commercial, China often understood the needs of a cash-starved Pakistan and offered credit loans along with deals.[53]

China's arms transfers to Pakistan between 1966 and 1980 exceeded US$630 million, which was over one-third of the total arms transferred to Pakistan during this period.[54] Vertzberger described the nature of China's arms assistance to Pakistan at the onset of the 1980s as follows:

> China served as a secure source of arms supply when other potential sources could not be relied on for continuous unimpeded access to their arms markets... Obtaining arms from China was considered a vital achievement of Pakistan's China policy in light of the flow of Soviet modern weapon systems and technology to India, especially since the latter has not been threatened by embargo as have Pakistan's supplies from the West on various occasions.[55]

By 1982, as a result of frequent US sanctions during the 1960s and 1970s, Chinese arms had become the backbone of Pakistan's weaponry, forming 75 per cent of its entire tank force and 65 per cent of its aircraft.[56] In August 1984, an Indian newspaper claimed that Pakistan had become the largest recipient of China's military aid after North Korea and China's ally, North Vietnam. The report also claimed that China had trained Pakistani soldiers and wanted to deepen military ties with Pakistan.[57]

THE CHANGING NATURE OF ECONOMIC RELATIONS

As mentioned earlier, China had changed its policy of economic assistance from grants to loans since the 1970s. Afterwards, most of Beijing's aid was in the form of 'soft loans, commercial credits with an element of grant'. Moreover, China began demanding sovereign guarantees from commercial banks while financing projects in Pakistan.[58] This 'commercial' dimension came to save as a prominent feature in Beijing's ties with Islamabad. Secondly, Chinese leaders, in their interaction with their Pakistani counterparts, began emphasising the importance of economic and trade ties for their overall relationship. This indicated that China's policy expanded the base of its relations which was thus far centred on strategic ties.

An important step towards economic relations was the establishment of a Joint Economic Committee during Zia's third visit to China in October 1982. The committee was aimed at enlarging cooperation in non-political areas such as industry, agriculture, science, and technology.[59] It was also empowered to review the progress of existing projects, identifying new ones, and giving recommendations to both governments.

HIGH-PROFILE VISITS

One of the hallmarks of Sino-Pakistan relations was a regular exchange of visits by the top-level leadership of the two countries. This feature became obvious from the mid-1980s onwards. To return Zia's October 1982 visit, Chinese President, Li Xiannian, arrived in Pakistan in March 1984. Earlier, he had visited Pakistan twice as vice-premier. As the head of state, he received a grand welcome in Pakistan. Zia presented Li with the Nishan-i-Pakistan, the highest civil award in the country.[60] The Afghan war, especially the unprecedented number of refugees and their social, economic, and political impact on Pakistan; Cambodia, which was important for Chinese policy; and the Iran-Iraq war were discussed during the visit. Li applauded Pakistan's humanitarian assistance to over three million Afghan refugees. He stated that in order for the Afghan and Cambodian issues to be settled politically, all foreign troops must leave unconditionally.[61] Zia explained the difficulties Pakistan had been facing as a result of Afghan refugees and his efforts to end the Iran-Iraq war. Both sides expressed a 'complete identity of views' on bilateral relations and international issues.[62]

In June 1985, China's Defence Minister, Zhang Aiping, made an eight-day visit which was the first visit by a Chinese defence minister since the establishment of diplomatic relations.[63] During his stay, Zhang expressed appreciation for Pakistan's positive contribution to peace in Asia and its stand on Afghanistan. He also called for an immediate withdrawal of foreign forces from the country.[64] Pakistan's media gave wide coverage to Zhang's visit, and analysts highlighted its importance to Sino-Pakistan defence cooperation and to regional security.[65]

Pakistan also played a role in Sino-Saudi relations. In 1985, Pakistan arranged a meeting in Islamabad between the Saudi Ambassador to the US, Prince Bandar Bin Sultan, and the Chinese diplomats. This mirrored Pakistan's role in helping improve China's ties with another conservative Muslim state, Iran. According to Dutta, this was the first contact between China and Saudi Arabia. Later, in March 1988, Beijing and Riyadh signed an agreement under which China supplied around 35 CSS-2 Intermediate Range Ballistic Missiles (IRBM) to Saudi Arabia. This was the first time China provided IRBMs to another country.[66] These contacts led to the establishment of full diplomatic relations between China and Saudi Arabia in 1990.

On the other hand, Pakistan continued to experience political changes. As a result of February 1985 elections in Pakistan, Muhammad Khan Junejo, Zia's handpicked leader, took the oath as prime minister. By the end of the year, Zia lifted martial law and thus ended more than seven years of direct military rule in Pakistan. Prime Minister Junejo started a new tradition of paying the first foreign visit to the PRC as a 'tribute' to the special relationship with China.[67] Some of his successors continued this tradition. Prior to Junejo's visit, Pakistan dispatched its Finance Minister, Mahbub-ul-Haq, to explore a way to expand trade and economic ties.[68] Haq's words clarified the growing importance of economic and trade ties for the overall relationship between the two countries, 'Politically China is the oldest and [the] most firm ally of Pakistan. We would like to ensure that in the economic field too, it becomes our firm and permanent ally…' In the context of economic ties, he stressed the need for energy cooperation, to which in the coming years China responded by extending assistance for nuclear power plants and dams.[69]

During his stay in China in November 1985, Junejo stated that Sino-Pakistan relations were not only important for both countries but were also a source of peace in the region and the world.[70] This expression reappeared in future statements as well and indicated the continued dominance of the strategic factors in their relations. In addition to this, the two sides discussed bilateral ties, the situation in Afghanistan, Indo-Pakistan relations, the Gulf War, and the tension in the Middle East. China reasserted its support for Pakistan as well as its desire for peace in South Asia.[71] At the same time, the Sino-Soviet thaw was changing China's tone towards the US-USSR détente. It was in this context that Li expressed his desire for the success of the upcoming summit talks between them.[72] This was in contrast with China's earlier stance under which it denounced the US-Soviet détente. This reflected the PRC's changing perception of, and intention to improve, its relations with both superpowers.

During Junejo's visit, China agreed to increase imports from Pakistan such as scrap from the ship-building industry, iron and steel products, urea, fruits, and vegetables.[73] Beijing also promised to install two turbines at the Jamshoro hydroelectric project, offered help in the expansion of the Heavy Mechanical Complex and the Heavy Forge and Foundry, gave a credit loan of US$10.86 million, and most importantly agreed to build the Heavy Electrical Complex (HEC).[74]

In April 1986, the Chinese Vice-Minister for Machine-building Industries, Zhao Mingsheng, visited Pakistan to participate in the opening of the HEC and a power plant at Guddu; both the projects were started with China's assistance. During the visit, Zhao offered Chinese help to start new industrial projects and expand some of the existing projects.[75] In September 1986, both sides signed an agreement on cooperation in the peaceful use of nuclear energy, which had safeguards from the International Atomic Energy Agency (IAEA). Pakistan stated that the agreement should put an end to 'irresponsible rumours' about China's support to the country's nuclear programme. However, the Indian Prime Minister called the project a threat to peace in South Asia.[76]

In June 1987, Chinese premier, Zhao Ziyang, made his second visit to Pakistan within six years. The visit came amidst strains in Sino-Indian relations over India's granting of statehood to Arunachal Pradesh, which China claimed in its entirety, and the 'not-so-good' relations between India and Pakistan. Against this backdrop, Beijing showed a warmer tone towards Pakistan. This time, it was Zhao who repeated Junejo's earlier statement saying that Beijing-Islamabad relations were not only beneficial for the two countries but were also a source of peace and stability in the region. He meant that no one would be allowed to disturb this 'peace and stability'—assumedly a veiled reference to India. Zhao reiterated China's commitment to remain a 'trustworthy' friend of Pakistan regardless of what happened in the world. The PRC promised an interest-free loan worth US$2.7 million for small and medium-sized projects.[77] Zhao also extended support to the South Asian Association for Regional Cooperation (SAARC).[78]

Throughout the Afghan war, Pakistan remained in constant contact with China. Prior to signing the Geneva Accords, Pakistan sent its Foreign Minister, Zain Noorani, to China for 'consultation' in February 1988. After signing the Geneva Accords, Prime Minister Junejo himself flew to Beijing to brief the Chinese leadership about the deals. Upon his return from China on 29 May 1988, Zia dismissed the Junejo government.[79] However, to ensure that this domestic purge would not affect two-way ties, Zia sent the new Foreign Minister, Yaqub Khan, to China. During the visit, Chinese Foreign Minister, Qian Qichen, reaffirmed his country's traditional friendship, its support for the new political set-up in Pakistan, and its efforts to bring peace to Afghanistan.[80]

PAKISTAN'S NUCLEAR PROGRAMME DURING THE AFGHAN WAR

A significant consequence of the Afghan war was Pakistan's clandestine development of nuclear weapons in which it also received 'useful' help from China. Pakistan intended to develop a nuclear programme after its defeat in the 1971 war with India. The Indian nuclear test, in May 1974, proved to be a 'tipping point' in this pursuit.[81] Although it is hard to pinpoint when exactly China's assistance to Pakistan's nuclear programme started, as the topic is shrouded in secrecy, such support most probably began in the mid-1970s, reaching its peak during the Afghan war. By the late 1980s, Pakistan had reportedly acquired nuclear capability.[82] Some Western sources claimed that China's support included technical assistance, designs of nuclear weapons, supply of weapons-grade uranium, ring magnets necessary for reprocessing uranium, the sharing of information, nuclear power plants, missiles, and missile components.[83]

According to Garver, China's 'significant assistance' started during the 1980s and continued into the mid-1990s. Around 1982, Beijing reportedly helped Pakistan overcome some technical difficulties in uranium enrichment at its Kahuta plant. In 1983, China allegedly provided a design for a 25 kiloton nuclear weapon that was a copy of the bomb China used in its fourth nuclear test in October 1966.[84] During the same period, China sold Pakistan tritium—an isotope of hydrogen used for enriching fission explosions—via a private German company.[85] In November 1985, the Soviets claimed that Pakistan planned to conduct a nuclear test in Xinjiang.[86]

During the 1980s, Islamabad overcame most hurdles in acquiring nuclear weapons. Although the US raised concerns, it did not take any major steps to stop Pakistan from it progressing down the nuclear path. The US President continued to issue an annual certificate that was required for the US military and economic assistance to Pakistan, stating that the country did not possess nuclear weapons. In early 1989, Acting Deputy Assistant Defence Secretary, Frederick C. Smith, while admitting that Pakistan had acquired nuclear capability, reiterated the continuation of an on-going six-year, multi-billion dollar package of US military and economic aid to Pakistan, and that President George H. W. Bush '[would] continue to be able to make the annual certification that Pakistan does not possess a nuclear explosive device'. He said that stopping aid to Pakistan could be counter-productive and would reduce the US' ability to influence Pakistan's nuclear policy. He further stated, 'from a military point of view, Pakistan's desire to buy more US F-16 jet fighters is reasonable and justified to maintain approximately the current air balance with India'.[87] However, the US commitments soon dissipated. In 1990, a year after the Soviet withdrawal from Afghanistan, Washington imposed partial sanctions in response to Pakistan's nuclear and missile programme. These fluctuations in US polices, also mentioned at other places in this book, created a negative image of the US in Pakistan despite its solid economic and military assistance.

China's role in Pakistan's nuclear and missile programme has remained a subject of debate. No doubt, Beijing provided useful help to Islamabad, however, it appears that aid given is often overstated to the extent of making China the prime reason behind it. To a great degree, Pakistan's nuclear programme was assembled in parts. Founding scientists (e.g. Dr A. Q. Khan) were trained and smuggled from Europe. Islamabad gained financial help from some Arab countries while it exchanged information with North Korea and perhaps even Iran. Pakistan put together all these fragmented parts to build nuclear weapons. As Rizvi stated, without proper infrastructure and a team of experts and scientists, Pakistan could not have achieved results. Hence, China's help was very useful but Pakistan's nuclear programme was not totally dependent upon it. Secondly, commercial aspects, since the early 1980s, also served as a factor behind China's assistance rather than mere strategic considerations.

SINO-INDIAN TIES

During the 1980s, parallel with these developments in Sino-Pakistan relations, China and India continued to improve their relationship. Between 1981 and 1988, both the sides completed eight rounds of border talks. As a result of their growing rapprochement, in December 1988, Indian Prime Minister, Rajiv Gandhi, made a historic visit to China. According to Garver, Rajiv Gandhi's visit was equivalent, in terms of its political and symbolic significance, to Richard Nixon's 1972 visit or Mikhail Gorbachev's 1989 visit to China. It was the first visit in thirty-four years by an Indian Prime Minister since Nehru visited China in 1954. Both sides held extensive talks on a wide range of topics of mutual concern. In his meeting with Rajiv Gandhi, Deng Xiaoping said, 'Let both sides forget the unpleasant period in our past relations, and let us treat everything with an eye on the future.'[88]

In a joint communiqué, it was stated that China and India had decided to settle the border issue through peaceful means, and to establish a joint working group on the boundary question and on economics, trade, and scientific technology. In response to Chinese concerns, India reiterated that Tibet was an autonomous region of China and it would not allow Tibetans to engage in anti-China activities.[89] As the communiqué showed, Pakistan did not figure—at least publicly—in the talks.[90] The visit began a new chapter in China-Indian relations.

PAKISTAN AND CHINA'S POST-ZIA TIES

In August 1988, Pakistan's President, Zia ul-Haq, died in a plane crash. In the following November 1988 elections, the Pakistan People's Party (PPP) led by Benazir Bhutto won a majority and formed the government. The new Prime Minister, Benazir Bhutto, continued the tradition of her predecessor and made her first foreign visit to China in February 1989. She stated that the purpose of the visit was to establish personal contacts between the new leadership in the two countries.[91] On arrival at the Great Hall where premier Li Peng personally received her, she was given a 19-gun salute.[92] She briefed the Chinese leaders about the improvement in Indo-Pakistan relations after the SAARC summit held in Islamabad. She stated their relationship with China was a 'cornerstone' in Pakistan's foreign relations, and extended an invitation to Li to visit Pakistan. Islamabad and Beijing signed two agreements. Keeping in view political feuds among different political parties of Pakistan, Deng offered advice to Benazir Bhutto, 'Various political parties in Pakistan and the Pakistan people are all our friends. I hope they get united to develop Pakistan instead of haggling over past resentment. This is the hope or a suggestion from a friend of Pakistan.'[93] As future events showed, his suggestion was not taken seriously. By this time, the situation in Afghanistan had become disturbing. Although the Soviet withdrawal had become a reality, civil war among different factions had destroyed the prospect of peace. An unstable Afghanistan had direct implications for China. Against this backdrop, premier Li expressed his concerns to Bhutto about the situation in Afghanistan and hoped for a broad-based coalition government there.[94]

PAKISTAN'S SUPPORT TO CHINA: THE TIANANMEN SQUARE INCIDENT

In June 1989, on the orders of top Chinese leadership, the PLA suppressed the pro-democracy demonstration in and around Tiananmen Square in Beijing. Approximately one hundred individuals, mostly students, were killed. A large section of the international community condemned China's actions and imposed punitive sanctions, many of which continue till today. The incident proved to be one of the most severe diplomatic setbacks to China since the start of the reforms and opening up policy. At this juncture, when China was once again isolated, Pakistan stood by it.[95] As Hussain stated, 'Pakistan was one of the few major countries which publicly expressed solidarity with China in the aftermath of the June 1989 crackdown on pro-democracy protesters at Tiananmen Square.'[96] Islamabad termed the happenings inside China as its internal affair. Within days of the incident, Pakistan's Ministry of Foreign Affairs dispatched a delegation to show its solidarity with the Chinese government. In a meeting with the delegation, premier Li Peng stated, 'In times of difficulty, it is very clear who are true friends.'[97] Shortly afterwards, on 29 June, Pakistan's Prime Minister, Benazir Bhutto, called in Chinese Ambassador, Tian Ding, and told him, 'Pakistan will be united with China at any time.' She extended her warm greetings and good wishes to the Chinese leaders, and expressed her satisfaction at the restoration of normality in China. She repeated the invitation to premier Li to visit Pakistan. Ambassador Tian thanked the government and the people of Pakistan for their support in a time of 'temporary difficulties'.[98]

Islamabad's support of Beijing continued in the aftermath of Tiananmen. In September 1989, the Pakistani Foreign Minister supported a Japanese proposal which suggested that the international community should not isolate China because of the Tiananmen Square incident.[99] Pakistan gave a rousing welcome to the visiting Chinese premier, Li Peng, in November 1989, to show its solidarity. This was the first visit by a top Chinese leader outside China since the PLA's actions in Tiananmen.[100] In September 1990 Pakistani President Ghulam Ishaq Khan presided over the inaugural session of the Asian Games held in Beijing at China's request.[101]

Pakistan's pro-China stance defied dominant world opinion led by the West. As eminent writer, Burke, noted concerning Pakistan's foreign policy, 'Islamabad has strong ties with China, and Washington's complaint with Beijing following the crushing of the "democracy movement" in June 1989, is not echoed in Islamabad. Pakistan will not cooperate with US efforts aimed at sanctioning China.'[102]

Islamabad did not join any forum to condemn, isolate, or sanction Beijing over the Tiananmen Square incident. This policy of Benazir Bhutto's government was in sharp contrast to the tradition of her party, which had long struggled against the tyrannical military regime of General Zia for the restoration of democracy. However, she did not support similar democratic standards for the Chinese people—perhaps, if there had been any other government, it would have taken a similar position. Pakistan's stance won the goodwill of the Chinese leadership. In fact, both sides had developed a policy of non-interference in each other's internal affairs which helped them strengthen their relationship.

In November 1989, Li Peng during his visit briefed Benazir on Sino-Indian relations following Rajiv's China visit. He assured her that improvement in Sino-Indian relations was neither at the cost of Pakistan nor would it affect Sino-Pakistan relations.[103] The PRC agreed to build a 300 MW nuclear power plant, Chashma-I, and continued to meet Pakistan's defence needs. It was China's first nuclear reactor to be sold to another country.[104] Later, in December 1991, both sides signed an agreement worth US$300 million under which the Shanghai Nuclear Engineering Research and Design Institute designed the main part of the plant which started operating in 2000.[105]

Pakistan considered the acquisition of a nuclear power plant an accomplishment in the context of a severe energy crisis. The deal came following France's refusal to provide a nuclear reprocessing plant and other Western countries' stringent policies towards offering any nuclear technology to Pakistan.[106] Furthermore, the plant accorded significant prestige and complemented Pakistan's clandestinely developed nuclear weapons programme. In fact, except for the IAEA's safeguarded reactors, Pakistan's civilian and military programmes were intertwined to such a degree that diversion from the former to the latter could be done easily.[107] Earlier, the China National Energy Corporation had also sold two mini reactors for research purposes which went into operation in November 1989 and February 1990.[108]

During Li's visit, an official in Pakistan's Ministry of Foreign Affairs stated that Islamabad was ready to play a role in restoring Sino-US relations which had been cool since the Tiananmen Square protests. It appears that Pakistan made this offer in light of its earlier experience in Sino-US rapprochement in 1971 and because by that time, Pakistan had good relations with both powers.[109] Nonetheless, neither China nor the US approached Pakistan for such help.

It was also reported that during Li Peng's visit, China provided a loan which was used for Pakistan's rocket development programme. Within weeks of Li's departure, General Ding Hanggao, head of China's State Commission for Science, Technology, and Industry for National Defense arrived in Pakistan. The two sides signed a Memorandum of Understanding (MoU) to increase joint procurement, research, development in the national defence industry, and development in electronics and computer technology for a ten-year period.

LONG TERM COSTS OF CREATING THE MUJAHIDEEN

The Soviets finally pulled out of Afghanistan in February 1989. During the Afghan war in the 1980s, the US and Pakistan, along with allies (especially from the Middle East), had recruited thousands of fighters from Pakistan, Afghanistan, the Middle East, the Gulf, and even a small number from China. These mujahideen were trained in camps inside Pakistan and Afghanistan by the CIA and the Pakistani military.[110] The US, Saudi Arabia, China, and various Islamic countries provided billions of dollars, weapons, and other assistance to fight this war.[111] Most of this money was channelled through the Pakistan Army and its spy agency, the Inter-Services Intelligence (ISI).

While pursuing an anti-Soviet policy, these states ignored the possible consequences of the army of jihadis they were preparing. Soon after the Soviet withdrawal in 1989, all of these states, and even the world at large, began to face the consequences of this policy which will be discussed in the next chapter. In later years, Islamic militancy became a serious challenge to Sino-Pakistan relations.

CONCLUSION

As a result of its post-Mao reforms and modernisation, China expanded the nature and scope of its relations with South Asian countries. In particular, the PRC began to stabilise ties with New Delhi. During this period, China returned to a neutral stance on the Kashmir issue and stopped issuing rhetorical statements in favour of Pakistan during India-Pakistan disputes. This, however, did not lead to a reduction in the PRC's 'special' relations with Pakistan. Beijing continued its support to Islamabad's nuclear and missile programme, and remained Pakistan's most reliable arms supplier and source of economic assistance. The Soviet invasion of Afghanistan brought the US, China, and Pakistan closer to each other, bringing a new level of cooperation between them. Most importantly, veiled by the Afghan war, Pakistan clandestinely developed its nuclear programme for which China provided aid. Another important development, which started in this period, was a change in China's assistance policy from grants to loans in both economic and military fields. A commercial aspect began to influence Sino-Pakistan relations. Islamabad became not only a strategic partner but also a huge market for Chinese goods and arms. Both sides continued regular contacts, extended support to each other's viewpoint, and adhered to the policy of non-interference. Issues such as the Soviet invasion of Afghanistan, Vietnam's invasion of Cambodia, the Gulf War, and the situation in the Middle East figured regularly in Sino-Pakistan consultations. Islamabad reciprocated Beijing's assistance by supporting the PRC on Taiwan, Tibet, human rights, the Tiananmen Square incidents, and facilitating Beijing's ties with Muslim countries.

This period came to an end with an important change. The Soviet Union completed its withdrawal from Afghanistan in May 1989. This shattered the US-Pakistan-China cooperation, leaving the unresolved issue of thousands of armed and trained mujahideen. Additionally, in 1989, wide-scale protests in Indian-held Kashmir led to a new phase of tension between India and Pakistan. These developments took place parallel to the improvement of Beijing's ties with New Delhi and Moscow. China's response to these developments and how they affected Sino-Pakistan relations are discussed in the next chapter.

Notes

1. Shaheen Akhtar, 'Pak-China Economic Relations: Forging Strategic Partnership in the 21st Century', *Regional Studies*, vol. XIX, no. 3 (Summer 2001), 46.
2. The US, anti-Soviet front in Afghanistan was quite large in countries where Saudi Arabia had a far greater role than China. However, because of the theme of this book, the focus will remain on the role of US, Pakistan, and China.
3. Different sources mention different dates for Pakistan's acquisition of nuclear weapons. In December 1985, Pakistani scientist, A. Q. Khan, claimed that his country could detonate a nuclear device on a week's notice. In 1986, US intelligence sources stated that Pakistan was only 'two screwdriver turns' from assembling the weapons. In 1987, A. Q. Khan again stated that the country was able to make a bomb. For details, see Mark Fitzpatrick (ed.), *Nuclear Black Markets: Pakistan, A. Q. Khan and the Rise of Proliferation Networks*, a Net Assessment (London: IISS, 2007), 22.
4. 'Message of greetings from President General Mohammad Zia ul-Haq to the Prime Minister of the People's Republic of China and the United States', on 17 December 1978, in *Foreign Affairs Pakistan*, vol. V, nos. 9 & 10 (September–October 1987), 61.
5. Mohan Ram, 'Karakoram Highway', *Economic and Political Weekly*, vol. 13, no. 26 (1 July 1978), 1058.
6. 'Speech by the Chinese premier Mr Geng Biao at the banquet given by CMLA, June 16, 1978', in *Foreign Affairs Pakistan*, vol. V, nos. 5 & 6 (May–June 1978), 79.
7. Ibid.
8. Mishra, *Rapprochement Across the Himalayas*, 53.
9. 'Prime Minister Morarji Desai's news conference at Ahmadabad, 23 October 1978', in R. K. Jain, *China-South Asia Relations: 1947–1980*, vol. 1 (New Delhi: Radiant Publishers, 1981), 483.
10. 'Indian notification on import and export trade with Tibet Region of China, 7 November 1978', ibid. 484.
11. Amardeep Athwal, *China-India Relations: Contemporary Dynamics* (London and New York: Routledge, 2008), 24.
12. *Keesing's Contemporary Archives* (1981), 31153.
13. Mishra, *Rapprochement Across the Himalayas*, 54.
14. Ibid.
15. In addition to the outbreak of Sino-Vietnam war, the Soviet invasion of Afghanistan also affected, in some ways, China-India normalisation of ties. The Soviet move increased Pakistan's importance to both China and the US.

Secondly, unlike the majority of the international community, New Delhi did not condemn the Soviet invasion and continued its close ties with Moscow. At that time, the Chinese leadership was preoccupied with the Soviet threat, and New Delhi's closer ties with Moscow were not so pleasant for Sino-Indian rapprochement.

16. Shah Alam, 'Iran-Pakistan Relations: Political and Strategic Dimensions', *Strategic Analysis* (October–December 2004), 535.
17. Sujit Dutta, 'China and Pakistan: End of a "Special Relationship"', *China Report*, vol. 30, no. 125 (1994), 130.
18. 'Premier Hua Guofeng's message to President Gen. Zia ul-Haq appealing to grant clemency to Mr Bhutto, 10 February 1979', in R. K. Jain, *China South Asian Relations: 1947–1980*, vol. 2 (New Delhi: Radiant Publishers, 1981), 185.
19. It also appears from this statement that China had made 'several' requests for Bhutto's clemency. 'Quarterly Chronicle and Documentation', *The China Quarterly*, no. 79 (September 1979), 679. According to a former Chinese Ambassador to Pakistan, China sent seven requests to Zia for this purpose.
20. Hasan-Askari Rizvi, *Pakistan and the Geostrategic Environment: A Study of Foreign Policy* (London: Macmillan, 1993), 147.
21. A. Z. Hilali, 'China's Response to the Soviet Invasion of Afghanistan', *Central Asian Survey*, vol. 20, no. 3 (2001), 329.
22. Some Pakistani scholars argue that Pakistan faced no threat from the Soviet invasion, and the military regime of General Zia ul-Haq exaggerated the threat for personal gains. Interview of Ayesha Siddiqa in Geomentary—*Mere azeez hum watano* [my dear countrymen]: Story of the 3rd martial law, Geo TV (21 October 2011).
23. These relations existed only until the Soviet's withdrawal from Afghanistan. After the Soviet withdrawal, the US imposed sanctions against China and Pakistan for their cooperation in nuclear and missile technology. From the early 1990s to 2001, Pak-US relations remained strained. Devin T. Hagerty, 'China and Pakistan: Strains in the Relationship', *Current History*, vol. 101, no. 656 (September 2002), 287–8.
24. Mushahid Hussain, 'Pakistan-China Defence Cooperation: An Enduring Relationship', *International Defence Review*, vol. 26, no. 2 (February 1993), 109.
25. John K. Cooley, *Unholy Wars: Afghanistan, America and International Terrorism* (Sterling, Va.: Pluto Press, 1999), 66.
26. Hilali, *China's Response to the Soviet Invasion of Afghanistan*, 337.
27. Ibid. 339. Also see footnote on page 350.
28. According to Milt Bearden, the CIA's head in Pakistan from 1986 to 1989, the US and Saudi Arabia alone provided about US$ 3.5 billion for Afghanistan

and Pakistan. Cited in Jessica Stern, 'Pakistan's Jihad Culture', *Foreign Affairs*, vol. 79, no. 6 (November–December 2000), 121.

29. Lillian Craig Harris, 'China's Islamic Connection', *Asian Affairs: An American Review*, vol. 8, no. 5 (May–June 1981), 291 and 300.
30. Hilali, *China's Response to the Soviet Invasion of Afghanistan*, 327.
31. *Beijing Review*, no. 6 (11 February 1980), 8–9, in ibid. 341.
32. Thomas Perry Thornton, 'Between the Stools?: US Policy towards Pakistan during the Carter Administration', *Asian Survey*, vol. 22, no. 10 (October 1982), 969.
33. William L. Richter, 'Pakistan: A New "Front-Line" State?', *Current History*, vol. 81, no. 475 (May 1982), 205.
34. S. M. Burke, *Pakistan's Foreign Policy: An Historical Analysis* (London: Oxford, 1973), 447–8. Under the Reagan Administration in mid-1981, Pakistan and the US reached an agreement under which the US provided US$3.2 billion aid to Pakistan, half economic and half military. In the defence sector, the US agreed to sell on a cash basis, 40 F-16 fighter aircraft at the total cost of US$1.1 billion. See also Richter, 'Pakistan: A New "Front-Line" State?', 205–6.
35. Mahmud, 'Sino-Pakistan Relations: An "All-Weather Friendship"', 17.
36. Hilali, *China's Response to the Soviet Invasion of Afghanistan*, 335.
37. *Xinhua General News Service* (3 May 1980), accessed via LexisNexis Academic.
38. 'Quarterly Chronicle and Documentation', *The China Quarterly*, no. 83 (September 1980), 624.
39. China viewed the Soviet friendship treaties with India, Vietnam, Mongolia, and Afghanistan; the increased Soviet troops on the Sino-Soviet border; and the Vietnam-backed and Soviet supported HengSamrin government in Cambodia as a part of the Soviet strategy to encircle China.
40. *Beijing Review*, no. 19 (12 May 1980), 4.
41. For instance, in October 1980, in an interview with the correspondent of *Beijing Review*, Zheng Fangkun, Zia opposed foreign intervention in Cambodia. 'Beijing Review's Interview with Pakistan President Zia ul-Haq', *Beijing Review*, no. 45 (10 November 1980), 9–11.
42. *Beijing Review*, no. 19 (12 May 1980), 19.
43. *Xinhua General News Service* (3 May 1980), accessed via LexisNexis Academic.
44. 'Quarterly Chronicle and Documentation', *The China Quarterly*, no. 87, (September 1981), 571.
45. 'Speech by vice-premier Li Xiannian at a banquet, 21 January 1979', Jain, *China South Asia Relations: 1947–1980*, 184.
46. John W. Garver, 'Sino-Indian Rapprochement and the Sino-Pakistan Entente', *Political Science Quarterly*, vol. III, no. 2 (Summer 1996), 327.

47. Ghulam Ali, 'China's Kashmir Policy: Back to Neutrality', *IPRI Journal*, vol. V., no. 2 (Summer 2005), 50–1.
48. *Dawn* (20 October 1982), as cited in Zubeida Mustafa, 'Pakistan's Foreign Policy—A Quarterly Survey', *Pakistan Horizon*, vol. XXXV, no. 4 (1982), 5–7.
49. Khalid Mahmud, 'Sino-Pakistan Relations: An "All-Weather Friendship"', *Regional Studies*, vol. XIX, no. 3 (Summer 2001), 17.
50. China's opening up had a double advantage. From the West, it could acquire high technology while it could sell its weapons to the Third World. Chinese weapons remained low in quality but they were far cheaper than those from the developed countries. Steven I. Levine, 'Sino-American Relations: Practicing Damage Control' in Samuel S. Kim (ed.), *China and the World: Chinese Foreign Policy Faces the New Millennium* (Colorado: Westview Press, 1998), 103.
51. Robert Wirsing, 'The Enemy of My Enemy: Pakistan's China Debate', *Asia-Pacific Centre for Security Studies, Special Assessment* (December 2003), 3.
52. Jabin T. Jacob, 'China-Pakistan Relations: Reinterpreting the Nexus', *China Report*, vol. 46, no. 217 (2010), 219.
53. SIPRI Yearbook 1985 (London: Taylor & Francis, 1985), 356.
54. Yaacov Vertzberger, 'The Political Economy of Sino-Pakistani Relations: Trade and Aid 1963–82', *Asian Survey*, vol. XXIII, no. 5 (May 1983), 647–8.
55. Ibid. 648.
56. Military Balance 1981–1982 (London: The International Institute for Strategic Studies), 86, as cited in Latif Ahmed Sherwani, 'Review of Sino-Pakistan Relations (1981–85)'. *Pakistan Horizon*, vol. XXXIX, no. 1 (First Quarter 1986), 97–8.
57. *The Times of India* (Bombay, 22 August 1984), cited in ibid. 97–8.
58. Khalid Mahmood, 'Economic Dimension of Pakistan China Relations', in *Proceedings of One-Day International Seminar on Pakistan-China Relations in Changing Regional and Global Scenario* (Jamshoro: Area Study Center for Far East & South East Asia, University of Sindh, 29 September 2005), 75.
59. *Beijing Review*, vol. 25, no. 44 (1 November 1982), 9.
60. Many Chinese officials and military personnel received Pakistan's civil and military medals including the highest, the Nishan-i-Pakistan. However, there was no reference found, at least during the time this book was written, that any Pakistani had received a Chinese medal.
61. *Beijing Review*, vol. 27, no. 11 (12 March 1984), 6.
62. Official statements on Talks between the President General Mohammad Zia ul-Haq and President Li Xiannian of China, on 6 March 1984, in Joint Communiqués 1977–1997 (Islamabad: Ministry of Foreign Affairs Government of Pakistan, n.d.), 133–4.
63. *The Muslim* (editorial), (Islamabad, 3 July 1985).

64. Rafique Afzal, *Pakistan Year Book, 1985–1986* (Karachi, Lahore: East and West Publishing Company, 1985), 205.
65. *The Muslim* (editorial), (Islamabad, 3 July 1985). Also see Yasmin Qureshi, 'Pakistan Foreign Policy: A Quarterly Survey', *Pakistan Horizon*, vol. XXXVIII, no. 3 (1985), 10–11. Abdur Razzaq Khan Abbasi, 'Thirty Five Years of Pakistan-China Relations', *Strategic Studies*, vol. IX, no. 4 (Summer 1986), 32.
66. Dutta, 'China and Pakistan: End of a "Special Relationship"', 130. Also Mushahid Hussain, 109.
67. *China Daily* (18 November 1985).
68. Fauzia, 'Pakistan Foreign Policy: A Quarterly Survey', *Pakistan Horizon*, vol. XXXVIII, no. 4 (Fourth Quarter 1985), 15–16.
69. *Pakistan Time* (30 September 1985) and *Jang* (30 September 1985).
70. Atique, 'Pakistan Foreign Policy: A Quarterly Survey',15–16.
71. Ibid.
72. The summit was held in Geneva in November 1985 between Reagan and Gorbachev.
73. Sherwani, 'Review of Sino-Pakistan Relations (1981–85)', 104.
74. Atique, 'Pakistan Foreign Policy: A Quarterly Survey', 17.
75. *Japan Economic Newswire* (22 April 1986).
76. 'Quarterly Chronicle and Documentation', *The China Quarterly*, no. 108 (December 1986), 769.
77. *Keesing's Contemporary Archives*, vol. XXXIII (November 1987), 35515.
78. *Pakistan Times* (24 June 1978) and *Dawn* (23 June 1987).
79. The Geneva Accords were signed in April 1988 between Pakistan and Afghanistan with the United States and the Soviet Union as guarantors to end the war in Afghanistan. Junejo's move to sign these accords led to a rift between his government and President Zia ul-Haq. The Pakistani Army was against signing any deal without first ensuring the installing of a pro-Pakistan government in Kabul. These differences led Zia to dismiss Junejo's government in May 1988.
80. Rafique Afzal, *Pakistan Year Book, 1988–1989* (Karachi, Lahore: East West Publishing Company), 281–2.
81. Following the Indian nuclear test, Bhutto called a cabinet meeting in which he officially decided to launch a nuclear weapons programme, which until that time was only a 'hedging option'. Fitzpatrick, *Nuclear Black Markets*, 16.
82. China joined the NPT in 1993 and its assistance to Pakistan continued for a year, ending around 1994. John W. Garver, 'The Future of Sino-Pakistani Entente Cordiale', in Michael R. Chambers (ed.), *South Asia in 2020: Future Strategic Balances and Alliances* (Carlisle: Strategic Studies Institute of the US

Army War College, 2002), 404. Some Western analysts alleged that China's support continued in other forms afterwards as well.

83. Ibid. Also see Dutta, 'China and Pakistan: End of a "Special Relationship"', 141–2.
84. *Financial Times* (14 August 1984); *Nucleonics Week* (23 May 1991), 1, as cited in Garver, 'The Future of the Sino-Pakistani Entente Cordiale', in Michael, *South Asia in 2020*, 403.
85. Ibid.
86. *Nawa-e-Waqt* (Urdu language daily from Rawalpindi), (7 November 1985).
87. *Dawn* (13 April 1989).
88. Wang Hongyu, 'Sino-Indian Relations', *Asian Survey*, vol. 35, no. 6 (January 1995), 546.
89. For the full text, see 'Sino-Indian Joint Press Communiqué' (Beijing, 23 December 1988), Ministry of Foreign Affairs of the People's Republic of China, <http://www.fmprc.gov.cn/eng/wjdt/2649/t15800.htm>.
90. Ibid.
91. *Beijing Review*, vol. 32 nos. 7 & 8 (13–26 February 1989), 10–11.
92. Mohammed Ahsen Chaudhri, 'Pakistan Foreign Policy: A Quarterly Review', *Pakistan Horizon*, vol. XLII, no. 2 (April 1989), 22–4.
93. *Beijing Review*, vol. 32, nos. 7 & 8 (13–26 February 1989), 7.
94. Ibid. 6–7.
95. The US and the Western world immediately reacted to the incident. The US suspended all military sales and contacts, and cancelled high-level meetings with China. Canada recalled its ambassador, while France and the Netherlands froze diplomatic ties. Belgium, Germany, and Mexico banned visits. Great Britain postponed talks on the return of Hong Kong, and the planned visits of Prince Charles and Princess Diana were called off. See Jim Abrams, 'China's Harsh Repression Leads to Diplomatic Isolation', *The Associated Press* (23 June 1989), accessed via LexisNexis Academic.
96. Mushahid Hussain, 'Pakistan-China Defence Cooperation: An Enduring Relationship', 110.
97. Ibid.
98. 'Pakistan always standing with China, B. Bhutto declares', *The Xinhua General Overseas News Service* (29 June 1989), accessed via LexisNexis Academic.
99. 'Asian News; Pakistan Supports Tokyo's Policy on China', *Japan Economic Newswire* (27 September 1989), accessed via LexisNexis Academic.
100. Li had emerged in a power struggle with former premier Zhao Ziyang during the crackdown. Zhao was sympathetic to the protesters and this led to his downfall, while Li advocated a hard line. *The Associated Press* (14 November 1989).

101. 'Quarterly Chronicle and Documentation', *The China Quarterly*, no. 124 (December 1990), 776.
102. Burke, *Pakistan's Foreign Policy*, 468.
103. 'Li says U.S. "owes a debt" to China', *United Press International* (16 November 1989), accessed via LexisNexis Academic.
104. 'Li Peng: China to offer Pakistan Nuclear Power Plan', *Xinhua General News Service* (16 November 1989).
105. *Asia Pulse* (28 October 1999).
106. Staff Study, 'Pakistan's Foreign Policy: Quarterly Survey—October to December 1989', *Pakistan Horizon*, vol. 43, no. 1 (January 1990), 1–2.
107. Fitzpatrick, *Nuclear Black Markets*, 15.
108. John W. Garver, 'Sino-Indian Rapprochement and the Sino-Pakistan Entente', *Political Science Quarterly*, vol. 111, no. 2 (1996), 334–5.
109. Staff Study, 'Pakistan's Foreign Policy: Quarterly Survey—October to December 1989', *Pakistan Horizon*, vol. 43, no. 1 (January 1990), 1–2.
110. The CIA and the ISI jointly recruited over 35,000 Muslim radicals from 40 Islamic states. Tens of thousands of others came to study in Pakistani madrasas (seminaries) which proliferated during the 1980s. Collectively over 100,000 foreign Muslim radicals were directly inspired by the Afghan jihad. Ahmed Rashid, 'The Taliban: Exporting Extremism', *Foreign Affairs*, vol. 78, no. 6 (November–December 1999), 31. Also see C. Christine Fair, 'Pakistan's Relations with Central Asia: Is Past Prologue?', *The Journal of Strategic Studies*, vol. 31, no. 2 (April 2008), 206.
111. According to Milt Bearden, the CIA's head in Pakistan from 1986 to 1989, the US and Saudi Arabia alone provided about US$ 3.5 billion for Afghanistan and Pakistan. Cited in Jessica Stern, 'Pakistan's Jihad Culture', *Foreign Affairs*, vol. 79, no. 6 (November–December 2000), 121.

4

China's Policy of Balance and Stability (1990–2001)

By the beginning of the 1990s, China's policy of reforms and liberalisation as well as its strategy of maintaining relative neutrality, vis-à-vis Indo-Pakistan disputes, including Kashmir, further deepened. At the same time, China's relations with its two giant neighbours, India and the Soviet Union, began to improve. By the end of the 1980s, China had hosted two important summit level meetings in Beijing. In December 1988, Indian Prime Minister Rajiv Gandhi paid a historic visit to China. A few months later, in May 1989, the Soviet Head of State Mikhail Gorbachev arrived in Beijing. These visits proved to be a turning point in Beijing's ties with New Delhi and Moscow. As a result of this improvement in relations with the Soviet Union, China's policy of support to the Afghan mujahideen changed. After Gorbachev's visit, Beijing informed Islamabad that it would stop military assistance to Afghan guerrillas, arguing that after the Soviet withdrawal, the situation in Afghanistan was no longer a liberation movement. Beijing insisted that the Afghan people should resolve their differences by themselves.[1] The Soviet withdrawal brought an abrupt end to the US-Pakistan-China cooperation against the Soviet invasion. Thereafter, there was a major shift in ties between Washington and Beijing, and all Chinese support to the mujahideen halted while Pakistan continued to back them. These divergent policies had the potential to complicate Islamabad's relations with both China and the US.

After the Soviet withdrawal, Pakistan lost its strategic significance in US foreign policy. Pakistan's nuclear and missile programme, which was overlooked previously, emerged at the centre of US-Pakistan relations. The 1990 Pressler Amendment imposed economic and military sanctions on Pakistan, freezing most of their arms sales to Islamabad. Pakistan remained subject to US sanctions during most of the 1990s. The US sanctions negatively affected Islamabad while relations with their arch-rival, India, became tense after the 1989 uprising in Indian-held Kashmir.

During the nineties, China faced the dilemma of pressing forward with its rapprochement with India without leaving its traditional ally, Pakistan, isolated in the face of US sanctions and confrontation with India. As an analyst noted, 'Chinese arms transfers to Pakistan continued through the 1990s (marked by an expansion in licensing and end-user agreements on favourable attitude terms), facilitated, once again, by America's capricious attitude towards Pakistan. Whatever the merit of this American decision, it once again thrust Pakistan into China's embrace by default.'[2]

PAKISTAN SEEKS CHINESE SUPPORT OVER KASHMIR

To recap, from the mid-1960s to the late 1970s, China had staunchly supported Pakistan's stance that the people of Kashmir should be given the right to self-determination to decide their future. During the 1980s, China's position shifted from its support for the implementation of the United Nations' resolution to that of declaring Kashmir a 'bilateral' issue, which India and Pakistan should resolve through peaceful means. Then from 1990 onwards, China stopped extending its support for the implementation of the UN resolutions and also 'declined to support Pakistan's efforts to bring the Kashmir issue before the United Nations'. Moreover, 'Beijing also began expressing private disapproval and public non-endorsement of some of Islamabad's more assertive efforts to challenge India'.[3]

Pakistan's unease was natural; China was the only big power that had provided categorical support on the 'core' issue of Kashmir, which remained at the centre of Pakistan's defence and foreign policies. A shift in Beijing's policy, away from a pro-Pakistan stance, created unrest in Pakistan. To convince China to review its decision as well as discuss the latest uprising in Indian-held Kashmir, Pakistan's Prime Minister Benazir Bhutto sent a special envoy, Iqbal Akhund, to Beijing in February 1990. Chinese premier, Li Peng, appealed to India and Pakistan to settle the dispute through negotiations.[4] There was no reference to the UN resolutions. The envoy returned without any Chinese assurance of support. Within days of Iqbal's trip, China's Defence Minister came to Pakistan. Although the Minister praised Sino-Pakistan relations including their defence ties, Islamabad's support of the Afghan people's struggle against foreign aggression, and Pakistan's role in maintaining regional stability;[5] he did not take any position concerning the on-going Indo-Pakistan tension over Kashmir. In March 1990, Chinese Foreign Minister, Qian Qichen, visited India while Indo-Pakistan relations were still tense. According to an Indian analyst, in his talks with Indian officials, Qian had 'indicated' China's disapproval of the internationalising of the Kashmir issue.[6]

China's limited support on the Kashmir issue did not mean an overall reduction in bilateral relations between China and Pakistan who continued to exchange regular high-level visits and strong defence ties. Therefore, Beijing avoided being embroiled in the world's most complicated issues. In May 1990, Wan Li, Chairman of the Standing Committee of the National People's Congress (NPC), visited Pakistan. In September the same year, the President of Pakistan, Ghulam Ishaq

Khan, visited China to preside over the opening ceremony of the Asian Games. In terms of the military relationship, China and Pakistan signed a ten-year Memorandum of Understanding (MoU) in 1990 on defence, covering cooperation in weapons procurement, research and development, and military production with the transfer of technology. Both sides also agreed to jointly build Pakistan's first Main Battle Tank (MBT) and the K-8 trainer aircraft.[7]

Pakistan's domestic politics witnessed yet another change. In August 1990, Benazir Bhutto's government was dismissed by President Ghulam Ishaq Khan. As a result of the October 1990 elections, Nawaz Sharif became the next prime minister. In February 1991, he embarked on a trip to China. Chinese leaders told Nawaz they regarded the change of government in Pakistan an internal matter and that relations between the two countries would continue to grow no matter who held power in Islamabad.[8] The visit to China was also linked to Nawaz's Gulf peace mission. Both sides focused on the Gulf war; demanded the withdrawal of Iraqi forces from Kuwait, respect for Iraq's borders, provision of a greater role for the regional Muslim states, and opposition to the use of force. Nawaz stated that China and Pakistan had 'complete understanding' on the Kashmir issue and that the dispute should be settled through peaceful means 'in accordance with international agreements and the Simla Accord';[9] Nawaz was 'completely satisfied' with the visit, which in his opinion was 'most rewarding and constructive'.[10] Notably, the reference to the Kashmir dispute came from Nawaz and not from the Chinese side. Beijing continued to avoid publicly confirming a Pakistani stance but at the same time did not refute the Pakistani statements.

In October 1991, there were reciprocal visits on both sides. During Chinese President, Yang Shangkun's, visit to Pakistan, both sides signed an agreement for economic and technological cooperation; China provided an interest-free loan worth US$10 million, and assistance to the Afghan refugees in Pakistan. Yang termed his visit 'a complete success'.[11] Later in that month, Nawaz Sharif went to China with a 40-member delegation.[12] The visit was aimed at 'furthering economic cooperation between the two countries'. On the political front, China supported Pakistan's proposal to establish a Nuclear-Weapon-Free Zone in South Asia.[13] The two sides raised their concern over the US policies, especially its new world order and 'growing interference in other countries' domestic affairs under the pretext of protecting human rights and encouraging disarmament'. Their joint opposition to 'hegemonic' US attitudes might have been in reaction to Washington's June 1991 sanctions against them, which were imposed in response to China's assistance to Pakistan's nuclear and missile programme. In the context of US arms sanctions on Pakistan, China promised to fulfil Pakistan's military needs.[14]

Parallel to two-way visits, Beijing continued its overtures towards New Delhi. In December 1991, Chinese premier, Li Peng, visited India. This was the first visit in 31 years by a Chinese premier. Beijing and New Delhi signed agreements on the resumption of trade, the reopening of consulates in Bombay and Shanghai, and cooperation in space sciences and technologies. India conveyed its concerns to China about 'external inputs' to Pakistan's nuclear and missile programme, while China raised its concerns at anti-China Tibetan activities in India. New Delhi reiterated its stance that Tibet was an autonomous region of China and assured it that no anti-China activity would be allowed on its territory.[15] There are not many details regarding Beijing's response to New Delhi's concerns over support for Islamabad's nuclear and missile programme. In May 1992, Indian President, R. Venkataraman, visited China. This was the first visit by a head of state from either side. In September 1993,

Indian Prime Minister, Narasimha Rao, went to China. The most important outcome of Rao's visit was the signing of an agreement on the Maintenance of Peace and Tranquillity along the Line of Actual Control (LAC).[16]

In 1992, Pakistan expanded the Heavy Rebuild Factory (HRF) and renamed it Heavy Industries Taxila (HIT). The HRF had been established in the late 1970s, with China's economic and technical assistance, to rebuild Chinese T-59 tanks. In the following year, it was expanded and enlarged to contain various workshops and units.[17] It later became Pakistan's first tank rebuilding complex and produced two Main Battle Tanks (MBT)—Al-Khalid and Al-Zarar—armoured personnel carriers, tank guns, and a large array of components used in related arms industries. The HRF became one of the largest defence facilities and was considered the backbone of the Pakistan Army. In the Air Force, the most important outcome of Sino-Pakistan joint cooperation was the completion of the K-8 trainer aircraft. In 1999, Pakistan presented the aircraft at the Paris Air Show.

Another issue that China and Pakistan began to face, during the 1990s, was the former's support for the latter's nuclear and missile programmes. Beijing intended to continue providing assistance to Islamabad's arms programmes but this could damage China's relations with Washington. As mentioned before, proliferation had emerged as a major issue in US-Pakistan relations. Secondly, as the US drew China into the Nuclear Non-Proliferation Treaty (NPT) and the Missile Technology Control Regime (MTCR), it became increasingly difficult for Beijing to continue assisting Pakistan. As Dutta put it, 'Clandestine cooperation in these two critical areas cannot be ruled out [but] it would also face the risk of exposure, international condemnation, and sanctions.'[18] However, by the time of the implementation of the nuclear non-proliferation regime, Pakistan had reached an advanced stage in its missile programme.

The US, which had imposed sanctions on China in 1991, removed them in 1992 as China agreed to abide by the MTCR.[19] Shortly afterwards, Washington again accused Beijing of transferring M-11 missiles to Pakistan.[20] Besides this, China reportedly helped Pakistan build a factory to make its own missiles. This facility was completed, according to reports, in the mid-1990s.[21] In May 1993, the US stated it had a 'mounting pile of information' proving that China had transferred M-11 missiles to Pakistan. Finally, in August 1993, the US imposed two-year limited sanctions on the Chinese Ministry of Aerospace and the Pakistani Ministry of Defence.[22]

China's reaction to this spate of sanctions was quite strong. Deputy Foreign Minister, Liu Huaqiu, summoned the US Ambassador, J. Stapleton Roy, and lodged a 'strong protest' calling the US measures a 'naked hegemonic act' which 'brutally violated the norms governing international relations'. China threatened to pull out of the Missile Technology Control Regime (MTCR) and hold the US responsible for all 'consequences'. Beijing stated that the sanctions were not based on any principle but were designed to appease a domestic audience. It claimed that the real threat to regional security was not M-11 missiles but the US sale of 150 F-16 aircraft to Taiwan.[23]

In response to US sanctions, the number of military-related visits between Pakistan and China increased. In December 1993, the Chief of the General Staff of the People's Liberation Army (PLA), General Zhang Wannian, visited Pakistan and signed a deal to extend credit to Pakistan for the procurement of defence equipment. However, the amount of credit and the nature of weapons were not disclosed. Pakistan stated that the agreement would 'further promote mutual cooperation and strengthen the bonds of friendship between the armed forces of the two countries'.[24] Shortly afterwards, Pakistan's Defence Minister went to China.

Once again, Benazir Bhutto assumed power in Pakistan. Within days of her oath taking ceremony, she flew to China, in October 1993, in continuation of the tradition to visit China as the first official trip abroad.[25] During her stay, the issue of the US sanctions was an important topic of discussion. She stated that the US sanctions were based on 'erroneous information' as their two countries had not violated the guidelines of MTCR. Both sides called on the US to remove the 'unjustified' sanctions.[26] She briefed the Chinese side on the upcoming Indo-Pakistan talks at the Foreign Secretary level and on the situation in Kashmir. Pakistan reiterated its support of China regarding Taiwan, Tibet, and the return of Hong Kong. Both sides expressed their concern at their low-scale economic and trade ties, and stressed the need to establish joint ventures and to encourage domestic businesses to invest in each other's country.[27] Benazir Bhutto made another visit to China in September 1995 to address the United Nations Fourth World Conference on Women. In an interview with the *Beijing Review*, she praised the progress made by Chinese women, calling them a model for women in third world countries, including Pakistan. She also committed to increased exchanges between women from the two sides.[28] There was, however, not much progress in this area.

In 1994, Pakistan, which had denied the receipt of any missiles from China, stated that it had received short-range missiles but they were within the limits of the MTCR. An official at Pakistan's Embassy in the US stated that the country had informed the Clinton Administration about the delivery of M-11 missiles. He argued that with India's development of the Prithvi Missile, which was capable of reaching all of the major cities in Pakistan, his country was left with no choice. He expressed Pakistan's readiness to accept a zero-missile regime in South Asia.[29] India felt that was unacceptable.

In November 1994, Pakistan completed the Chinese-funded Heavy Electric Complex (HEC) at an estimated cost of US$30 million.[30] The HEC, which obtained technology from a Chinese firm, manufactured and supplied grids and equipment to Wapda and KESC (top state-owned power companies of Pakistan). Overall, HEC production contributed towards self-sufficiency in power generation and strengthened the capital engineering goods base in Pakistan.[31]

The PRC's assistance in mega projects, and in some infrastructure-related areas in Pakistan, did not improve trade and economic ties between the two sides. Two-way trade remained low, especially when considering their close diplomatic and political relations. Chinese leaders, having seen the positive outcome of economic reforms in their country, consistently emphasised to their Pakistani counterparts the importance of increasing trade and economic ties. Given this context, the subject of low economic and trade ties dominated discussions during Pakistani President, Farooq Ahmad Leghari's, visit to China in December 1994. In a meeting with Farooq Leghari, Chinese President, Jiang Zemin, underlined the growing importance of trade and economic factors in international relations, hoping that their two countries would expand their cooperation in science, technology, and trade. He promised to address the issue of Pakistan's trade deficit with China.[32]

There were several visits by defence delegations from the two sides during the mid-1990s. In July 1994, Chinese Defence Minister, Chi Haotian, visited Pakistan and reaffirmed his government's support for Pakistan in the region and internationally.[33] The visit was in response to earlier visits to Beijing by Pakistan's Defence Minister and the

Pakistani Chief of Army Staff. In September 1994, Pakistan's Chief of Air Staff, Air Marshal Farooq Feroz Khan, visited China to receive the first batch of K-8 jet trainers, jointly produced by the two countries. China also trained Pakistani pilots and technicians relating to this project. In 1995, two high-level military delegations from China and one from Pakistan exchanged visits.[34] The frequency of military visits showed that defence cooperation remained significant to their overall relationship and was not affected by China's improving ties with India.

CHINA'S NEW SOUTH ASIAN POLICY

In December 1996, Chinese President, Jiang Zemin, visited four South Asian countries—India, Pakistan, Bangladesh, and Nepal. During this tour, China demonstrated its 'balanced' policy towards South Asia more clearly.

By the time Jiang's visit took place, Beijing and New Delhi had further stabilised their relations. Jiang began his tour in India. Normally, visiting leaders in India were received by the Prime Minister or the President at the forecourt of the *Rashtrapathi Bhavan* (the President's House) but Indian Prime Minister, H. D. Deve Gowda, received Jiang at the airport as a special gesture. This was the first time a Chinese President visited India. Prior to Jiang's arrival, the statement given by the Chinese Ambassador to India—that his country was against internationalisation of the Kashmir dispute—had helped create a conducive environment for talks. The two sides signed four agreements; the most important being the treaty to maintain peace and tranquillity along their border. In a joint statement, the two sides pledged 'non-use of military capability against each other'.[35] President Gowda claimed that the visit was the beginning of a new era in Sino-Indian relations.[36]

Jiang was counted amongst the most influential Chinese leaders. Earlier, powerful leaders such as Mao Zedong or Deng Xiaoping had not visited Pakistan. Thus, Jiang's visit to Pakistan was 'an opportunity for Pakistan to play host to a Chinese president who could actually call the shots'.[37] However, the outcome fell far short of expectations. Pakistan's political instability struck the first blow. A month before Jiang's arrival, Pakistani President, Farooq Ahmad Khan Leghari, using his constitutional power, dissolved Benazir Bhutto's government. Hence, the caretaker government that received the Chinese president was in office for the transitional three month period, and had no political mandate to make important deals with China. Furthermore, the National Assembly (the power yielding body) was dysfunctional; Jiang addressed Pakistan's Senate, the upper house. In his speech, he proposed a five-point plan to improve relations with South Asian countries. These five points included increasing exchanges, enhancing mutual respect, promoting cooperation, properly handling disputes, and fostering unity. Jiang only made a short reference to China-Pakistan relations, while devoting most of his speech to relations with, and between, the South Asian countries.[38]

What disappointed Pakistanis was that, in his speech, Jiang did not mention the Kashmir dispute, which used to be at the core of Pakistan's foreign policy. In an indirect reference to the Kashmir issue, Jiang stated, 'If some issues cannot be resolved, then they should be temporarily shelved so that they do not have a wrong or bad effect on relations between countries.'[39] Jiang's advice was contrary to Pakistan's policy of 'internationalising' the Kashmir dispute. It was the host caretaker, Pakistani Prime Minister, Meraj Khalid, who stated in his response that the Kashmir issue was the main cause of conflict in the region.[40]

A section of the Pakistani press raised its voice over Jiang's omission of the 'core issue' from his speech. Later, in an attempt to limit the damage, the Pakistani Foreign Minister commented that Beijing's support on the Kashmir dispute had not dwindled, adding that Jiang spoke in the context of China's own experience with India, which was different from Pakistan's.[41] It was clear, as future events showed, that the PRC had greatly disentangled itself from the Kashmir imbroglio. During the visit, the two sides signed agreements regarding narcotics control, economic and technological cooperation, private sector cooperation, and maintaining Pakistan's consulate general in Hong Kong after its return to China. Beijing also provided a RMB50 million grant to Pakistan.[42]

A day after Jiang's departure, it was announced that China had agreed to supply a second nuclear power plant, Chashma-II, to Pakistan.[43] The plant cost US$860 million (PKR51.46 billion) of which China provided US$350 million.[44] Both Chashma-I and Chashma-II were pressure water reactors, with 300MW capacity and a 40 year life span.[45] China also supplied enriched fuel to be used in the plants. Later, in November 1997 during his visit to the US, Jiang resisted US pressure over the supply of nuclear power plants to Pakistan. He stated that his country would not compromise its commitments to Pakistan over the peaceful use of nuclear technology.[46]

In February 1998, Pakistani Prime Minister, Nawaz Sharif, made his third visit to China. On that occasion, China's Vice-Premier, Wu Bangguo, again pointed out that trade and economic relations between the two sides remained well below their potential.[47] Although Pakistan was China's largest trade partner in South Asia, overall bilateral trade remained very low.[48]

Parallel with the growing cooperation between Beijing and Islamabad, 'serious differences' also emerged over the support of Pakistan-based militant groups to the separatist movement in Xinjiang and the creation of the Taliban in Afghanistan. In fact, even during the late 1980s, when the Afghan war was in progress, China complained to Pakistan about the support of some Islamic groups for Xinjiang separatists. However, such concerns were conveyed quietly through diplomatic channels.[49] In early 1990, Beijing sent complaints through diplomatic channels again, concerning the activities of some Islamic groups in Xinjiang. According to a Pakistani official, China raised its concerns more loudly two years later, in 1992, and 'described this phenomenon as an interference in its internal affairs'.[50] This was the first open complaint from the PRC regarding this issue. Meanwhile, China closed the Karakoram Highway to tourists for months and curtailed traffic from Pakistan to stop the possible infiltration of Islamic militants into China.[51]

Along with concerns of Islamic militants' infiltration into Chinese territory, the emergence of the Taliban in Afghanistan, which was supported by Pakistan's military authorities, alerted Beijing. According to a Pakistani analyst, Beijing's decision to establish the Shanghai Five, which later turned into the SCO, was an indicator of China's alarm over the rise of militant religious fundamentalism in Afghanistan. Beijing termed the Taliban as promoters of 'terrorism' in the region, and accused secessionist elements from China's predominantly Muslim province of Xinjiang of training fighters in Afghani camps. They claimed that some religious parties in Pakistan also had a nexus with Islamic militants in Xinjiang.

Though China condemned 'international terrorism', it did not react to the rise of the Taliban with the same harsh manner displayed by the Americans. Beijing abstained from voting on the UN Security Council resolution or imposing sanctions against the Kabul regime. Instead, it used back channel diplomacy to talk to the Taliban. Pakistan facilitated the visit of several Chinese delegates to Kabul although 'no tangible results' were achieved.[52] In response to growing Chinese concern at the rise of militancy, Pakistan reassured China that no religious group from Pakistan would be allowed to meddle in Xinjiang. Islamabad also used its clout with the Taliban to ask them to refrain from interfering in China's internal affairs. Pakistan despatched the chief of Jamaat-e-Islami Qazi Hussain Ahmed to China in June 2000 to assure its hosts that all religious parties in Pakistan were committed to maintaining their friendship with China.[53]

MATURING NEUTRALITY

China's neutral policy, and the separation of its relations with Pakistan from its ties with India, that was launched by the post-Mao leadership, was demonstrated during Jiang's visit to South Asia. The policy was further deepened as was visible in the period that saw the nuclearisation of South Asia, the Kargil conflict, and the Indo-Pakistan military standoff.

NUCLEARISATION OF SOUTH ASIA

On 11 and 13 May 1998, India conducted five nuclear tests. Concurrently, on the second day of testing, *The New York Times* published a letter, from Indian Prime Minister, Atal Bihari Vajpayee, to the US President, Bill Clinton, in which Vajpayee expressed deep concern at the deteriorating security environment in India's neighbourhood. Vajpayee argued that a direct safety threat from China led his government to conduct nuclear tests. He expected that the US would understand Indian security needs and its decision to carry out the tests.[54]

A study of the events showed that China was provoked by the contents of the letter rather than the nuclear tests themselves. At the first test, even though China expressed its 'deep concern', the overall Chinese reaction was 'rather restrained'.[55] According to Garver, China's response to the first series was 'subdued' and 'implied approval of the tests'.[56] Generally, it takes some time for Chinese leaders to reach a consensus on how they are to respond to a new development, which could be a reason behind Beijing's 'subdued' response. However, the 13 May testing, with the concurrent publication of the letter, provoked China.

Islamabad sent a delegation to Beijing for consultation before carrying out its own tests. China refused to provide a nuclear umbrella but assured that it would not impose sanctions should Pakistan decide to test a nuclear device. This, however, was not a special favour; China did not impose any sanctions against India.[57] When Pakistan conducted its tests, Beijing expressed its 'deep regret'. Though Beijing regarded Islamabad's tests as a reaction to Indian tests and made India responsible for triggering the nuclear crisis in South Asia, its reaction was no less intense than the one Beijing had shown on the first series of Indian explosions. Afterwards, China adopted an even-handed approach towards India and Pakistan. On 4 June, Beijing and Washington sponsored a meeting of the foreign ministers of the permanent members of the United Nations Security Council (UNSC) that adopted a joint communiqué, which pledged to prevent a nuclear arms race in South Asia.[58] Beijing was also at the forefront of passing the UNSC Resolution 1172, which treated India and Pakistan equally.[59] China adopted the same even-handed approach in the joint statement issued during the US President Bill Clinton's visit to China in June 1998,[60] as well as at other international forums where the nuclearisation of South Asia was discussed. Thus, despite India triggering the nuclear crisis in South Asia and the projection of

China as a threat, Beijing maintained a relatively balanced and neutral position towards India and Pakistan.

China did not allow the nuclear issue to obstruct bilateral relations with Pakistan (or India). This was clear from their two-way military and political relations. In February 1999, China's Defence Minister, General Chi Haotian, came to Pakistan with a 16-member military delegation. During the visit, Chi stated that Sino-Pakistan strategic relations were 'growing well' and would ensure peace in the region.[61] His visit was reciprocated by the Chief of Army Staff, General Pervez Musharraf, who went to China in May 1999. Earlier in April 1999, the former Chinese premier and then Chairman of the National People's Congress (NPC), Li Peng, headed a trade delegation to Pakistan. According to an Indian analyst, 'his visit to Pakistan within one year of the Chagai [the site where Pakistan conducted nuclear explosions] tests indicated that Sino-Pakistan relations were not affected by Pakistan going nuclear'. The visit aimed at increasing economic ties, and the PRC provided aid for various development projects and for the import of machinery from China.[62] Li assured Pakistan's Prime Minister, Nawaz Sharif, that friendship with Pakistan was a 'permanent feature' of China's foreign policy. Nawaz admired China's invaluable support at 'critical times', and expressed 'understanding and sensitivity' towards Pakistan's security concerns. It was an implied reference to China's recent role during the nuclear crisis. [63] There was no Chinese response to this. In return, Nawaz endorsed China's proposal for the establishment of a multi-polar world which, according to Nawaz, would contribute to the 'relaxation in global tension and promotion of peace and development'.[64] Nawaz did not miss the opportunity to add that a just and final settlement of the Kashmir dispute between India and Pakistan, on the basis of the UN resolutions, was essential for regional peace.

Most importantly, during Li's visit, both sides 'played down' their differences over the Kosovo war and the Taliban. In a rare circumstance; Pakistan and China held divergent views on the 1999 Kosovo war. Islamabad expressed its support for the Muslims of Yugoslavia and mobilised the Organisation of Islamic Cooperation (OIC) on this issue. It also did not oppose the NATO air strikes against the Milosevic government. China, on the other hand, considered airstrikes a dangerous precedent for foreign intervention and opposed the US-led NATO operation in Kosovo. One of NATO's strikes accidently hit the Chinese Embassy in Belgrade, killing three Chinese individuals. This incident further provoked a Chinese reaction. Understandably, Islamabad and Beijing were on opposite sides on the Kosovo war. Secondly, a few months prior to Li's visit, Beijing had once again raised its concerns to Islamabad regarding the support of Pakistani militants to the Xinjiang separatist movement. However, as an Indian analyst stated, during Li's visit, both sides did not let this 'minor irritant' affect their 'otherwise "strong" friendship'.[65]

INDO-PAKISTAN CONFLICT IN KARGIL (1999)

The Kargil conflict was a low intensity war between India and Pakistan that took place, in May–July 1999, in the Kargil district of Indian-controlled Kashmir. India accused the Pakistan Army of infiltrating militants and paramilitary forces across the Line of Control. The incident led to a low-scale conflict between the two sides. Most scholars agree that although Sino-Indian relations had not fully recovered from the nuclear tests, Beijing disapproved of Pakistan's actions and showed considerable neutrality. According to a Pakistani analyst, the Chinese were 'upset' and 'made it known to Pakistan that they did not favour confrontation between India and Pakistan'.[66] As

Hagerty stated, 'China refused to condone Islamabad's provocation; China's rhetoric was slightly warmer toward Pakistan than India, but its official diplomatic position was neutral.'[67] According to a Chinese scholar, 'China not only took a neutral position but also played the role of an informal mediator by hosting separate visits for the Pakistani and Indian foreign ministers.'[68] An Indian analyst, while acknowledging China's neutrality and its meaningful diplomacy in defusing the Indo-Pakistan tension, stated:

> ...what apparently placed China at the centre stage in the international response to the recent Kargil conflict was also the series of high-level visits from both India and Pakistan that made China appear as the most important external actor in finding ways and means to terminate the Kargil conflict. Even if that may not be fully true, yet, China's continued commitment to its posture of neutrality over this fourth Indo-Pak conflict definitely made the leadership in Beijing so much more noticeable and so much more effective in facilitating the Pakistan decision to seek an honourable retreat from Kargil. But above all, what made China's response unique was its contrast with all its responses during the earlier Indo-Pakistani conflicts when China had openly supported and sided with the Pakistanis.[69]

The visits to China by Pakistan's Prime Minister Nawaz Sharif and Foreign Minister Sartaj Aziz during the height of the crisis, did not win any major support. Instead, official Chinese statements issued at various occasions urged both India and Pakistan to resolve the issue through peaceful means. On the other hand, China's references to 'bilateral settlement' in line with the Lahore Declaration[70] and its considered stance on non-interference by outsiders, in some ways, were unfavourable to Pakistan's position.[71] China's balanced neutrality pleased India and helped in thawing Sino-Indian relations that had been tense since India's nuclear tests.[72] China's message to Pakistan was clear. It could expect Beijing to continue strong bilateral relations, including the cultivation of defence arrangements with Islamabad, but China would neither back nor condone any move by Pakistan to confront India, or any other country. In some ways, China's policy towards Pakistan was similar to that of the US towards its allies in East Asia, e.g. Taiwan and the Philippines. The US sold weapons to Taiwan but did not want it to provoke China. Similarly, the US had an alliance with the Philippines but did not want Manila to recklessly draw the US into a conflict.

In October 1999, China celebrated the Golden Jubilee of its founding. Pakistan was the only country that was officially invited to participate. Pakistan also announced week-long celebrations to commemorate the occasion. Speaking at a forum as part of those celebrations, Pakistan's Minister of Information, Mushahid Hussain, stated that the PRC was a 'guarantor of peace and a hindrance to Indian hegemonic designs in the region'. In his return speech, Chinese Ambassador, Lu Shulin, opposed 'hegemonism' in all forms but did not name any country.[73] Most probably, Mushahid's remarks were his own idea, not China's. As in the past, Beijing neither confirmed nor denied this. A confirmation could affect China's relations with India while a denial could do the same with Pakistan. Several Pakistani newspapers published supplements on China's national day.

In 1999, Pakistan started pilot production of the Al-Khalid tank produced at the Heavy Mechanical Complex (HMC). Both the tank and the HMC were built with China's assistance.[74] Afterwards, Pakistan displayed the tank at defence exhibitions and marketed it to the Third World and Middle Eastern countries. China also helped Pakistan build its Aeronautical Complex (PAC) for overhauling and building aircraft and their parts.[75] The PAC worked closely with China National Aero-Technology Import Export Corporation (CATIC), China Nanchang Aircraft Manufacturing Company (CNAMC), and Chengdu Aircraft Industrial Group. In the late 1990s, the PAC started joint work on a Super-7 aircraft (called the Chengdu FC-1 in Chinese).[76] The US sanctions on Pakistan, during the 1990s, stopping the supply of F-16 aircraft and parts led Pakistan to find an alternative. According to reports in the wake of the US' first round of sanctions, in the early 1990s, Pakistan decided to include a large quantity of relatively low quality Chinese fighters in its air squad.[77]

MILITARY GOVERNMENT IN PAKISTAN AND RELATIONS WITH CHINA

In October 1999, the Pakistan Army toppled Nawaz Sharif's government and seized power. Unlike some Western capitals that raised concern over the issue of democracy, China called this coup, and the new regime's trial of the deposed prime minister on the charges of high treason, an internal affair. Zhu Bangzao, the spokesperson of China's Ministry of Foreign Affairs, stated that developments in Pakistan were not of China's concern.[78]

Like his predecessors, the new military ruler of Pakistan, General Pervez Musharraf, gave Pakistan's relations with China priority. In January 2000, within four months of his military coup, he flew to Beijing to reconnect with Pakistan's 'trusted' friend. Selecting China as his first visit outside the Islamic world was significant. He knew that no other major power would receive him as he had just assumed power by overthrowing a democratically-elected government. Musharraf received 'exceptionally warm, courteous, and detailed attention and hospitality'.[79] More important for the General was that he received

China's support for his government and assurance of the continuity of traditional friendship between their two countries. Both premier Zhu Rongji and President Jiang Zemin reiterated China's policy of non-interference in Pakistan's internal affairs. Premier Rongji told Musharraf that China's support for Pakistan would continue regardless of the developments on the international scene or inside Pakistan. 'The internal affairs of Pakistan are its internal issue and China will never interfere. We respect the choice of the Pakistani people', Zhu stated.[80] Chinese leaders assured Pakistan that in the new century, relations between the two sides would continue to grow.[81] During the visit, neither side raised the issue of the Taliban or of Pakistan-based militant groups, or support for the separatist movement in Xinjiang, at least publicly. The success of the visit enhanced Musharraf's confidence in dealing with internal political opponents as well as in foreign relations.

At the time of Musharraf's visit, Indo-Pakistan and Sino-Indian relations were not in a good state and Beijing tried to avoid taking sides. A spokesperson of China's Ministry of Foreign Affairs, Zhu Bangzao, stated, 'China sincerely hopes that India and Pakistan will effectively implement the UN Security Council Resolution 1172, prevent the further escalation of the arms race in the region, and work together to preserve peace and stability in the region.'[82] On the Kashmir issue, he added, 'We hope that they (India and Pakistan) can through peaceful consultations handle properly various differences. We hope they can become good neighbours, good friends, good partners.'[83] An editorial in an Indian newspaper termed China's stance 'mature and neutral' and a 'victory for India' in the context of stressful Beijing-New Delhi ties over the Dalai Lama issue.[84] The editorial described the reason behind the change in China's policy towards India and Pakistan:

> This is not because of any special diplomatic initiative by the latter [India]. It is just that China wants to project itself as a world player and not a country embroiled in local and regional conflicts. It is on a look-West mission and wants to occupy an exalted position in the group of near-developed nations. On the one hand, it is keen to join the WTO [which Beijing did in 2001] and on the other, wants to increase its exports to the USA and other Western countries. Under these circumstances, it has been trying to sidestep Asian irritants.[85]

Following Musharraf, in June 2000, Qazi Hussain Ahmed, the head of Jamaat-e-Islami (a conservative Islamic political party) visited China to defuse China's concerns regarding the Taliban in Afghanistan and Pakistan-based militant groups' support to Xinjiang's separatists. Qazi assured the Chinese leaders that his country had no intention to fan insurgency in Xinjiang, and he even suggested that China could use Pakistan as a conduit for talks with the Taliban.[86]

In May 2001, Chinese premier, Zhu Rongji, visited Pakistan and held meetings with the Chief Executive, General Pervez Musharraf. Both leaders agreed to enhance economic cooperation, especially in the areas of agriculture, infrastructure, and information technology.[87] Pakistan and China signed six agreements; the most important was the latter's willingness to finance the Gwadar deep seaport.[88]

Gwadar is located in Pakistan's south-western province of Balochistan. It is about 460 kilometres west of Karachi, and 70 kilometres east of the Iranian border, close to the Strait of Hormuz and the Persian Gulf. Pakistan decided to build a port at Gwadar during the 1960s but could not start the construction due to lack of funds. General Pervez Musharraf's military regime considered the construction of the port important for both economic and strategic reasons and requested China to finance it. Out of the total cost of

US$248 million required for the first phase, China provided US$198 million (US$50 million grant, US$50 million commercial credit, and US$98 million Chinese state credit), while Pakistan met the remaining cost of US$50 million. Also during Zhu Rongji's visit, China provided a US$200 million loan to Pakistan for the construction of the 653 kilometre Makran Coastal Highway (National Highway 10 or N10).

CONCLUSION

In Pakistan, there were frequent changes of governments but relations with China remained traditionally strong. This indicated that a consensus on its China policy existed in Pakistan. In spite of China's insistence for economic and trade ties, no progress could be achieved mainly due to Pakistan's lack of economic reforms, frequent changes of government, and India-centric policies. China's policy to expand its ties, with South Asia in general and with India in particular, entered a new stage. Beijing successfully separated its relations with Islamabad from its relations with New Delhi, and distanced itself from Indo-Pakistan disputes. This relatively neutral policy was unequivocally pronounced during Jiang's South Asian tour, and was further demonstrated during the nuclearisation of South Asia and the Kargil conflict. However, China's ties with India were not at the cost of relations with Pakistan. Most of the changes in China's policy were a result of overall restructuring in foreign relations rather than an attempt to merely please India. Pakistan accepted this change in China's policy as a fait accompli. Despite Chinese and Pakistani approaches differing over Pakistan-based Islamic militants' support of separatist elements in Xinjiang, Taliban's ascendency to power in Afghanistan, and the Kosovo war; they did not allow these incidents to affect two-way relations. Hence, while

Islamabad remained under partial US sanctions, China filled the gap and provided military assistance in defence sectors. Joint production in aircraft and other defence sectors led Pakistan to attain a degree of self-sufficiency and access to Chinese technology. Both sides, as usual, supported each other's policies, maintained regular visits, and did not interfere in each other's internal affairs. These factors strengthened the overall relationship.

Notes

1. Mushahid Hussain, 'Pakistan-China Defence Co-operation: An Enduring Relationship', *International Defence Review*, vol. 26, no. 2 (February 1993), 110.
2. Isaac B. Kardon, 'China and Pakistan: Emerging Strains in the Entente Cordiale', *Project 2049 Institute* (Arlington, Virginia, 25 March 2011), 17, <https://project2049.net/documents/china_pakistan_emerging_strains_in_the_entente_cordiale_kardon.pdf>.
3. John W. Garver, 'The Future of the Sino-Pakistani Entente Cordiale', in Michael R Chambers (ed.), *South Asia in 2020: Future Strategic Balances and Alliances* (Carlisle: Strategic Studies Institute of the US Army War College, 2002), 399–400.
4. 'Quarterly Chronicle and Documentations', *The China Quarterly*, vol. 122 (June 1990), 369.
5. Foreign Broadcast Information Service (hereafter FBIS), (22 February 1990).
6. Keshav Mishra, *Rapprochement Across the Himalayas: Emerging India-China Relations* (New Delhi: Kalpaz Publications: 2004), 68–9.
7. Sujit Dutta, 'China and Pakistan: End of a "Special Relationship"', *China Report*, vol. 30, no. 125 (1994), 146.
8. *Beijing Review*, vol. 34, no. 10 (11–17 March 1991), 5.
9. Statement by Prime Minister Nawaz Sharif at a Press Conference in Beijing at the conclusion of his visit to China, 28 February 1991, in *Pakistan Horizon*, vol. 44, no. 2 (April 1991), 201–3.
10. Ibid.
11. 'Quarterly Chronicle and Documentation', *The China Quarterly*, no. 129 (March 1992), 283.
12. Nawaz termed his visit 'homecoming' while Chinese leaders described their visits to Pakistan as 'calling on relatives'. *Beijing Review*, vol. 34, no. 10 (11–17 March 1991), 5.

13. 'Quarterly Chronicle and Documentation', *The China Quarterly*, no. 133 (March 1993), 206.
14. *South China Morning Post* (Hong Kong, 9 October 1992).
15. Mishra, *Rapprochement Across the Himalayas*, 70.
16. Pakistan 'hoped' that the Sino-Indian border accord would defuse tension in the region. *Asian Recorder* (1993), 23452.
17. *Xinhua General News Service* (29 November 1979). Also see BBC summary of World Broadcasts (12 December 1979).
18. Dutta, 'China and Pakistan: End of a "Special Relationship"', 145–6.
19. *Asian Recorder* (1993), 23418.
20. According to an analyst, Beijing's decision to supply missiles to Pakistan might have been in a reaction to the 'US decision to supply 150 F-16 war planes to Taiwan over China's vociferous objections'. Ahmad Faruqui, 'The Complex Dynamics of Pakistan's Relationship with China', *IPRI Journal*, vol. 1, no. 1 (Summer 2001), <http://www.ipripak.org/journal/summer2001/thecomplex.shtml>.
21. Douglas Waller, 'The Secret Missile Deal', *Time* (30 June 1997).
22. Ibid.
23. Michael Dillon, *Xinjiang-China's Muslim Far Northwest* (London & New York: Routledge, 2009), 137; Also see *Asian Recorder*, 23409–10.
24. 'China Plans Pakistan Credit toward Weapons Purchases', *The New York Times* (5 December 5 1993). Also see *Asian Recorder* (1995), 24895.
25. China was among the first countries to extend warm congratulations to Benazir Bhutto for her second time as Prime Minister of Pakistan. *Asian Recorder* (1993), 23535.
26. *AFP* (29 December 1993), accessed via LexisNexis Academic.
27. *Beijing Review*, vol. 37, no. 2 (10–16 January 1994), 4–5.
28. Ibid. vol. 38, no. 29 (26 September–1 October 1995), 21.
29. *The Washington Post* (8 September 1994).
30. *Japan Economic Newswire* (17 November 1994).
31. Ibid. Also see Hussain Ahmed Siddiqui, 'Pak-China Cooperation in Engineering Sector', *Business Recorder* (1 October 1999).
32. *Beijing Review*, vol. 37, no. 2 (10–16 January 1994), 5.
33. 'Quarterly Chronicle and Documentation', *The China Quarterly*, no. 140 (December 1994), 1238–9.
34. Muhammad Ishaque Fani, 'Pak-China Security Relations and Mutual Ventures', *JRSP*, vol. 46, no. 2 (2009), 85–6.
35. Dipanker Banerjee, 'Jiang's visit helps to improve ties with India', *The Straits Times* (Singapore, 30 December 1996), accessed via LexisNexis Academic.

36. *Deutsche Presse-Agentur* (1 December 1996), accessed via LexisNexis Academic.
37. Andrew Small, *The China-Pakistan Axis: Asia's New Geopolitics* (London: C. Hurst & Co., 2015), 48.
38. The full text of Jiang's speech in Pakistan's Senate (Upper House) on 2 December 1996 is available at <http://www.fmprc.gov.cn/eng/wjb/zzjg/yzs/gjlb/2757/2758/t16111.htm>.
39. Ibid.
40. 'China denies helping Pakistan go nuclear', *United Press International* (1 December 1996), accessed via LexisNexis Academic.
41. *Deutsche Presse-Agentur* (1 December 1996), accessed via LexisNexis Academic.
42. 'China denies helping Pakistan go nuclear', *United Press International* (1 December 1996), accessed via LexisNexis Academic.
43. 'China ready to supply Pakistan second nuclear power plant', *Agence France Presse* (5 December 1996).
44. The plant started power generation in May 2011.
45. Chashma-I will complete its life span in 2040 while Chashma-II will end in 2050.
46. Fani, 'Pak-China Security Relations and Mutual Ventures', 87–8.
47. 'Quarterly Chronicle and Documentations', *The China Quarterly*, no. 154 (June 1998), 470.
48. *Beijing Review*, vol. 37, no. 50 (12–18 December 1994), 5.
49. According to a Pakistani scholar, China first raised its concern to Pakistan during the Junejo government (1985–88). Interview with Hasan-Askari Rizvi, Lahore, April 2011.
50. As cited in 'Chronology of Events', *Pakistan Horizon*, no. 4 (October 1992), 70.
51. Dutta, 'China and Pakistan: End of a "Special Relationship"', 129.
52. Khalid Mahmud, 'Sino-Pakistan Relations: An "All-Weather Friendship"', *Regional Studies*, vol. XIX, no. 3 (Summer 2001), 23.
53. Ibid.
54. For the full text of the letter, see 'Nuclear Anxiety; India's Letter to Clinton on the Nuclear Testing', *The New York Times* (13 May 1998), <http://www.nytimes.com/1998/05/13/world/nuclear-anxiety-indian-s-letter-to-clinton-on-the-nuclear-testing.html?scp=1&sq=Vajpayee%27s%20letter%20to%20Clinton%2013%20May%201998&st=cse>.
55. Jing-dong Yuan, 'India's Rise after Pokhran II: Chinese Analyses and Assessments', *Asian Survey*, vol. 41, no. 6 (November–December 2001), 979.
56. John W. Garver, 'The Restoration of Sino-Indian Comity following India's Nuclear Tests', *The China Quarterly*, no. 168 (December 2001), 867.

57. *The New York Times* (21 May 1998), <http://www.nytimes.com/1998/05/21/world/chinese-delegation-seems-to-deny-pakistan-a-nuclear-umbrella.html?scp=128&sq=China+Pakistan&st=nyt>.
58. Garver, 'The Restoration of Sino-Indian Comity following India's Nuclear Tests', 872.
59. For the full text of the UNSC Resolution 1172, see <http://daccess-dds-ny.un.org/doc/UNDOC/GEN/N98/158/60/PDF/N9815860.pdf?OpenElement>.
60. 'Sino-U.S. Presidential Joint Statement on South Asia' (Beijing, 27 June 1998), <http://www.nti.org/db/china/engdocs/sasiasum.htm>.
61. Mahmud, 'Sino-Pakistan Relations: An "All-Weather Friendship"', 27.
62. Bhartendu Kumar Singh, 'Li Peng's Visit to Pakistan: An Analysis', *Institute of Peace and Conflict Studies* (22 April 1999), <http://www.ipcs.org/article/china/li-pengs-visit-to-pakistan-an-analysis-186.html>.
63. *Dawn* (10 April 1999).
64. Ibid.
65. Singh, 'Li Peng's Visit to Pakistan: An Analysis'.
66. Mahmud, 'Sino-Pakistan Relations: an "All-Weather Friendship"', 24.
67. Hagerty, 'China and Pakistan: Strains in the Relationship', 288.
68. Sun Shihai, 'China-Indian Relations in the 21st Century', *Institute of Asia Pacific Studies, CASS*, <http://www.casas-pkucis.org.cn/ZuiXinCG/showcontent.asp?iD=32>.
69. Swaran Singh, 'The Kargil Conflict: Why and How of China's Neutrality', *Strategic Analysis* (October 1999), 1083–4.
70. The Lahore Declaration was signed at the conclusion of a historic summit between Indian Prime Minister Atal Bihari Vajpayee and Pakistani Prime Minister Nawaz Sharif, in Lahore in February 1999.
71. Satyabrat Sinha, 'The Strategic Triangle: India-China-Pakistan', *China Report*, vol. 40, no. 221 (2004), 224.
72. Lisa Curtis, 'China's Credentials on the Global Stage at Stake in the Current Crisis in Pakistan', *Jakarta Globe* (27 May 2009), <http://www.thejakartaglobe.com/opinion/chinas-credentials-on-the-global-stage-at-stake-in-the-current-crisis-in-pakistan/277638>.
73. Mahmud, 'Sino-Pakistan Relations: an "All-Weather Friendship"', 27–8.
74. *Deutsche Presse-Agentur* (8 August 1999).
75. Pakistan Aeronautical Complex, Kamra, <http://www.pac.org.pk/index.html>.
76. Haris Raqeeb Azeemi, '55 Years of Pakistan-China Relationship', *Pakistan Horizon*, vol. 60, no. 2 (April 2007), 122.
77. *Asian Recorder*, vol. XXXIX, no. 1 (19–25 March 1993), 23005.
78. *Agence France Presse* (18 January 2000), accessed via LexisNexis Academic.

79. *People's Daily* (online), (21 January 2000).
80. *Agence France Presse* (18 January 2000).
81. Ibid.
82. The Security Council adopted the resolution on 6 June 1998, asking India and Pakistan to sign the Comprehensive Nuclear-Test-Ban Treaty (CTBT) and the Nuclear Non-Proliferation Treaty (NPT), and to find a mutually acceptable solution to the vexed Kashmir issue. *The Tribune* (Chandigarh, 19 January 2000), <http://www.tribuneindia.com/2000/20000119/main4.htm#top>.
83. Ibid.
84. *The Tribune* (Chandigarh, 20 January 2000), <http://www.tribuneindia.com/2000/20000120/edit.htm>.
85. Ibid.
86. Faruqui, 'The Complex Dynamics of Pakistan's Relationship with China'.
87. Fazal-ur-Rehman, 'Pakistan-China Economic Relations: Opportunities and Challenges', *Strategic Studies,* vol. 2 (Islamabad, 2006), <http://www.issi.org.pk/journal/2006_files/no_2/article/a3.htm>.
88. Ministry of Foreign Affairs of the People's Republic of China (14 April 2001), <http://chinaembassy.org.nz/eng/topics/3755/3756/3770/3771/t19280.htm>.

5

China's Renewed Interest in Pakistan—Relations Post-9/11

The repercussions of the September 2001 terrorist attacks on the US left deep imprints on the regional and international environment. These attacks not only affected China and Pakistan individually but also influenced their bilateral relations. In retaliation to 9/11, the US President, George W. Bush, launched a global War on Terror (WoT). The US invaded Afghanistan in 2001 and Iraq in 2003. Pakistani military ruler, General Pervez Musharraf, joined the WoT. This, once again, revived US-Pakistan relations which had been in a lull since the 1990s. US economic and military assistance began to pour into Pakistan on a large scale. To escape the US onslaught in Afghanistan, a large number of al-Qaeda and Afghan Taliban crossed into Pakistan's tribal areas; this added to the challenge of terrorism. To address this menace, Pakistan and China launched counter-terrorism cooperation.

Parallel to the deepening ties with Islamabad, Beijing continued the policy of relative neutrality towards Indo-Pakistan disputes by projecting itself as a mediator and stabiliser. It played the role of facilitator in defusing Indo-Pakistan tension which remained tense since Kargil. While recognising China's 'constructive role', the US Secretary of State, Colin Powell, stated, 'Beijing was not trying to be a spoiler but, instead, was trying to help us alleviate tensions and convince the two parties to scale down their dangerous confrontation…'[1] In

May 2002, President Jiang reassured a visiting US Congressional delegation of Chinese impartiality.[2] Later, Jiang held separate meetings with Pakistani President, Pervez Musharraf, and Indian Prime Minister, Atal Bihari Vajpayee, on the side-lines of a conference in Almaty and urged restraint.[3]

According to a Chinese scholar, Beijing played a role in President Pervez Musharraf's handshake with Prime Minister Vajpayee at the Summit of the South Asian Association of Regional Cooperation (SAARC) that was held in Kathmandu in January 2002. In the wake of attacks on the Indian parliament, India had banned Pakistani flights over its territory. To attend the summit, Musharraf flew via China, where he made a stopover. It was during this stay that the PRC leadership suggested he take the initiative and meet Vajpayee. Musharraf was cautious as it would be a cause much of embarrassment if Vajpayee refused to reciprocate. The Chinese leaders replied that were that to happen it would disgrace India, not him. They cited a similar example from their interaction with the US during an early phase of the Cold War.[4] Musharraf acted upon the advice and shook hands with Vajpayee. The handshake broke the ice between India and Pakistan.

POLITICAL RELATIONS THROUGH HIGH-PROFILE VISITS

Regular visits at top-level leadership remained the key feature of Sino-Pakistan relations in the post-9/11 period. This trend increased with the change of leadership in both Pakistan and China, in 2002–03. In November 2002, Mir Zafarullah Khan Jamali of the Pakistan Muslim League-Q (PML-Q), a pro-military political party, became the prime minister. In China, Hu Jintao replaced Jiang Zemin as president while Wen Jiabao succeeded Zhu Rongji as prime minister. Within four months of his assumption of power, Jamali embarked on a visit to China. He was the first foreign dignitary to be received by China's new leadership.

During Jamali's stay, the two countries signed four accords on nuclear energy, railways, tourism, and economic cooperation. China agreed to set up another nuclear power plant in Karachi and provided US$9 million grant under the Sino-Pakistan economic and technical cooperation agreement. Both sides shared identical views on Iraq, where the situation had worsened in the wake of the US invasion. Both leaders opposed the US occupation of Iraq, not only over the incorrect premise of the invasion—that Iraq possessed weapons of mass destruction—but also from the standpoint of their national policies. They expressed their concern over human casualties, urged an immediate end to the war, and demanded a political solution within the framework of the United Nations (UN). There was a general perception in Pakistan that Iraq was another Islamic country which had become a victim of US aggression. China, on the other hand, was becoming increasingly concerned about the US military interventions, especially the ones in its neighbourhood.[5] Apart from congruence on international issues, Prime Minister Jamali could not obtain China's support on the Kashmir dispute beyond Beijing's usual verbal appreciation of Islamabad's efforts to resolve the issue through peaceful means.

On the economic front, during Musharraf's November 2003 visit, China and Pakistan signed the Joint Declaration (on the Direction of Bilateral Relations) and a Preferential Trade Agreement.[6] This was a comprehensive agreement which identified major areas of future cooperation between the two sides. Musharraf also attended the second annual conference of Boao Forum for Asia (BFA), which emerged as an additional platform for Beijing and Islamabad to review their bilateral relations.[7]

In Pakistan, Jamali was replaced with Shaukat Aziz as prime minister. He visited China in December 2004—less than four months into his term—making it the second visit by a Pakistan's prime minister in eight months. The two sides signed eight documents. China agreed to restart work on the Gomal Zam Dam, which had been halted following attacks on the Chinese engineers, and finalised details about setting up another nuclear power plant in Pakistan. In his meeting with the Chinese leaders, Aziz expressed his apprehension about the proposed UN reforms. Pakistan feared that if and when the UN reforms were carried out, India might gain a permanent seat in the United Nations Security Council (UNSC). Due to its traditional rivalry with New Delhi, Islamabad was worried that an Indian seat in the UNSC, with or without veto power, would decisively tilt the regional balance of power in favour of India. Aziz later informed the media that President Hu completely agreed with him on the subject of the UN reforms.[8] Like Pakistan's unilateral statements on the Kashmir dispute and India, the statements regarding the UN reforms also came from the Pakistani side. There was no clear Chinese position on the issue of India's quest for a permanent seat in the UNSC.

As a matter of reciprocity, Pakistan continued its backing of China on important matters such as Taiwan and human rights. Whenever cross-strait relations were tense or the Taiwan issue was in the international limelight, Pakistan issued pro-China statements. Responding to such a situation in August 2002, Islamabad stated that it firmly believed in the One China policy, which would never change.[9] In March 2005, when China passed its anti-secession law to prevent Taiwan from declaring independence, Pakistan was among the first few countries to endorse it.[10] This policy has continued ever since.

TREATY OF FRIENDSHIP, COOPERATION, AND GOOD NEIGHBOURLY RELATIONS

In April 2005, Chinese premier, Wen Jiabao, spent three days in Pakistan during his eight-day visit of four South Asian countries: Pakistan, Bangladesh, Sri Lanka, and India. During Wen's stay, Beijing and Islamabad signed 22 agreements covering a wide range of areas including a Treaty of Friendship, Cooperation, and Good Neighbourly Relations.[11] Although this treaty received little attention, Article 4 was significant in regard to their future relations:

> Neither signatory shall join any alliance or bloc detrimental to the other side's sovereignty, security and territorial integrity; or take any action of this nature, including signing any treaty of this nature with a third country. Neither signatory shall permit any third country to use its territory to impair the other signatory's national sovereignty, security and territorial integrity.
>
> Neither signatory shall permit the establishment in its territory of any organisation or body that can impair the other signatory's sovereignty, security and territorial integrity.[12]

China and Pakistan stated that the treaty would institutionalise the spirit of 54 years of friendship, giving it a new direction.[13] An India-based analyst said that the agreement 'binds the two nations to desist from "joining any alliance or bloc which infringes upon the sovereignty, security and territorial integrity of the other sides"'.[14] These remarks capture the spirit of the treaty well.

To understand the necessity of such an unprecedented treaty, it is important to comprehend the context in which it was conceived. The treaty came in the wake of rapidly growing US-Pakistan ties after

Islamabad had embraced America's WoT. In 2004, the US granted Pakistan the status of a major non-NATO ally. As a part of cooperation on the WoT, Pakistan reportedly provided military bases and shared high-level military information with the US. According to some media reports, Pakistan had started accepting unconditional US demands. The Pakistani embassy in the US granted a large number of visas to US citizens, most of whom were reportedly from intelligence sources. As a result, the US presence and influence in Pakistan increased considerably.

Initially, China supported the US WoT, and Beijing was among the first countries to express its sympathies and help. Beijing was, reportedly, also behind Islamabad's decision to join the WoT. However, as the WoT unfolded, it exposed the US intention to entrench itself, for a long-term stay with a heavy military presence, in China's neighbourhood. This concerned Beijing, which not only began to distance itself from the WoT but initiated a strategy to deal with the US presence nearby. China knew of Pakistan's vulnerability: heavy dependence on the US and Western financial institutes such as the World Bank, the IMF, and the Asian Development Bank for economic assistance. In those circumstances, Islamabad could fall, wittingly or unwittingly, into the Western orbit. China might have feared a replica of the Cold War situation when Pakistan had an alliance with the US parallel to close ties with China. It was probably this assessment that prompted Beijing to include Article 4 in the treaty to ensure that Islamabad's ties with Washington, or any other country, did not go beyond a point that worried China. The part of the treaty that stipulates that neither party would allow the establishment of 'any organisation or body' that could harm the 'sovereignty, security and territorial integrity of the other', it appears, was related to the Uighur sanctuaries in Pakistani tribal belts. Thereby, through this agreement, China put its demands in black and white.

The treaty, which was not 'targeted' against any third country, was to remain valid for 20 years and could be further extended with mutual consent.

During Musharraf's next visit to China in 2006, both sides signed 41 agreements: 13 at a state level and others between traders and entrepreneurs of the two countries. At that time, the subject of the UN reforms was an important issue. The burgeoning Indo-US ties with Washington's open backing of India's plea for a permanent seat in the UNSC concerned Pakistan. Musharraf, therefore, raised the matter with Chinese leadership; both sides expressed understanding. Pakistan also stated its desire for full membership status of the Shanghai Cooperation Organisation (SCO).[15]

It was in this context that Musharraf offered Pakistan as a trade and energy corridor. He suggested an alternate route to the Strait of Malacca through which the PRC handles the bulk of its oil supplies and trade.[16] The proposal came in the context of the two countries' plans to expand the Karakoram Highway (KKH) and construct a road and pipeline alongside it. China had already completed the first phase of the Gwadar port and was engaged in developing an infrastructure, especially roads, within Pakistan to link the KKH with seaports in the country. With the completion of these projects, Pakistan hoped that it could become a trade and energy corridor. As a Pakistani expert stated, 'Pakistan has been making concerted efforts to highlight the strategic importance of the [Gwadar] port, while proposing to link it with Central Asia, Afghanistan, and China's western province of Xinjiang Uighur Autonomous region, through KKH.'[17] The proposed corridor could also support the modernisation of China's western region. However, instead of Pakistan's vocal stance on the issue, China adopted a subdued approach. Without making any public announcement, Beijing continued to prepare the ground and waited for the right time to make the implementation of this project public knowledge. It was in 2013 that Beijing started actively pursuing the goal of completing the China-Pakistan Economic Corridor (CPEC) that will be discussed in Chapter 6.

China's intentions for establishing a corridor were also made clear from its investment in similar, infrastructure related mega projects. In June 2006, China's State-owned Assets Supervision and Administration Commission (SASAC) signed an MoU with the Pakistan Highway Administration to upgrade and expand the KKH, incurring the cost of about $795 million, with the lion's share coming from China. Under this renovation scheme, the road was expanded while bridges and tunnels were improved, and snow galleries were constructed. The two countries planned to upgrade the road so that it could remain open all year round.[18] In Hartpence's words, 'It [was] set to become a key artery of commercial exchange between China's northwestern region and South Asia, and [would] further integrate Pakistan's economy with northwestern China's.'[19]

In line with this plan, China completed its feasibility report on the construction of a Karakoram railway line and pipeline. This 700 kilometre long, proposed rail track will connect Kashgar (Xinjiang, China) with Havelian (Rawalpindi, Pakistan) through the Khunjrab Pass. It will eventually extend to the Gwadar Port. Chinese engineers completed an initial study of the project in 2008;[20] the project involved one of the most challenging terrains in the world. Despite the formidable nature of the work involved, analysts did not rule out its completion, considering China's previous success in finishing mega projects.[21]

Continuity of high-profile visits remained the hallmark of Sino-Pakistan relations. In November 2006, China's President, Hu Jintao, came to Pakistan with a large delegation. This was the first visit in ten years by a Chinese president. Earlier, Chinese President, Jiang Zemin, had visited Pakistan in December 1996. An analysis of the tone and contents of the statements Hu made during his stay in Pakistan show that his statements were clearly stronger than the ones made by his predecessor. Hu termed Pakistan an 'indispensable partner for cooperation in peace and promised unremitting efforts to further boost these relations'. He stated, 'The Chinese can leave gold, but not the friendship with Pakistan', and proposed five steps to further promote Sino-Pakistan relations through strategic cooperation, win-win business ties, cultural and social exchanges, cooperation in international affairs, and exchanges among civilizations.[22] He also made a live address to the people of Pakistan, the second foreign head of state to do so.[23]

President Musharraf conferred the Nishan-i-Pakistan, the highest civilian award, on President Hu in recognition of his visionary leadership and contribution to strengthening Pakistan-China relations. Commenting on his visit, Hu said he was touched by the 'outpouring of brotherly affection' from the people of Pakistan.[24] Both sides signed 18 MoUs including a Free Trade Agreement (FTA), a Five Year Development Programme on Trade and Economic Cooperation under which they identified 62 new projects,[25] and established a Joint Investment Company (JIC) to encourage Chinese businessmen to invest in Pakistan. Pakistan was the second country, after Chile, to sign an FTA with China.[26]

In April 2007, Pakistani Prime Minister Aziz attended the Boao Forum for Asia. On said occasion, both sides signed 13 documents and reiterated their determination to strengthen their relationship, to fully implement the FTA, and to fight against 'East Turkestan' separatists and cross-border crimes.[27] During the visit, Aziz inaugurated Pakistan's Consulate General in China's southwestern Sichuan Province.[28] This was Pakistan's fourth diplomatic mission in China. Earlier, Pakistan had established an embassy in Beijing and consulates in Hong Kong and Shanghai.

In 2008, General Pervez Musharraf's regime ended. The Pakistan People's Party (PPP) formed a coalition government with Syed Yousuf Raza Gilani as its prime minister. Six months later, in September 2008, the co-chairperson of the PPP, Asif Ali Zardari, the widower of Benazir Bhutto, replaced Musharraf as president. Founded in the late 1960s by Zulfikar Ali Bhutto, the PPP often claimed credit for Pakistan's close ties with China. Thus, after assuming power in 2008, the Party leadership decided to carry forward the legacy of strong ties with Beijing.

Like his predecessors, Prime Minister Gilani extended support to China on matters dealing with Tibet, Xinjiang, human rights, and Taiwan. In particular, he backed Beijing on the 2008 Olympics torch relay and during the July 2009 Xinjiang demonstrations. In March 2008, a few months before the Beijing Olympic Games, protests erupted in Tibet against the Chinese regime and soon turned violent. The demonstrations came in the wake of attacks on the Olympics torch relay, which passed through different cities around the world, including Islamabad. For the prestige of its 'all-weather' friend, the Pakistani authorities took extraordinary measures to ensure the safety of the torch relay.[29] The President and the Prime Minister participated in the ceremony, which was held in Islamabad, to welcome the torch.[30] Later, Prime Minister Gilani congratulated the Chinese leaders for successfully organising the Olympic Games which, in his opinion, would long be remembered as the most splendid sporting event in history.[31]

In regards to human rights, Pakistan continued to stand by China; for example, Islamabad's stance in the UN Human Rights Council, where all member states review their human rights record once every four years. In its January 2009 session, when some Western countries criticised China's policies towards Tibetans and Uighur Muslims, Pakistan's representatives in the UN supported China's policies towards its minorities, deeming them an internal matter.[32]

Most importantly, Islamabad also backed China's crackdown on demonstrators in Xinjiang in July 2009, which led to the death of nearly 200 people. Pakistan was the first country to issue a statement in support of China. Not only this, Islamabad used its clout in the Islamic world to prevent certain countries from taking the issue of violence in Xinjiang to the Organisation of the Islamic Conference (OIC). This, according to the Chinese Ambassador to Pakistan, Luo Zhaohui, saved Beijing from embarrassment.[33]

President Asif Ali Zardari made ten visits to China during his five-year term. Some of the sojourns, however, were described as 'working visits' or in a 'private capacity' in which he did not meet the top Chinese leadership. He claimed that the purpose of the visits was to study the economic development of China and then apply that knowledge to Pakistan. His first visit in October 2008 came in the context of Pakistan's deepening financial crisis and the Indo-US nuclear deal.[34] No details regarding what China offered to Pakistan were released but a spokesman of China's Foreign Ministry stated, 'As a long friend of Pakistan, China understands it is facing some financial difficulties... we're ready to support and help Pakistan within our capability.'[35] Chinese entrepreneurs reportedly offered to invest US$5 billion in Pakistan's defence, banking, oil exploration, and mining sectors—to develop Thar coal and to build the Bhasha and Kohala dams.[36] The two sides signed a total of 12 agreements including a deal between the China Great Wall Industry Corporation (CGWIC) and the Pakistan Space and Upper Atmosphere Research

Commission (SUPARCO) to launch the Pakistan Satellite Communication Paksat-1R.[37]

The second most important visit from the Chinese side was of premier Wen Jiabao in December 2010. During Wen's stay, the two sides signed dozens of agreements and MoUs worth US$35 billion—the largest deal that Pakistan had ever signed with another country. Importantly, there was no pact related to military relations.[38] The joint statement released stated that Sino-Pakistan bilateral cooperation not only served the fundamental interests of the two countries, it also contributed to peace and development in the region and beyond. China promised to assist Pakistan in post-flood reconstruction and altogether offered US$410 million in the form of loans and assistance. Both sides also agreed to cooperate on issues dealing with Afghanistan, climate change, food and energy security, and UN reforms. Pakistan termed China the 'bedrock' of its 'foreign policy and national consensus' while China described Pakistan as an 'important member state of the region', which played a 'vital role in safeguarding peace, security, and stability'.[39] It was obvious from the statement that China was far more important to Pakistan than vice versa.

EMERGING DIFFERENCES IN US-PAKISTAN TIES

Parallel to the revival of US-Pakistan relations triggered by 9/11, US-India relations also grew faster, and culminated in a strategic partnership that was symbolised by the inking of the Indo-US nuclear deal in 2008. To remove obstacles in the deal, 'the US orchestrated a waiver for India in the Nuclear Suppliers Group, allowing it to legally import civilian nuclear technology'.[40] Pakistan, a key partner in the WoT and a major 'non NATO ally', demanded a similar deal which Washington flatly refused. The US policy of supporting India suited neither Pakistan nor China. Mistrust that had already started accumulating in US-Pakistan ties started to grow further. This once again led Pakistan towards China, which for its own reasons had already expanded the base of its ties with Islamabad.

Relations between Pakistan and the US turned sour over Operation Neptune Spear conducted by US Naval commandos to kill Osama Bin Laden, hiding in Abbottabad, Pakistan. The US reprimanded Pakistan's failure to capture the most wanted terrorist and began to question its role in the WoT. Pakistan, on the other hand, protested the unilateral action and the violation of its sovereignty. Although Islamabad-Washington cooperation in the WoT continued, mistrust persisted on both sides. If the operation was conducted unilaterally, as some media reports stated, it exposed the weaknesses of Pakistan's air defence system, which failed to detect US helicopters that flew from Afghanistan and managed to penetrate Pakistani territory for quite some time without being intercepted.[41]

It was in this context that Pakistan's Prime Minister flew to China in May 2011. Although the visit coincided with the year-long celebrations of the sixtieth anniversary of their diplomatic relations, the aftermath of the 2 May incident dominated their discussions. Some observers perceived that Pakistan was playing the China card to put pressure on the US.[42] On the other hand, as in the past, Beijing did not abandon its 'all-weather' friend in a time of crisis. In a meeting with Gilani, Chinese President, Hu Jintao, rejected recent international criticism and appreciated Pakistan's outstanding contribution in the fight against terrorism. He termed Gilani an 'old friend' whose visit gave a new boost to their friendship. Importantly, China agreed to deliver 50 JF-17 fighter jets to Pakistan on an emergency basis.[43] This injected confidence in Pakistan's Air Force that was under pressure since the operation. In a joint statement, China stated that

Pakistan's tremendous efforts and the great sacrifices it had made in the WoT should be recognised and its 'sovereignty, independence, and territorial integrity should be respected'. This provided breathing space to Pakistan's government that was under mounting public pressure over America's violation of the country's sovereignty. Additionally, during the visit, the PRC agreed to construct another mega project, the Faisalabad-Karachi-Gwadar motorway. The EXIM Bank of China provided finance for this multi-billion dollar project.[44] This motorway would become a part of the greater trade and energy corridor.

While Gilani was in China, the Chief of the General Staff of the PLA, Chen Bingde, was on a week-long visit to the US. The Chinese officials reportedly told Gilani that they had taken up Pakistan's concerns over the 2 May incident in meetings with US officials, urging them to respect Pakistan's sovereignty. Gilani informed the media that the Chinese officials had told their US counterparts that 'there should be no harm to the Pakistani sovereignty and the US should understand and appreciate [the] concerns of Pakistan'.[45] If Gilani's claim was true, China had taken a strong stance in favour of Pakistan. Some observers termed China's position during the crisis as a clear tilt towards Pakistan.[46] Sections of the media published reports that China had even warned that an attack on Islamabad would be considered an attack on China. However, there was no official confirmation of these reports.

NEW LEADERSHIP AND THE CONTINUITY OF HIGH PROFILE VISITS

In 2013, both China and Pakistan underwent leadership transition. In March, China's legislature appointed Xi Jinping as the president of the country and Li Keqiang as the premier. A few months later,

Pakistan also witnessed a change of leadership. As a result of the May 2013 elections, Nawaz Sharif of the Pakistan Muslim League-N (PML-N) became prime minister of the country for a historic third term. The new leadership on both sides not only continued the legacy of close relationship with each other but also took measures to further improve them.

Continuity of high-profile visits remained the hallmark of this relationship. Chinese premier, Li Keqiang, visited Pakistan in May 2013. Pakistan was the second leg of premier Li's South Asian tour; he directly flew there from India. President Asif Ali Zardari assured his guest that China would remain the pillar of Pakistan's foreign policy. Nawaz Sharif, Prime Minister-in-line, also met with premier Li. It was during this visit that the two sides laid the foundation of CPEC.

In July 2013, Nawaz flew to China for his first visit abroad. On that occasion, the two countries signed pacts on economic and technical cooperation, training courses for textiles, flood relief, disaster management, and the provision of equipment for eradicating polio from Pakistan. The Communist Party of China and the PML-N also signed an agreement for party-level cooperation. China also agreed to revive work on the Nandipur power plant. In a joint statement, the two sides reiterated their aim to devise 'people-centric' policies aimed at mitigating poverty, promoting social and economic development, and diminishing the roots of conflict.[47] Nawaz held extensive talks with the Chinese leaders to overcome crippling energy crises in the country.

Nawaz also visited Shanghai and Guangzhou via train and explored the prospects of a high-speed rail network in Pakistan. In Shanghai, he addressed the Pakistan-China Energy Forum, which was attended by the heads of over 50 prominent companies. Nawaz also ordered the fixation of a China Cell that was converted into a secretariat to implement the MoUs signed between the two countries and monitor the progress of CPEC.

The most outstanding boost to the recent phase of relations came with Chinese President, Xi Jinping's, visit to Pakistan. The visit was postponed a few times due to political demonstrations in Pakistan but finally took place in April 2015. It added a new dimension to Sino-Pakistan relations. As Xi's plane entered Pakistan's air space, a formation of eight JF-17 escorted the aircraft. Top political and military leadership were present at the airport to receive him. The same protocol was adopted at the time of his departure.

President Xi stated that both countries faced common threats and should stick together to deal with them. He lauded Pakistan's role in the fight against terrorism; promised to enhance Pakistan's capabilities in this fight; and expressed firm support to maintain Pakistan's sovereignty, territorial integrity, and national dignity. Pakistan extended its support to China in its fight against separatism, and its stance on Taiwan and Tibet.

The two sides signed 51 agreements worth US$46 billion as China's investment in Pakistan. According to the joint statement, 'The two sides believed that the Silk Road Economic Belt and the 21st Century Maritime Silk Road initiatives represent a new model of regional and South-South cooperation, which will offer new opportunities for Asia's rejuvenation and the common prosperity of all countries.' It added, 'The two sides decided to speed up the second round of talks on the Pakistan-China free trade agreement and are ready to open up the banking industry wider to each other under the Pakistan-China agreement on trade in services.' Both sides agreed to expand cooperation in civil nuclear energy under IAEA safeguards, in space technology, and maritime research; and committed to expand their existing trade from US$15 billion to US$20 billion in the next few years.[48]

COOPERATION ON COUNTERTERRORISM

In the history of bilateral relations between China and Pakistan, the issue of terrorism—the support of Pakistan-based militant groups to Uighur separatists, and from 2004 onwards some targeted attacks on Chinese workers in Pakistan—emerged as the most daunting challenge that had the potential to affect their relations. In the past, China conveyed its concerns about the militant groups' support to separatists privately. In the wake of 9/11, especially after the launch of the WoT, China began to adopt a more open stance. As an analyst noted, 'The Chinese government sought to link the crackdown on the Uighur movement as part of the global war on terror.'[49] Hence in the post-9/11 period, terrorism emerged at the centre of Sino-Pakistan relations and was discussed at almost every bilateral engagement between their top-leadership.

It was in this context that within days of 9/11, Chinese President, Jiang Zemin, dispatched a special envoy to Pakistan to discuss the new situation with General Pervez Musharraf.[50] In December 2001, Musharraf visited China where he strongly supported Beijing's efforts to combat separatism in Xinjiang. At the request of Chinese leadership, Musharraf held a meeting with the Imam of the Grand Mosque of Xian and other Muslim leaders, urging them to be patriotic and work for the betterment of China.[51] Musharraf said, 'Islam is a religion of peace and we don't believe in any violence and therefore you, being a part of China, have to be very patriotic and all Muslims in China should work for the good of China.'[52] According to Fazal, 'This was… the first time that a Pakistani leader went public in support of the Chinese policies to curtail Muslim separatists in Xinjiang.'[53] During his visit, Musharraf took China into confidence on his decision to join the WoT. Later, Musharraf banned a number of religious organisations in Pakistan. These measures helped curb terrorism to some extent. Beijing termed Musharraf's steps as courageous, which according to China were widely popular in Pakistan.[54]

In November 2003, Musharraf went to China for the third time. On this occasion, Chinese President, Hu Jintao, urged that the two sides should enhance cooperation in non-traditional security areas such as drug trafficking, cross-border crimes, and fighting the 'three evil forces' of 'terrorism, separatism, and extremism'. Both the countries signed two interrelated agreements, one on counterterrorism and the other on the extradition of criminals. These pacts addressed some of China's concerns about the links between the Pakistani militant groups and Uighur separatists in Xinjiang. Under the extradition treaty, Pakistan was obliged to return any Uighur separatists if caught on its territory.[55] In the following years, Islamabad extradited several Uighurs who were arrested in its tribal areas. *Dawn* commented on the treaty:

> The two governments have resolved to fight, what President Hu called, 'three forces'—those of extremism, ethnic separatism, and terrorism. Even though he was not specific, President Hu was obviously referring to the activities of separatist groups in China's Xinjiang province. Pakistan's role in denying sanctuary to the separatists has been crucial in China's successful handling of the situation... As China's friend and as a country which borders on China's Xinjiang province, it is in Islamabad's interest to ensure conditions of peace and tranquillity in its neighbourhood.[56]

In the mid-2000s, terrorism manifested itself in another ugly way. A series of targeted attacks on the Chinese workers in Pakistan started. The first incident took place, in May 2004, in which a remote-controlled bomb fixed in a parked car exploded when a vehicle carrying twelve Chinese engineers, working on the Gomal Zam Hydroelectric Project, passed by it. Three Chinese engineers lost their lives while others suffered injuries. Following the incident, the Chinese company stopped work on the project. A few months later, in October 2004, two Chinese engineers along with their guard were kidnapped in South Waziristan, Pakistan's Tribal Agency bordering Afghanistan. Abdullah Mehsud, a Taliban operative who was allegedly linked with al-Qaeda, had ordered the abduction of the Chinese workers. He was among the 26 prisoners released from the infamous Guantanamo Bay prison by the US in March 2004. Mehsud offered to release the Chinese workers if, as a quid pro quo, two Uzbek militants taken by Pakistan were also released, and the military operation launched by the Pakistan Army against foreign militants and Al-Qaeda operatives in FATA was halted. When the negotiations collapsed, military commandos raided the terrorist hideouts in which one engineer was rescued unhurt, while the other sustained fatal injuries.

After the second attack, China publicly demanded the safety of its workers and action against Uighur sanctuaries inside Pakistan. In response, Islamabad increased its crackdown on foreign militants, especially the Uighur separatists hiding in its tribal areas. The major breakthrough came in October 2004 when the Pakistan Army killed Hassan Mahsum in an operation. Thirty-nine year old Hassan led the East Turkestan Islamic Movement (ETIM) and was one of China's most wanted 'terrorists'.[57] In addition, the Pakistani law enforcement agencies killed, arrested or extradited a number of Chinese separatists from its tribal areas.

The execution of Hassan did not end the issue of terrorism. A few more attacks on Chinese technicians were in the offing. Four days before Musharraf's February 2006 visit to China, three Chinese were gunned down in Hub, Balochistan, by the Balochistan Liberation Army. It was the third attack on Chinese workers in Pakistan. Beijing, which had been less assertive before, put great pressure on Islamabad to 'catch the terrorists, ensure the safety of the Chinese there, and properly handle the aftermath'.[58] Musharraf assured his Chinese counterpart that Pakistan would take all necessary measures to arrest the culprits and bring them to justice. Subsequently, Pakistan tightened security for the Chinese workers in the country.[59]

As the menace of terrorism expanded, China devised a comprehensive counterterrorism strategy with Pakistan. Beijing increased coordination between relevant bodies; started sharing information; provided financial assistance, equipment, and weapons to increase Pakistan's capacity in the fight against terrorism; and engaged the leadership of Pakistan's religious parties.

CHINA'S ENGAGEMENT WITH PAKISTANI ISLAMIC PARTIES

China was cognizant of the role of religious parties in Pakistani politics and their influence on militant groups. Beijing started engaging some of the Islamic parties to get their support for its Xinjiang policy. In February 2009, a delegation of the Jamaat-e-Islami (JI) led by its head, Qazi Hussain Ahmed, visited China at the invitation of the Communist Party of China (CPC). During the visit, Qazi stated that China's role was necessary for regional peace and security. The two parties signed an agreement to further enhance party-level exchanges.[60] *The Times of India* claimed that the Chinese leaders had entered an informal agreement with the JI, stating that the latter would not support separatists in Xinjiang.[61] The JI also issued a statement in which Qazi urged President Zardari to develop closer ties with China and make efforts to free Pakistan from the 'clutches' of the US.[62]

Following Qazi, a delegation led by Maulana Fazal-ur-Rahman, head of Jamiat Ulema-e-Islam (JUI), visited China at the invitation of the CPC in April 2010. The delegation signed an MoU for cooperation with the CPC and visited China's troubled Xinjiang province.[63] Again in March 2015, a JUI delegation, led by its head, undertook a week-long visit of China at the invitation of CPC. Upon his return, Fazal stated that the Pakistan-China relationship was remarkable, and his party will endeavour 'to strengthen the relationship'.[64] JUI is a predominantly Pashtun Deobandi sect of Sunni Muslims, whose organisational structure and support relies heavily on a large madrasa network.[65] The leaders of the JI and JUI have some influence, directly and indirectly, on militant groups. It is quite likely that these visits will convey a message to the Islamists that China is a friendly country whose interests should not be jeopardised, nor should Uighur separatists be supported.[66]

In monetary terms, China provided moderate assistance to Pakistan on counterterrorism. In June 2009, Beijing sanctioned US$290 million in aid, specifically for fighting terrorism. This help came at a time when the Pakistan Army's military offensive against the Pakistani Taliban was in full swing. In December 2009, China supplied explosives and weapon detector scanners to Pakistan, and trained the police to use them. These scanners were installed at entry points of major cities and helped detect vehicles carrying explosives.[67] Between June 2009 and May 2010, China's aid to counterterrorism activities in Pakistan exceeded US$470 million.[68]

Pakistan, on the other hand, continued to back China's Xinjiang policy. In August–September 2011, President Zardari visited China. The visit had come in the wake of demonstrations in Urumqi following a terrorist attack in the remote region. Initially, some local Chinese officials alleged that the terrorists might have obtained training in a Pakistani camp. Although the stated purpose of Zardari's visit was to attend the inauguration of the China-Eurasia Expo held in Urumqi to attract Chinese investment, the underlying aim was to assuage Chinese disquiet and send a message to the Muslims in Xinjiang to be loyal to the Chinese authorities. As later events showed, Beijing appeared to be satisfied with Islamabad's assurances. In a meeting with Zardari, Chinese vice-premier, Li Keqiang, stated, 'China and Pakistan are true friends who have faced trials and tribulations together and are strategic partners who trust each other.'[69] The Chairman of Xinjiang's regional government declared that violent actions of individual terrorists would not affect the 'all-weather' friendship between the two countries.[70] The President of Pakistan also met local officials and heads of Chinese companies investing in Pakistan. Zardari assured his hosts of Pakistan's support against Uighur separatists, and thanked China for supporting Pakistan over the controversy with the US following the killing of Osama bin Laden.[71] Zardari's visit managed to alleviate China's concerns. These events suggest that Pakistan and China could successfully manage the issue of Uighur separatism.

DEFENCE COOPERATION

The defence and military ties between China and Pakistan in the post-9/11 period further expanded. As Pakistan had remained under military rule for several years, the Army naturally emerged at the centre of bilateral relations. Some salient features include joint military exercises, the start of security talks and strategic dialogues, and joint defence production.

JOINT MILITARY EXERCISES

The first exercise between armies from the two sides was held in August 2004 with the goal of enhancing the anti-terrorism capabilities of their law enforcement agencies. The three-day drill code, named 'Friendship-2004', was conducted in Xinjiang in which over 200 soldiers from both sides participated. It was the first time that a foreign army took part in a military exercise on Chinese soil. The second drill, 'Friendship-2006', was held in December 2006 in Abbottabad, Pakistan. Over 400 soldiers participated in this eight-day exercise. This was the first time that the People's Liberation Army (PLA) engaged in a military exercise on Pakistani territory.[72] The third exercise was held in July 2010 in China's Ningxia Hui Autonomous Region,[73] and the fourth in November 2011 near Islamabad. The fourth exercise was 'unusually large' and was aimed towards counterterrorism and low-intensity conflict environments.[74] Though Pakistan and China stated categorically that the exercise was not targeted against any third country, Indian media reported it as 'dangerous for India'.[75]

The first naval exercise between the two navies was held in 2003. It was also the first of its kind by the PLA Navy with a foreign country. China also participated in two multi-national naval exercises organised by Pakistan in the Arabian Sea: 'AMAN-2007' held in March 2007 and 'AMAN-2011' held in March 2011.[76] In April 2011, the Chinese and Pakistani ships, on anti-piracy duty off the Somali coast, conducted a joint anti-piracy exercise. In September 2014, Beijing and Islamabad started their first bilateral naval exercise that encompassed 'the entire spectrum of multifaceted maritime operations involving surface, air, and special forces'.[77]

Like their armies and navies, the air forces of the two countries have also carried out joint exercises. In March 2011, the Pakistan Air Force (PAF) and Chinese PLA Air Force (PLAAF) conducted their first joint air exercise code-named 'Shaheen-1' in Pakistan. The exercise coincided with the sixtieth anniversary of the establishment of their diplomatic relations.[78] It was the first time that PLAAF deployed its combat aircraft in Pakistan, and joined its counterpart in operational aerial manoeuvres for a few weeks. An analyst termed it another milestone in Beijing's ties with Pakistan. Thereafter, these exercises have been held annually—the site alternates between the two countries—without fail, demonstrating their commitment to defence cooperation. When Shaheen-III was held in Pakistan in May 2014, Pakistan used its JF-17 aircraft, which was jointly built by the two sides. The Indian concerns over these exercises could be measured from the following comments:

> Although China and Pakistan have framed their recent security cooperation in terms of counter-terrorism, air exercises are generally provocative given that air assets, especially fighters, are seldom deployed against small terror outfits that often use sub-conventional guerrilla tactics. The Shaheen series of exercises have thus received considerable attention in New Delhi and Washington.[79]

Two aspects of the Sino-Pakistan joint exercises are worth mentioning. First, the joint exercises started only in the wake of post-9/11, and were limited in scope and confined to counterterrorism. In about a decade, not only has the scope of those exercises increased, they have also been expanded to all branches of their armed forces. This qualitative and quantitative increase was, it seemed, in response to the catalytic developments in the region triggered by 9/11. Secondly, Pakistan proved to be the first foreign country with whom three branches of the Chinese armed forces conducted exercises.

STRATEGIC DIALOGUES, AND DEFENCE AND SECURITY TALKS

Another trend that emerged in the post-9/11 years was the move to institute two separate mechanisms of consultation: 'Defence and Security Talks' and 'Strategic Dialogues'. Despite close military relations between China and Pakistan, there had been no regular mechanisms to discuss their strategic and military ties. This realisation, prompted by 9/11, led them to give a formal shape to their defence relationship.

The Defence and Security Talks were led by the military leadership and were aimed at coordination between the two armed forces. The Strategic Dialogues were held by political leaders and dealt with broader strategic issues including matters pertinent to their armed forces. Since its first session in March 2002, the two sides have held a total of eight rounds of Defence and Security Talks.[80] The areas covered included military-to-military cooperation, regional security, collaboration between defence industries of the two countries, joint training, and counterterrorism.[81] Strategic Dialogues were less frequent but were held at a higher level. They were led by political leadership, and covered a wide range of strategic issues. The Strategic Dialogues were generally led by a Foreign Secretary from Pakistan's side and an Assistant Foreign Minister leading the Chinese delegation, aided by civil and military bureaucrats. By July 2015, six rounds of the Strategic Dialogues had been held. Not much information has been released about these discussions but clearly this mechanism has given Sino-Pakistan's strategic cooperation a formalised structure.

JOINT PRODUCTION IN THE DEFENCE SECTOR

In the defence sector, there were at least four main joint production programmes during this period: the JF-17 aircraft, naval frigates, Fast Attack Craft (FAC) missile boats, and submarines. These projects were jointly started in China where Pakistani experts received training. After initial production, the projects were shifted to Pakistan along with a transfer of technology. The JF-17 Thunder, a light-weight multi-role combat aircraft, was jointly developed by Chengdu Aircraft Corporation and the Pakistan Aeronautical Complex (PAC). The Pakistan Air Force (PAF) received two aircraft in March 2007 and 2009. After that, production was undertaken in Pakistan. Both sides have been developing jets on commercial lines with an eye on the potential market in the Third World and the Middle East.[82] The warplane is equipped with modern technological features, and is capable of carrying both conventional and nuclear weapons. Notably, it is a good substitute for the US F-16, the sale of which was suspended for several years due to sanctions imposed against Pakistan.

In April 2005, the two countries signed a deal worth US$600 million, under which China provided four Type 22 frigates and six Z-9c helicopters. The agreements covered all the associated equipment, systems, and transfer of technology. Three of the frigates were built in China while the fourth at the Karachi Shipyard and Engineering Works (KSEW).[83] By September 2010, China had supplied three frigates while Pakistan built the fourth in the next few years.[84] Pakistan also signed an agreement with China to acquire two Fast Attack Crafts, one to be built by China Ship Industry Corporation and the other by KSEW.[85] Most recently, they have signed deals for the sale of eight Chinese submarines, worth US$6 billion, to Pakistan along with the transfer of technology. Once finalised, it will be the largest deal in the history of the two countries.

ECONOMIC, ENERGY, AND INFRASTRUCTURAL COOPERATION

After 9/11, the two countries institutionalised their economic relations by signing a series of agreements: the Early Harvest Programme (EHP), the reduction of tariffs on a long list of items, the Free Trade Agreement (FTA) in 2006, Pak-China Industrial and Business Exhibition, and accords to activate their banking sector and introduce currency swap. Furthermore, China assisted Pakistan in mega projects, space technology, and the energy sector.

Along with building infrastructure, China provided economic assistance to support Pakistan's moribund economy. According to a Pakistani diplomat, 'Apart from agreeing to roll over the deposit of $500 million to support Pakistan's balance of payments, during 2000–02, China committed $700 million for projects under implementation and $800 million for new projects.' During this period, Beijing's cumulative loans and investments in Pakistan amounted to $4 billion while two-way trade exceeded $2 billion.[86]

The leadership of the two countries pushed the hitherto inactive banking sector to facilitate their economic, business, and trade ties.[87] In July 2007, the China Development Bank and Pakistan's Ministry of Finance established the Pak-China Investment Company Limited (PCICL), which was registered with the Securities and Exchange Commission of Pakistan. The two governments also facilitated their counterparts in different areas to enter bilateral agreements. For example, the Shanghai Stock Exchange signed a pact with the Karachi Stock Exchange, the Habib Bank of Pakistan with the City Bank of Urumqi, and the National Bank of Pakistan with China Development Bank.[88] In May 2011, the Industrial and Commercial Bank of China (ICBC) opened branches in Islamabad and Karachi, and showed interest in expanding the network to other parts of Pakistan.[89] In addition, the Pakistan Chamber of Commerce and Industry, along with China, entered numerous agreements to boost economic ties.[90] The growing involvement of the financial and banking sectors had the potential to help improve their economic relations, which continue to lag behind their political and diplomatic ties.

During Musharraf's April 2008 visit, the Chinese leaders promised to encourage state-owned companies to invest in Pakistan to boost its economy. They also agreed to increase youth exchanges between the two sides to pass the friendship on to new generations. Musharraf extended Pakistan's support for the Olympic Games and backed Beijing's stance on Tibet.[91] This was Musharraf's last visit to China; four months later, he resigned in the face of an impeachment threat.

In the post-9/11 period, China increased its investment in mega projects in Pakistan with dual economic and strategic impact. Beijing provided US$198 million for the construction of the strategically important Gwadar Port and US$200 million for the Makran Coastal Highway. In 2002, China Harbour started work on the first phase of the Gwadar seaport and completed it in 2005, ahead of schedule.[92] At some points during the construction, nearly 500 Chinese worked almost round the clock. According to an analyst, the Gwadar port was 'one of the latest chapters in the storied "all-weather" friendship'.[93] The inauguration ceremony, which was delayed due to 'security reasons', finally took place in March 2007. As part of greater Gwadar plan, the two countries also planned to build an international airport, a military garrison, oil storage facilities, and oil refineries. Another important project that was completed with China's help was the 653 kilometres long Makran Coastal Highway (National Highway 10 or N10), which ran along the coast of the Arabian Sea and connected Karachi with Gwadar.[94] The road reduced the travelling distance between Karachi and Gwadar considerably. Previously, it took several days to reach Gwadar from Karachi; now it is a seven-hour drive. The fishing industry has also received a boost after the completion of the highway.[95] From a geostrategic point of view, it connected Pakistani ports and major cities along the coast.

China also assisted in the development of Pakistan's railways. Through two deals worth US$20 million and US$62 million, signed in 2002 and 2003 respectively, China supplied 52,000 metric tonnes of railway material and 1,300 double capacity freight coaches. Two-thirds of the coaches were built at the Lahore Moghalpura Railways workshop with transferred technology.[96] In late 2008, Pakistan Railways finalised another deal to purchase 75 Chinese locomotives.[97] Generally speaking, Chinese technology was not as high in quality as the West's in railways as well as many other areas. On occasion, Chinese locomotives and coaches faced many technical faults.[98] Nevertheless, the low price, availability, and the element of technological transfer were compelling factors to continue business with China.

SPACE TECHNOLOGY COOPERATION

China-Pakistan cooperation in space technology was another emerging feature of their mutual relations. This cooperation has dual commercial and military applications. The two countries have been cooperating on climate, basic space, and atmospheric and earth sciences.[99] China appears to be the only country that has transferred technology to Pakistan in the space sector.[100]

During the first decade of the 2000s, Sino-Pakistan cooperation in space technologies entered a new phase. In September 2009, Beijing provided a US$222 million soft loan for the completion of its satellite.[101] The following year, EXIM Bank of China provided a RMB86.5 million concessional loan to complete this project.[102] As a result, on 11 August 2011, Pakistan launched its Telecommunication Satellite Paksat-1R from China's Xichang Satellite Launch Centre (XSLC). Following its launch, the China Great Wall Industry Corporation (CGWIC) handed over ground control facilities to the Pakistan Space and Upper Atmosphere Research Commission (SUPARCO). The satellite replaced the Paksat-1, which completed its 15 year life span in November 2011, and introduced a range of new services including broadband internet, digital TV distribution/ broadcasting, remote/rural telephony, emergency communications, tele-education, and tele-medicine.

Since space sciences and rocket development are closely related areas, military applications of cooperation in space technology could not be ruled out. SUPARCO is closely linked with the Kahuta Research Laboratories (KRL) of Pakistan, which is one of the organisations responsible for Pakistan's missile programme. According to media reports, SUPARCO cooperated with the KRL in making Pakistan's Hatif and Shaheen missiles. During the 1990s, when the US imposed sanctions on Pakistan, SUPARCO was one of the organisations which was affected by those sanctions.[103]

ENERGY SECTOR

China's investment in the energy sector exceeds all other areas of investment. It seems determined to help Pakistan overcome power shortages. Beijing's help in building nuclear power plants and several dams was particularly significant for an energy-starved Pakistan. In 2013, China started work on two nuclear power plants—Chashma-III and Chashma-IV, each with a 300 MW capacity—at Chashma Nuclear Power Complex where two plants built by China were already operational. Most recently, in a landmark deal, China agreed to sell two more nuclear power plants with a combined capacity of 2,000 MW to be set up in Karachi, KANUPP-2 and KANUPP-3. China National Nuclear Corporation (CNNC) and Pakistan Atomic Energy Commission (PAEC) plan to sign an agreement to conduct a joint study to finalise design modifications and other details.[104]

China intends to build more nuclear power plants in Pakistan. However, Beijing's joining of the Nuclear Suppliers Group (NSG) has complicated the situation.[105] As a member of the NSG, any further nuclear deal with Pakistan requires China to gain the group's approval, as seen in the case of the Indo-US nuclear deal in September 2008. Until recently, China took the position that all those plants were 'grandfathered' in the past when Beijing was not a member of the NSG. How this alters China's position if it wishes to deliver more nuclear power plants to Pakistan remains to be seen.

Additionally, the two sides have been expanding their cooperation in hydropower generation. In June 2009, China signed an MoU with Pakistan for an investment of US$700 million to construct twelve small and medium size dams in Pakistan. In August 2009, they signed another MoU in which China's Three Gorges Project Corporation agreed to provide economic and technical assistance for the construction of 7,000 MW Bunji Dam in Gilgit-Baltistan.[106] Besides nuclear and hydropower projects, Pakistan completed several thermal power units with China's assistance.[107]

COMMERCIAL ASPECTS OF THE RELATIONSHIP

In its relations with Pakistan, China also gained commercial benefits and access to Pakistan's natural resources. For example, in the nuclear sector, China has been building 40 per cent of the world's total nuclear power plants (mostly inside China), and intends to increase its share of the global nuclear energy market. Beijing plans to present its cooperation with Islamabad as a showcase to other developing countries, which offer a huge market for the sale of nuclear power plants. According to an observer, 'China's nuclear industry executives, on the other hand, see abundant opportunities to expand their business overseas and want to use their experience with Pakistan's Chashma nuclear complex to leverage other contracts abroad.'[108] Another analyst says that, 'It also provides a workplace for China's nuclear industry to gain experience in building nuclear power plants abroad, an endeavour that the Chinese in the future very much want to do.'[109] A segment of the Western media also claimed that it was China, not Pakistan, that was 'pushing ahead with nuclear energy cooperation' using 'outdated nuclear technology'.[110] Regardless of these comments, the nuclear power plant deals benefited both sides, especially Pakistan that was in dire need of energy.

In return, Beijing got access to some of Pakistan's natural resources through these treaties. Chinese companies were engaged in various projects in Pakistan and signed contracts for important resources—

such as the Saindak copper and gold mines in the Chagai District, the Duddar lead and zinc mining project in Lasbela, vast telecom industry, and easy access to Pakistani markets.[111] Chinese companies also showed interest in oil, gas, and coal explorations in Pakistan. In 2003, China's largest copper producer, Jiangxi Copper Co. Ltd, began to operate the US$300 million Saindak copper mine project for a period of ten years. The mine produced about 16,000 tons of blister copper ore annually, all of which was purchased by China. According to an estimate, the mine has ore reserves of over 12 million tonnes. Similarly, the China Metallurgical Construction Group Corporation, with financial help from the China Development Bank, ran the Duddar zinc and lead mine with an estimated capacity of some 660,000 tonnes. The same company showed interest in modernising Pakistan Steel Mills, Pakistan's only integrated steel manufacturing plant.[112] The exploitation of Pakistani resources proved mutually beneficial. China gained access to raw materials while Pakistan received investments to develop various unexplored sectors.

MUTUAL SUPPORT IN NATURAL CALAMITIES AND MULTILATERAL FORUMS

In the broader framework of their 'all-weather' relationship, China and Pakistan have developed a tradition of helping each other during natural disasters. Although the scale of such help has been fairly moderate (especially from the Pakistani side except during the May 2008 earthquake in Sichuan, China), this reciprocal assistance has helped to create public goodwill on both sides. In October 2005, when a deadly earthquake hit Azad Kashmir and Khyber Pakhtunkhwa in Pakistan, Beijing immediately sent a 49-member international rescue team. Within three weeks, China's relief aid reached US$20.5

million. Beijing's help continued in the following months along with rehabilitation efforts in the affected areas.[113]

Islamabad reciprocated Beijing's gestures in a similar spirit. In May 2008, a powerful earthquake struck China's Sichuan province. Pakistan immediately sent a team of paramedical staff with a mobile hospital and medicines, dispatched 30,000 tents, food, lifesaving drugs, and other essential supplies. Touched by the quick and overwhelming response from Pakistan, Chinese President, Hu Jintao, specifically met the Pakistani team of doctors during his visit to the affected area. On said occasion, Hu stated that they symbolised the friendship that the Pakistani and Chinese people cherished.[114] It was this sentiment of goodwill that prompted the Chinese audience at the Beijing Olympics, in 2008, to give a standing ovation to the Pakistani sports delegates when it entered the stadium. Most interviewees (from China and Pakistan) called it a gesture of appreciation for Pakistan's help during the Sichuan earthquake as well as a tribute to this enduring relationship between the two countries. When in October 2008 an earthquake hit Quetta, the capital of Balochistan, China was the first country to send assistance.[115] China also extended its support to Pakistan during the 2010 floods (which affected over 20 million people) and the 2014 floods.

This mutual support was also demonstrated at multilateral forums. In June 2003, Pakistan became a member of the Association of Southeast Asian Nations (ASEAN) Regional Forum (ARF) with help from China.[116] Again in 2005, Pakistan's entry into the Shanghai Cooperation Organisation (SCO), as an observer, became possible with China's support.[117] Similarly, in November 2005, China became an observer of the South Asian Association of Regional Cooperation (SAARC) with Pakistan's support. Pakistan had lobbied hard since

India was reluctant to include China.[118] These are only a few examples and they reflect the existing goodwill on the two sides.

CONCLUSION

Despite changes in the regional security environment triggered by 9/11, China-Pakistan relations not only remained steadfast but became more structured. This was evident from the various agreements the two sides signed covering different sectors. To address the issue of terrorism, they shared information, conducted joint military exercises, and China extended assistance to Pakistan's counterterrorism efforts. Islamabad increased security measures for the Chinese workers, and took measures against Uighur sanctuaries in Pakistan's tribal areas. Although this issue could not be resolved fully, China was generally satisfied with the measures taken by Pakistan. China's help in building mega projects such as the Gwadar seaport, nuclear power plants, coal and zinc mines, highways, telecommunications, a satellite, railways, dams, and the ambitious trade and energy corridor contributed to Pakistan's long-term economic development. They further strengthened two-way relations and in return, China gained access to some Pakistani natural resources, won a reasonably large market, and obtained Pakistan's support on important issues such as Taiwan, Tibet, and human rights. From an economic and trade point of view, the signing of the FTA, the establishment of the Joint Investment Company, economic and industrial zones, and joint ventures addressed the issue of low economic and trade ties. Above all, the successful implementation of CPEC, as discussed in the next chapter, will further expand their cooperation, especially in economic, trade, and people-to-people contacts.

NOTES

1. *Dawn* (7 February 2002).
2. *The Press Trust of India* (29 May 2002).
3. *AFP* (6 June 2002).
4. An interview with a senior Chinese scholar working with Peking University, Beijing, June 2014.
5. In addition to the invasion of Afghanistan and military bases in some Central Asian States, Iraq was another US target. These developments worried China about the US' future intentions and military presence in its neighbourhood.
6. For full text of the Joint Declaration, see Ministry of Foreign Affairs of the People's Republic of China, <http://www.fmprc.gov.cn/eng/wjdt/2649/t40148.htm>.
7. Ibid.
8. *Dawn* (16, 17 & 19 December 2004).
9. Ibid. (11 August 2002).
10. *Pakistan Times* (16 March 2005).
11. Ibid. (11 April 2005).
12. For full text of the treaty, see BBC Monitoring Asia Pacific—Political, Supplied by BBC Worldwide Monitoring (6 April 2005), accessed via LexisNexis Academics.
13. Maqbool Ahmad Bhatty, 'The Security Dimension of Pakistan China Relations,' in Proceedings of One-Day International Seminar on Pakistan-China Relations in *Changing Regional and Global Scenario* (Jamshoro: Area Study Center for Far East & South East Asia, University of Sindh, 29 September 2005), 19.
14. D. S. Rajan, 'China: Revisiting the 2005 Friendship Treaty with Pakistan', *South Asia Analysis Group,* paper no. 2058 (10 December 2006), <http://www.southasiaanalysis.org/%5Cpapers21%5Cpaper2058.html>.
15. *Dawn* (22 February 2006).
16. Ibid. (22–23 February 2006).
17. Fazal-ur-Rehman, 'Prospects of Pakistan Becoming a Trade and Energy Corridor for China', *Strategic Studies*, vol. XXVII, no. 2 (Summer 2007), <http://www.issi.org.pk/old-site/ss_Detail.php?dataId=431>.
18. Although China and Pakistan refer the road as an 'all-weather' link, practically it is not so. The road was closed most of the winter due to heavy snow and bad weather conditions.
19. Hartpence, 'The Economic Dimension of Sino-Pakistani Relations', 587.
20. *Business Recorder* (16 December 2010), <http://www.brecorder.com/news/top-stories/1134627:chinese-prime-minister-to-open-icbc-branch-visit-begins-from-december-17.html>.

21. C. Raja Mohan, 'China plans Karakoram rail link to Pak and the Arabian Sea', *Indian Express* (6 July 2010).
22. *People's Daily* (online), (24 November 2006).
23. President Bill Clinton was the first head of state who made a live address to the Pakistani people during his visit to Pakistan in March 2000, *Daily Times* (25 November 2006).
24. *People's Daily* (26 November 2006).
25. 'Message from Minister for Finance, Revenue, Statistics and Economic Affairs', *Business Recorder* (18 December 2007).
26. *Dawn* (25 November 2005).
27. *People's Daily* (online), (18 April 2007).
28. Ibid. (19 April 2007).
29. *People's Daily* (online), (15 April 2008).
30. Ibid.
31. Ibid. (26 August 2008).
32. *Dawn* (10 January 2009).
33. *Daily Times* (5 September 2009).
34. By the time of Zardari's China visit, foreign reserves were rapidly depleting. Pakistan at that time needed 'approximately US$3–4 billion in the next quarter and $7–10 billion over the next year.' *Dawn*, 'Pak-China Friendship' (editorial), (16 September 2008).
35. *Dawn* (17 October 2008).
36. Ibid. (18 October 2008).
37. *Xinhua* (16 October 2008), <http://news.xinhuanet.com/english/2008-10/16/content_10206116.htm>.
38. Ghulam Ali, 'Wen Jiabao's visit to India and Pakistan reinforces stability and neutrality', *East Asia Forum* (21 January 2011), <http://www.eastasiaforum.org/2011/01/21/wen-jiabaos-visit-to-india-and-pakistan-reinforces-stability-and-neutrality/>.
39. Joint Statement between the People's Republic of China and the Islamic Republic of Pakistan, <http://pk.chineseembassy.org/eng/yingwenzhuanti/t780017.htm>.
40. Isaac B. Kardon, 'China and Pakistan: Emerging Strains in the Entente Cordiale', *Project 2049 Institute Arlington* (Virginia, 25 March 2011), 18.
41. B. Raman, 'All Eyes on Gilani's Visit to China', *South Asia Analysis Group*, paper no. 4493 (16 May 2011), <http://www.southasiaanalysis.org/%5Cpapers45%5Cpaper4493.html>.
42. Tanvir Ahmad Khan, 'Permanence in a world of flux', *The Express Tribune* (21 May 2011).
43. *Dawn* (21 May 2011).

44. The Exim Bank of China financed major joint projects such as Chashma Nuclear Power Plants, Karakoram Highway, and Saindak Gold and Copper Mining.
45. Ibid. (21 May 2011).
46. Interview with Professor Tahir Amin, November 2013, Islamabad.
47. *The Express Tribune* (6 July 2013), <http://tribune.com.pk/story/573220/nawazs-beijing-visit-trade-corridor-tops-mou-bonanza/>.
48. For full text of the 'Joint Statement between the Islamic Republic of Pakistan and the People's Republic of China on Establishing the All-Weather Strategic Cooperative Partnership', signed on 20 April 2015 in Islamabad, see *Silk Road Fund*, <http://www.silkroadfund.com.cn/enweb/23809/23814/27160/index.html>.
49. Abanti Bhattacharya, 'The Xinjiang Factor' in Swaran Sing (ed.), *Sino-Pakistan Strategic Relations: Indian Perspectives* (New Delhi, Manohar, 2007), 350.
50. Fazal-ur-Rehman, 'Targeted Attacks on Chinese: Myth and Reality', *Strategic Studies*, vol. XXVII, no. 4 (Winter 2007), <http://www.issi.org.pk/old-site/ss_Detail.php?dataId=451>.
51. Ahmad Faruqui, 'China Card Could yet Trump Musharraf', *Asia Times* (25 May 2002), <http://www.atimes.com/ind-pak/DE25Df02.html>.
52. Ibid.
53. Fazal-ur-Rehman, 'Targeted Attacks on Chinese'.
54. *People's Daily* (online), (21 December 2001).
55. *Dawn* (4 November 2003).
56. *Dawn* (5 November 2003), <http://www.dawn.com/news/1065228>.
57. In December 2003, China issued its first list of wanted terrorists that included four groups and 11 individuals. *BBC* (15 December 2003), <http://news.bbc.co.uk/2/hi/asia-pacific/3319575.stm>.
58. *People's Daily* (online), (16 February 2006).
59. In September 2009, China's Ambassador to Pakistan, Lou Zhaohui, in an interview with the Pakistani media stated that his country was fully satisfied at the security arrangements provided by the Pakistan government. *Daily Times* (5 September 2009).
60. *Geo TV* (Pakistan), (11 February 2009).
61. *The Times of India* (20 February 2009).
62. Ibid.
63. M. K. Bhadrakumar. 'US puts a stop to hyphenation', *Asia Times* (17 July 2010), <http://www.atimes.com/atimes/South_Asia/LG17Df03.html>.
64. *Dunya TV* (26 March 2015), <http://dunyanews.tv/index.php/en/Pakistan/270039-Fazlur-Rehman-urges-PM-to-include-neglected-areas->.

65. 'Islamic Parties in Pakistan', International Crisis Group, *Asia Report,* no. 216 (12 December 2011).
66. Ghulam Ali, 'China's Deepening Engagement with Pakistan on Counter-terrorism', *Central Asia Caucasus Analyst,* vol. 12, no. 10 (26 May 2010), <http://www.cacianalyst.org/?q=node/5333>.
67. *Associated Press of Pakistan* (5 December 2009).
68. Ibid.
69. *Dawn* (1 September 2011).
70. *Xinhua* (online), (7 March 2012).
71. B. Raman, 'Zardari in Urumqi: Focus on Chinese Role in Gilgit-Baltistan & Sino-Pakistan MaritimeCooperation', *South Asia Analysis Group*, paper no. 4675 (1 September 2011), <http://www.southasiaanalysis.org/%5Cpapers 47%5Cpaper4675.html>.
72. *People's Daily* (online), (11 December 2006).
73. See <http://english.peopledaily.com.cn/90001/90776/90883/7051015.html>.
74. *CNTV* (17 November 2011), <http://english.cntv.cn/program/asiatoday/20111117/112429.shtml>.
75. Vilani Peiris, 'Joint military exercise highlights growing Pakistan-China relations', World Socialist Website (28 November 2011), <http://www.wsws.org/articles/2011/nov2011/paki-n28.shtml>.
76. *China Daily* (8 March 2011), <http://www.chinadaily.com.cn/china/2011-03/08/content_12137816.htm>.
77. *Daily Times* (17 September 2014).
78. *The News,* <http://www.thenews.com.pk/NewsDetail.aspx?ID=12808>.
79. Ankit Panda, 'Pakistan, China Conclude Shaheen-III Air Exercise', *The Diplomat* (online), (29 May 2014).
80. *China Daily* (23 February 2011), <http://www.chinadaily.com.cn/china/2011-02/23/content_12068081.htm>.
81. Lutfullah Mangi, 'Pakistan and China: An Excellent Model for Relations Between Neighboring Countries', *Contemporary International Relations,* vol. 20, no. 6 (2010), 111–12. Also see *Dawn* (17 July 2003).
82. *Daily Times* (2 January 2009).
83. Pak Akhbar, <http://www.pakakhbar.com/military/navy.html>.
84. Ibid.
85. *Pakistan Observer* (21 September 2011), <http://www.pakobserver.net/201109/21/detailnews.asp?id=115288>. Also see *The Economic Times* (20 September 2011), <http://articles.economictimes.indiatimes.com/2011-09-20/news/30180297_1_pakistan-navy-admiral-noman-bashir-attack-craft>.
86. Abdul Sattar, *Pakistan's Foreign Policy 1947–2009: A Concise History* (Karachi: Oxford University Press, 2006), 276–7.

87. For example, during the 1990s, only two Pakistani banks, the National Bank of Pakistan and the Muslim Commercial Bank, had offices in China. 'China time-tested links benefit both sides'. *China Daily* (11 February 1998).
88. Sumita Kumar, 'The China-Pakistan Strategic Relationship: Trade, Investment, Energy and Infrastructure', *Strategic Studies*, vol. 31, no. 5 (September 2007), 774.
89. *Daily Times* (21 May 2011).
90. *The Express Tribune* (5 September 2011), <http://tribune.com.pk/story/244845/presidents-visit-exploring-new-business-opportunities-with-china/>.
91. Ibid. (14 April 2008).
92. It is very rare in Pakistan for a project to be completed ahead of time.
93. Zaid Haider, 'Balochistan, Beijing, and Pakistan's Gwadar Port', *Georgetown Journal of International Affairs* (Winter/Spring 2005), 96.
94. *Daily Times* (18 August 2002), <http://www.dailytimes.com.pk/default.asp?page=story_18-8-2002_pg5_1>.
95. Fishing is the main source of income for the people of this area. In the past, because of the long journey, fishermen could not transport fish to Karachi, the largest market for fish in the country.
96. *Daily Times* (12 February 2003).
97. The Economic and Commercial Counsellor's Office of the People's Republic of China in the Islamic Republic of Pakistan (4 January 2009).
98. *Dawn* (27 April 2005).
99. Syed Fazl-e-Haider, 'China, Pakistan cooperate in space', *Asia Times* (26 April 2007), <http://www.atimes.com/atimes/South_Asia/ID26Df01.html>.
100. Ibid.
101. *Geo TV* (19 September 2009), <http://www.geo.tv/9-19-2009/49449.htm>.
102. *The Nation* (Islamabad, 30 October 2010).
103. Federation of American Scientists, 'Space and Upper Atmosphere Research Commission (SUPARCO)', <http://www.fas.org/spp/guide/pakistan/agency/>.
104. *The Express Tribune* (11 November 2011), <http://tribune.com.pk/story/289908/energy-requirement-pakistan-to-buy-two-nuclear-power-plants-from-china/>.
105. The NSG is a group of 45 nuclear supplier countries, which seek to promote non-proliferation of nuclear weapons through the implementation of guidelines for nuclear exports and nuclear related exports, <http://www.nuclearsuppliersgroup.org/Leng/default.htm>.
106. *Pamir Times* (24 August 2009), <http://pamirtimes.net/2009/08/24/7000-mw-bonji-dam-next/>.
107. Kumar, 'The China-Pakistan Strategic Relationship: Trade, Investment, Energy', 777.

108. Syed Fazl-e-Haider, 'Pakistan plans nuclear power surge', *Asia Times* (online), (22 September 2010), <http://www.atimes.com/atimes/South_Asia/LI22Df02.html>.
109. Cited in 'China to sell outdated nuclear reactors to Pakistan', *Voice of America* (24 March 2011), <http://www.voanews.com/english/news/China-to-Sell-Outdated-Nuclear-Reactors-to-Pakistan-118572049.html>.
110. Cited in 'China to sell outdated nuclear reactors to Pakistan'.
111. Kerry B. Dumbaugh, 'Exploring the China-Pakistan relationship', *Roundtable Report* (VA: Centre for Naval Analysis, June 2010), 11.
112. Mathias Hartpence, 'The economic dimension of Sino-Pakistani relations: an overview', *Journal of Contemporary China*, vol. 20, no. 71 (2011), 593.
113. The Central People's Government of the People's Republic of China (30 October 2005), <http://www.gov.cn/english/2005-10/30/content_86761.htm>.
114. *Xinhua* (2 June 2008).
115. *China Gate* (31 October 2005), <http://www.chinagate.cn/news/2008-10/31/content_16692701.htm>.
116. *Dawn* (20 June 2008).
117. The Embassy of the People's Republic of China in the Islamic Republic of Pakistan (20 June 2008), <http:/pk.chineseembassy.org/eng/zbgx/t203370.htm>.
118. For a detailed discussion, see Ghulam Ali, 'China: Emerging Partner of SAARC', *Defence Journal*, vol. 11, no. 4 (November 2007).

6

China-Pakistan Economic Corridor

China and Pakistan have decided to establish the China-Pakistan Economic Corridor (CPEC) to connect China's Kashgar with Pakistan's Gwadar Port through a network of roads, proposed railway tracks, an energy pipeline, and fibre-optics. CPEC is generally considered an overland connection but in reality it has wider connotations. It aims to integrate Pakistan with China, to a certain degree, in the long term although it also faces various tangible challenges. The corridor is a mutually rewarding adventure, which if implemented successfully will serve both countries' political, economic, and geostrategic interests.

The idea of an economic corridor surfaced during the 2000s when construction work was started on the first phase of Gwadar Port. Pakistan's former military ruler, General Pervez Musharraf, repeatedly suggested that Pakistan could serve as a conduit for China. For example, during his visit to China in February 2006, he proposed transit facilities to China that would provide it access to energy sources. In an interview to *China Daily*, he stated, 'We are interested in setting up a trade and energy corridor for China.' He repeated his offer during his next visit in June.[1] China neither accepted nor declined the proposal. On the ground, however, China continued infrastructure development: the construction of Gwadar Port and the Makran Coastal Highway, modernisation of Karakoram Highway, and feasibility studies of various related projects. Later events proved that

Beijing had far wider aims than what Musharraf had in mind. China, however, avoided premature revelation and waited for the right time to announce its plans.[2]

The first move towards the implementation of CPEC came in March 2013 when China gained administrative control of Gwadar Port, previously handled by the Singapore Port Authority. In the following years, the contours of the project further emerged, especially during the exchange of high-profile visits between the two countries. For instance, in May 2013, when the Chinese premier visited Pakistan and formally proposed the idea of the establishment of the corridor. On that occasion, the two sides signed more than a dozen agreements, many of them dealing specifically with CPEC. Similarly, during Nawaz Sharif's next visit to China in November 2014, the two countries signed an agreement to establish the 2,000 kilometre road and rail link connecting the northwestern city of Kashgar to Gwadar, an MoU pertaining to the Lahore-Karachi Motorway, and a deal worth US$44 million for setting up a fibre-optic cable across their borders.[3]

A major boost to the corridor project came during the Chinese President, Xi Jinping's, visit to Pakistan in April 2015. It was then that China promised to invest US$46 billion in Pakistan. This investment was more than double the amount of all foreign direct investment (FDI) Pakistan had availed since 2008, and greater than the entire assistance Pakistan had received from the US since 2002.[4] To further elaborate the plan, President Xi proposed '1+4' cooperation structure in which CPEC was put at the centre; while Gwadar Port, energy, transport infrastructure, and industrial cooperation were regarded as its key components. During the visit, the two sides signed 51 agreements, out of which over 30 dealt with CPEC. For its smooth implementation, the two sides have divided the project into two categories: early harvest or short term projects, which would be completed in three to five years and long-term projects, which would be completed in ten to fifteen years.

The CPEC is part of China's grand 'One Belt, One Road' (OBOR) initiative. The OBOR will revive the ancient Silk Route by connecting over 60 Asian countries, Europe, and Africa with over three billion people. Although a number of projects are part of OBOR such as the 21st Century Maritime Silk Road, Central Asian Silk Road, Bangladesh, China, India, and Myanmar (BCIM) Corridor; CPEC is considered the 'flagship'. As China's foreign minister, Wang Yi, stated, 'If "One Belt, One Road" is like a symphony involving and benefiting every country, then construction of the China-Pakistan Economic Corridor is the sweet melody of the symphony's first movement.'[5] China has included CPEC in its fifteenth Five Year plan.

The importance of CPEC is based on some of its special features. Unlike other branches of OBOR, CPEC requires China to deal with only one country—namely Pakistan with whom China has maintained an 'all-weather' relationship. All of the other branches involve various countries. In many cases, participating countries have either disputes with other members, or even with China itself. For example, in BCIM, India has deep reservations over China's long-term designs. Some Indian analysts equate OBOR, and for that matter BCIM, with China's attempt to assert its influence in the region. Similarly, the Silk Route from Central Asia passes through different countries making it harder to reach a consensus among participating countries. Secondly, CPEC works as a bridge between land and sea routes. It provides China access to the Arabian Sea, the Indian Ocean, and beyond, through a 2,500 kilometre land route between China's Kashgar and Pakistan's Gwadar Port. No alternative can provide China as direct an access to the Indian Ocean as CPEC.

Thirdly, Pakistan's strategically significant Gwadar Port, whose administrative control was handed over to China in 2013 for forty years, is at the centre of CPEC. Gwadar Port's natural characteristics and location enhances CPEC's overall importance for both countries. Gwadar is a natural, deep-sea and all-weather port, located in western Karachi and in the southwestern region of Balochistan. It is at the juncture of three important regions: central, south, and west Asia; the Indian Ocean; and the Middle East. Its approximate distance from the Strait of Hormuz (through which 40 per cent of the world's oil passes) is 400 kilometres. It is 172 kilometres away from Iran's Chabahar Port and 710 kilometres from Dubai.

The port is linked with Pakistan's main cities and trading routes. It is nearly 470 kilometres away from Karachi, 1,066 kilometres away from Chaman, 892 kilometres away from Ratodero, and 966 kilometres away from Quetta, the capital of Balochistan. A 653 kilometre long Makran Coastal Highway, completed with China's assistance in 2004, connects Karachi with Gwadar via Pasni and Ormara. The Makran Coastal Highway is also linked to the rest of the country via the National Highway.

On the other hand, Gwadar is around 2,800 kilometres away from the Chinese city of Kashgar. To connect Kashgar with Gwadar, China has provided significant assistance for various infrastructural projects. This includes expansion of the Karakoram Highway, upgradation of roads within Pakistan, and building a network of new roads and highways. With Gwadar Port at the heart of the project, CPEC will serve some of China's core interests. It could complement the ongoing drive for modernisation of China's western regions.[6] It can help in addressing the separatist tendencies in the troubled Xinjiang region, which is much closer to Gwadar than to Shanghai.[7] Therefore, these realisations prompted China to focus on Xinjiang in the context of CPEC.[8]

The corridor could serve China's energy needs by providing a shorter and safer route. As China's economy continues to grow, its energy needs are growing, making it increasingly dependent on oil from the Middle East, Africa, and beyond.[9] According to estimates, 60 per cent of China's oil comes from the Gulf by ships travelling over 16,000 kilometres in 45–50 days. This long route is infested with pirates and is dominated by the US and Indian navies. The weather is not very kind either. Over and above that, it passes through the narrow Strait of Malacca before it reaches Shanghai Port. A disruption at the Malacca Strait could affect China's entire chain of energy imports. Against this, CPEC provides cost effective, shorter, and safer access to energy sources. It cuts the time to 10 days and the distance to a mere 5,000 kilometres. As the *China Daily* notes, 'CPEC will reduce China's routes of oil and gas imports from Africa and the Middle East by thousands of kilometres, making Gwadar a potentially vital link in China's supply chain.'[10]

Besides energy, China can expand its political and economic interests in the Middle East which is a region under US influence. Getting a foothold there will offer a major advantage to Beijing as China has already become one of the largest exporters to the region. China exchanges commodities with oil, stabilising its balance of payment. Besides energy, a number of Chinese firms are engaged in various developmental projects with thousands of employees.[11] Combined with Pakistan's historically close cultural and religious ties with the Middle East, CPEC could support China's interests in the region.

China-Pak Economic Corridor could potentially provide China access to the Indian Ocean—a vital route for oil transportation between the Atlantic and the Pacific. As an analyst noted, 'Securing a route to the Indian Ocean via the port of Gwadar will do the job nicely, and will also help China develop its military presence in the region, while playing a role in its "String of Pearls" strategy.'[12] China has already started developing a blue navy and has increased its naval presence in the open sea. In its annual report to Congress on 'Military and Security Developments in China', the US Department of State has indicated that Beijing is looking for naval facilities in countries with which it has good relations, such as Pakistan. Hence Gwadar could become China's naval base in the future.[13] With administrative control already in its hands, sitting at Gwadar could enable China to monitor sea lanes of communication along the Persian Gulf. In the context of modernisation regarding China's armed forces, developing a blue navy and increasing presence in open seas together strengthened this perception. Although China and Pakistan deny such speculations, given the close strategic relationship between the two countries spanning over decades and expanding naval cooperation in recent years, such possibilities could not be ruled out either.

For Pakistan, CPEC offers economic and strategic benefits; huge investment in energy, infrastructure, and industrial sectors. CPEC is expected to foster construction work which experts say will create new jobs and generate economic activity. This will also help tackle insurgency and terrorism by offering economic incentives to people discouraging them from turning to militancy.[14] Pakistan's energy shortfall has badly affected its economy. Keeping in view this fact, China gave top priority to the energy sector in recent deals. Out of US$46 billion, US$33 billion will be spent on energy related projects.[15] This is likely to add 10,400 megawatts of electricity at the cost of US$15.5 billion by 2018.[16] It will boost Pakistan's industrial and agricultural sectors. Pakistan expects that there will be a 15 per cent increase in its GDP by 2030, once CPEC is completed.[17]

The benefits of the corridor could spill over to adjacent countries including Iran, Afghanistan, the Central Asian States, and India. Iran has an abundance of energy while Pakistan and China seek access to it. Iran's nuclear deal with the US will ease Western sanctions against Tehran. Under the Iran-Pakistan-India pipeline deal, Iran has already completed a gas pipeline up to Pakistan's border. This could be extended to China as well. The Central Asian States, many of which are landlocked, have an abundance of energy. CPEC would provide connectivity to these states as well as to India. It is important to note that India's economic growth will largely depend on the energy imported from overseas while a large part can come via Pakistan. Although under the current spate of Indo-Pakistan tension, CPEC's extension to India is not on the table, one can hope that the situation will change some day. As an analyst noted, 'There are opportunities for India in CPEC and in OBOR. In the wake of the removal of sanctions on Iran, the IPI gas project could be revived.'[17] Trade and energy routes from India in the east of Pakistan towards Central Asia, Afghanistan, and Iran in the west are part of CPEC's grand design.

CPEC: THE FUTURE OF SINO-PAKISTAN RELATIONS

The China-Pakistan relationship has reached a point where traditional characteristics are being replaced by new realities. The relationship, when it originated back in the early 1960s, was based on, among other factors, shared security concerns vis-à-vis India and Pakistan's role in breaking China's isolation, and as a bridge between China and the Muslim world. Over the years, these aspects have lost their relevance. Most importantly, the central pillar of Sino-Pakistan's entente—the India factor—has gradually been losing its significance in this relationship. Since the 1980s, Sino-Indian ties have steadily improved. Apart from occasional media reports of 'incursions', hardly any skirmish has taken place on their border. On the other hand, trade between China and India has exceeded US$70 billion which provides additional incentives for the two sides to maintain a conflict-free relationship. Over a period of time, China's approach towards India has changed.

Similarly, Pakistan's role as a bridge between China and the Islamic world does not have the same relevance as it did during the heyday of the Cold War as Beijing has developed direct contacts with most Islamic states. It is true that Pakistan facilitated China's emergence from its isolation in world affairs. However, China is no longer isolated—it has become the second largest economy—and a major force to be reckoned with. Pakistan is not as central to China's strategy as it used to be.

Moreover, in spite of official efforts, the two-way trade between China and Pakistan could not move forward substantially. The situation is particularly dismal when compared with the burgeoning Sino-Indian trade. At the start of the century, China's trade with Pakistan and India was about over a billion US dollars. Fifteen years later, China's trade with India has exceeded US$70 billion, while trade with Pakistan is roughly US$15 billion. For China, economic and trade ties are becoming increasingly important in its foreign relations.

As a result, the major factors upon which the Sino-Pakistan entente was originally based are gradually fading away. If one removes CPEC from Sino-Pakistan relations, Pakistan is left with little advantage in its relations with China. In such a scenario, Sino-Pakistan relations may remain stable but without any significant component. Given these facts, the execution of CPEC is crucial to sustain durable ties.

CONCLUSION

China's investment in CPEC is the largest in the history of the two countries and is indicative of the high stakes Beijing has invested in Islamabad. It is a crucial component of China's OBOR initiative, and serves China and Pakistan's economic and strategic interests. CPEC can potentially complement China's modernisation of its western region to neutralise separatist tendencies through the economic uplift of Xinjiang, while gaining shorter access to the Indian Ocean, the Gulf, the Middle East, and beyond. CPEC appears to be the most effective way of diversifying China's exports and energy imports. For Pakistan, it will bring about an unprecedented level of investment leading to infrastructure development and job creation. Pakistan could generate revenue through the royalties it earns. Strategically, China's backing will enhance Islamabad's stature in regional politics. CPEC envisages a degree of Pakistani integration with China. At the moment, CPEC has commercial value. However, its strategic objectives cannot be ruled out in the long-run. Given the fact that Pakistan is gradually losing its traditional significance vis-à-vis China, the success of CPEC will determine the future direction of Sino-Pakistan relations.

NOTES

1. *China Daily* (22 February 2006), <http://www.chinadaily.com.cn/english/doc/2006-02/22/content_522558.htm> and Economic and Commercial Counsellor's Office of the Embassy of the People's Republic of China in the Islamic Republic of Pakistan (15 June 2006), <http://pk2.mofcom.gov.cn/aarticle/chinanews/200606/20060602444058.html>.

2. A possible reason behind China's low profile could be the fact of the US engagement in neighbouring Afghanistan, Iraq, and later the Middle East.
3. *The Express Tribune* (6 July 2013), <http://tribune.com.pk/story/573220/nawazs-beijing-visit-trade-corridor-tops-mou-bonanza/>.
4. *BBC* (22 April 2015), <http://www.bbc.com/news/world-asia-32400091>.
5. 'China Readies $46 Billion for Pakistan Trade Route', *The Wall Street Journal* (16 April 2015), <http://www.wsj.com/articles/china-to-unveil-billions-of-dollars-in-pakistan-investment-1429214705>.
6. As a result of reforms and opening up initiated under Deng Xiaoping in the late 1970s, China's coastal regions developed quickly lagging behind the hinterland western region. To address the rising gap, in 1999, the central Chinese government launched a plan to modernise its western region. Given its proximity, the corridor could work as Xinjiang's gateway to the outside world.
7. Pepe Escobar, 'Pakistan enters the New Silk Road', *Asia Times* (24 April 2015), <http://atimes.com/2015/04/pakistan-enters-the-new-silk-road/>.
8. The Chinese government considers that separatism can be handled through economic development and infrastructural growth in the region that will create new opportunities for locals. This might bring the disgruntled Uyghur population into mainstream national development. The CPEC could play a crucial role in this regards.
9. *Huffpost* (11 June 2015), <http://www.huffingtonpost.co.uk/muhammad-zulfikar-rakhmat/china-pakistan_b_7532434.html>.
10. *China Daily* (22 April 2015), <http://www.chinadaily.com.cn/world/2015 xivisitpse/2015-04/22/content_20503693.htm>.
11. *BBC* (22 April 2015), <http://www.bbc.com/news/world-asia-32400091>.
12. Muhammad Daim Fazil, 'The China-Pakistan Economic Corridor: Potential and Vulnerabilities', *The Diplomat* (29 May 2015), <http://thediplomat.com/2015/05/the-china-pakistan-economic-corridor-potential-and-vulnerabilities/>.
13. Annual Report to Congress, Military and Security Developments Involving the People's Republic of China 2015, <http://www.defense.gov/Portals/1/Documents/pubs/2015_China_Military_Power_Report.pdf>.
14. *BBC* (22 April 2015), <http://www.bbc.com/news/world-asia-32400091>.
15. *Aljazeera*, <http://www.aljazeera.com/programmes/countingthecost/2015/05/china-pakistan-economic-corridor-150502073929994.html>.
16. See <http://www.wsj.com/articles/china-to-unveil-billions-of-dollars-in-pakistan-investment-1429214705>.
17. 'The China-Pakistan Economic Corridor: India's Dual Dilemma', <http://www.chinausfocus.com/finance-economy/the-china-pakistan-economic-corridor-indias-dual-dilemma/#sthash.vqeVGxcR.dpuf>.

7

Factors of Durability

The preceding chapters have examined the growth of Sino-Pakistan ties from the beginning until recent times. In light of that, this chapter enlists the factors upon which this relationship is based. Arguably, the congruence of national interests is at the centre of this relationship. The prophetic saying that in international relations there are neither permanent friends nor enemies but national interests, explains to a great extent the rationale of this friendship. Generally, the relationship follows a traditional state-to-state pattern. There are, however, some distinct features as well.

GEOGRAPHICAL PROXIMITY

The first and foremost factor, which defines the contours of the China-Pakistan relationship, is geography. Both the countries have a 523 kilometre long common border that makes them neighbours. Pakistan's northern part, Gilgit-Baltistan (former Northern Areas) and Azad Jammu and Kashmir, are connected with China's Xinjiang Uighur Autonomous Region. This geographical proximity, after border demarcation in 1963, emerged at the centre of Sino-Pakistan relationship. The Chinese side argues that China attaches even greater importance to geography; countries with common borders are treated like neighbours and get better attention than those at a distance. This approach is referred to as good neighbourhood policy and has its roots, according to Chinese scholars, in Chinese history and culture.[1] Since ancient times, Chinese emperors maintained friendly relations with neighbours through the exchange of gifts; a tradition called the tribute system.[1] Leaders of modern China continued this policy. Exponents of this view credit China's good neighbourhood policy for successfully settling border disputes with most of its neighbours, including Pakistan. Consequently, geographical proximity coupled with China's desire for good relations with neighbours provided the foundation for Sino-Pakistan friendship. Since geography is a permanent feature, it will continuously influence their relationship.

PAKISTAN'S GEOSTRATEGIC LOCATION

Pakistan occupies an important geostrategic location in the region.[2] Besides China, it shares a border with India (2,912 kilometres), Afghanistan (2,430 kilometres), Iran (909 kilometres), and a 1,046 kilometre coastline running along the Arabian Sea.[3] This location is at the crossroads of three important regions—south, west, and central Asia—and is not far from energy rich Central Asian and Middle Eastern countries. An important communication network of roads, railways, air routes, and proposed energy pipelines also traverses the area. It was mainly Pakistan's geostrategic location which attracted US attention during the Cold War to help contain Communist expansion, during the 1980s to defeat the Soviets in Afghanistan, and post-9/11 for the War on Terror. In the early 1960s, as the Sino-Pakistan entente was established, China began to benefit from Pakistan's geostrategic location. China's decision to build the Karakoram Highway in the late 1960s, seemed to be taken in recognition of this geostrategic factor. After its upgradation and modernisation, it could be used the whole year round. This added a new dimension to this relationship. The recently announced CPEC is based entirely on geographic considerations. Pakistan's geographic location can potentially serve some of China's core interests. Given this realisation, China has intensified its multi-dimensional, multi-faced engagement with Pakistan. President Xi Jinping's promise of a US$46 billion investment—the largest in the history of the two countries—is an indication of Beijing's enhanced stakes in Pakistan, primarily based on geography.

THE INDIAN FACTOR

Many Western and Indian analysts argue that the Indian factor—India as a 'common enemy' of China and Pakistan—is the main pillar upon which this friendship is based. From this perspective, the myth of 'the enemy of my enemy is my friend' governs this relationship. The fact that the Sino-Pakistan entente emerged only in the wake of the 1962 Sino-Indian border war reinforces this argument. Since India has enduring political and territorial disputes with China and Pakistan, and has separately fought wars with them, it draws Beijing and Islamabad together on an anti-India platform. As a result, China's support to Pakistan on Kashmir, its tilt towards Pakistan during the Indo-Pakistan conflicts, the supply of weapons to Islamabad, and Chinese assistance to Pakistan's nuclear and missile programme were all India-centric. China followed this policy from the early 1960s to the 1980s. During the 1980s, China's new South Asian policy began to evolve under which Beijing started taking a relatively balanced view towards the Indian subcontinent. This approach matured in the following decades. China's new strategy is to stabilise relations with India without compromising ties with Pakistan. This has changed the role of the Indian factor in Sino-Pakistan relations. It appears that the Indian factor is gradually moving from a central to a peripheral position, at least from the Chinese perspective. However, since India continues to harbour territorial and political disputes with China and Pakistan, the Indian factor continues to stay in one form or another.

CHINA'S PLACE IN PAKISTAN'S NATIONAL SECURITY STRATEGY

China has supported Pakistan, not only in traditional security areas but also in the non-traditional ones, such as domestic crises, natural calamities, economic bankruptcy, terrorism, international isolation, and occasional US pressures. There are various examples but only few are cited. From the use of its first ever veto in 1972, in support of Pakistan, China has exercised this power on various other occasions. To please its ally, Beijing did not hesitate to use its power to bloc certain Indian resolutions, which demanded bans on particular Pakistan-based religious organisations. Islamabad seems confident that it could rely on China's veto whenever required.[4] Such expectations were not unrealistic given the close nature of their relationship.

China has also used its influence to hedge tacit US pressure e.g. during the 1990s, regarding Pakistan's nuclear and missile programme. On occasion, Islamabad has successfully used the China card. For instance, in May 2011, the US killed Osama bin Laden in Operation Neptune Spear on Pakistani territory. This soured Washington-Islamabad ties. Amidst the tension, Pakistan's prime minister flew to China, issued strong statements in support of Sino-Pakistan relations, and supplied 50 JF-17 aircraft on an urgent basis. A section of opinion in Pakistan believes that China's backing deters America's extreme measures as was seen in Afghanistan, Iraq, and recently in the Middle East. Otherwise, Pakistan's nuclear and missile programme, and terrorism were enough justification for hardliners in the White House to consider strong military action against Islamabad.[5]

The study also found that China made positive and encouraging statements whenever Pakistan was faced with a crisis. Such statements from a major power gave Pakistan the confidence to deal with challenges of all kinds. There were numerous instances when the country was left isolated. Take for instance the trial of the deposed prime minister, Nawaz Sharif, by a military dictatorship in 2000; General Pervez Musharraf's declaration of emergency in 2007; and the assassination of former prime minister, Benazir Bhutto. At those occasions, when most Western powers were highly concerned about the future of nuclear Pakistan, China's response was quite different. It termed these crises temporary difficulties, and expressed confidence in the government and the people of Pakistan to address them.[6] Likewise, during natural calamities, China proved to be among the first countries to come up with relief assistance.

China's overall support of Pakistan has become incomparable. No other country, neither from the Islamic bloc nor its Western allies, could match this support. Some wealthy Middle Eastern states would offer economic assistance to Pakistan but none of them had political clout in world politics. As an observer noted, 'Pakistan's Middle East allies have supplied it with oil, money, a training ground for its soldiers, and massive remittances from its migrant workers. But they have had little to offer in the form of a security guarantee [against traditional and non-traditional threats].' China thus, appears to be the only power that possesses economic, political, and military clout, and is a permanent member of the UN Security Council with veto power. Not only this, Beijing has used its influence in support of Pakistan. It is this backdrop which explains Pakistan's description of China as a 'pillar of its foreign policy'.

'EARLY' AND 'MUTUALLY AGREED' BORDER SETTLEMENT

It would not be wrong to argue that the border demarcation between China and Pakistan proved an important milestone in their relations. In March 1963, China and Pakistan signed a border agreement under which the two sides demarcated the undefined part of their border on mutually agreed terms. The agreement was signed within 12 years of the establishment of their diplomatic relations. This 'early' and 'mutually agreed' settlement left behind no territorial dispute, and paved the way for a smooth and friction-free relationship. The significance of the border agreement could also be measured from the fact that many major world conflicts are direct outcomes of overlapping border or territorial claims among contending states. Immediate and relevant examples are disputes between India and Pakistan, China and India, and among South China Sea disputes. In fact, the relationship which turned to be entente cordiale started in the wake of the border agreement.

ISLAMIC WORLD FACTOR

Pakistan's Islamic identity, large land size, and close ties with Muslim countries—an important role in the OIC—termed in this section as 'Islamic world factor', has played a role in strengthening the Sino-Pakistan relationship. Pakistan has protected and projected China's interests in the vast Muslim community by using its influence. While highlighting the importance of this factor, John Garver stated, 'there is far more to the Pakistan-China relations than common hostility towards India. There are distinct Muslim and Middle Eastern aspects to that relationship'.[7]

The Islamic world factor started from the early days of the Sino-

Pakistan relationship. The two countries began to project their Muslim populations in advancing two-way ties. The fact that China's Xinjiang Uygur Autonomous Region, with a Muslim majority population, borders Pakistan reinforces this factor. In 1953, China established the Islamic Association of China (IAC) that proved instrumental in promoting Chinese Muslims bonds with Pakistan. According to an analyst, Islamabad provided almost unconditional support and strategic depth to China in Islamic states.[8] Pakistan promoted China's interests in the Muslim world both at a bilateral level as well as from the OIC platform. Islamabad was mainly responsible for establishing China's diplomatic ties with Iran in the 1970s, and with Saudi Arabia. Until the establishment of diplomatic relations between China and Saudi Arabia, the Pakistani government facilitated pilgrimage for Chinese Muslims to Mecca. Those devotees used to apply for visas at the Saudi Embassy in Islamabad while Pakistan offered various services to them during their stay in the country. Besides this, many Chinese Muslims used to send their children to Pakistan for higher education, including Islamic studies, at academic institutions and seminaries.[9]

Pakistan also acted as a facilitator in promoting an understanding between Chinese and Islamic civilizations. This role was significant as there was limited interaction between the two sides until recent years. Beijing used to consult Islamabad whenever it sought advice regarding its relations with the Islamic world.[10] According to a Chinese scholar, being an 'atheist' country, China faces a quandary when it comes to dealing with Muslim states, especially their Arab rulers in the Gulf and the Middle East. China would often seek advice from Pakistan on this issue.[11] Many Islamic countries, especially from the Middle East, also lacked an understanding of China and would consult Pakistan. In this way, Pakistan became an intermediary for China and the Muslim world, which would not have been possible otherwise. Moreover, China projected its 'special' relations with Pakistan to other Islamic countries.[12]

Most importantly, Pakistan has been playing a role in preventing member Islamic states from criticising Beijing's policies towards Muslim minorities in Xinjiang and taking the issue to the OIC. As an observer noted, 'Islamabad offers Beijing important diplomatic backing in the face of Muslim-majority nations who might otherwise criticise China's handling of its Muslim population.'[13] The Xinjiang region is prone to clashes between Uighur separatists and local authorities. Some OIC members, especially Turkey, have raised the issue of Beijing's 'suppressive' policies. For instance, during the July 2009 riots in Xinjiang, in which over 197 people died and 1,000 were injured in clashes between the rioters and the government forces, some member countries wanted to take the issue to the OIC but Islamabad prevented it. Islamabad successfully lobbied with the member states of the OIC that the Uighur issue should be addressed to China bilaterally and not from the OIC platform. Had the OIC been involved in the matter, it could have caused a diplomatic setback to Beijing, even though OIC resolutions are not implementable. Most of the Chinese scholars who were interviewed referred to Pakistan's role in this incident. Hence, Pakistan's place in the Islamic world has attracted China's interest and contributed to strengthening their two-way relations.

THE US FACTOR

It also appears that the US has influenced the China-Pakistan relationship in some ways. As discussed in preceding chapters, Pakistan's dependence on US military and economic assistance had started from the early days of its inception. Both the countries had signed defence pacts during the 1950s; closely cooperated with each other against the Soviet invasion of Afghanistan, during the 1980s, and joined hands in the post-9/11 years. Yet, they could not develop a sustained relationship. In every phase, the US-Pakistan relationship was prompted by a specific strategic goal. Once it was achieved, relations turned lukewarm. In reality, both sides lacked any long-term, shared strategic vision, as exists in the case of China-Pakistan. The US-Pakistan relationship is much more conditional, transitional, and strategic-factor prompted. Pakistan's strategic interests in the region remain constant while the US' interests oscillate. Even their current cooperation on counterterrorism does not have a clear strategic goal.[14]

Research found that a disruption in US-Pakistan relations often pushed Islamabad towards Beijing. The literature in Pakistan shows that the majority looks at relations with China and with the US comparatively. By putting relations with these powers in juxtaposition, Pakistanis find the US an 'unreliable' partner that has 'betrayed' Pakistan on many occasions by leaving it in the lurch instead of extending a helping hand as an ally. The quick shifts in US policies from assistance to sanctions were perceived in Pakistan as glaring examples of expediency. Washington's sanctions before the outbreak of the Indo-Pakistan wars in 1965 and 1971, delaying the supply of F-16 aircraft for 15 years for which Pakistan had already paid, and negotiating a pact with India on nuclear technology in 2008 while refusing a similar deal to Islamabad even though Pakistan was a crucial partner in WoT,[15] were only a few examples frequently cited by writers in Pakistan.

A majority of Pakistanis consider China a 'reliable' partner that always fulfilled its commitments. Even though the two countries did not enter any military pact, Beijing never let Pakistan down during times of crisis. Since the start of their entente in the early 1960s, there has been no mistrust or downturn in their relations. Furthermore, most areas in which the US imposed sanctions, while China extended its help, are ones that have been close to Pakistan's national pride: the nuclear and missile programme and its defence, security, and strategic sectors. A majority of Pakistanis believe that China pursues long-term policies and does not adopt expedient measures, treats Pakistan equally and with respect, never dictates, or interferes in its internal affairs—quite contrary to the US approach towards Pakistan. This has built strong reserves of goodwill for China in Pakistan. Given the hostile nature of Indo-Pakistan relations, Pakistan needs permanent backing of a big power. This pushes Pakistan towards China while the Chinese find Pakistan a convenient ally to counter US influence in the region.

'DISTINCT' FEATURES OF THE RELATIONSHIP

Most of these factors can be found in other state-to-state relationships. There are, however, some distinct features attributed to Sino-Pakistan ties.

From the very start, China dealt with Pakistan from a long-term perspective while keeping in view the geography factor. Under this consideration, it showed restraint over some of Pakistan's unfriendly polices—such as its move to sign anti-communist and anti-China defence pacts with the US during the 1950s. At this apparently hostile Pakistani move, China showed restraint. It neither lodged any formal protest nor changed its policy vis-à-vis South Asia. This attitude was in sharp contrast to that of the Soviet Union's which, after Pakistan had joined the Baghdad Pact and SEATO, changed its South Asian policy, and came squarely on the Indian side. The mistrust that Moscow and

Islamabad developed during the 1950s could not be shed in decades. On the other hand, China's tolerance prevented grudges. Therefore, as the two sides made overtures to each other in the early 1960s, it did not take much time for them to develop good relations.

Terrorism is another area where China's long-term approach prevented negative impacts on the Sino-Pakistan relationship. Terrorism affected this relationship in two ways. First, starting in the late 1980s, some Pakistan-based militant groups began to facilitate Uygur separatists from China's Xinjiang region. Secondly, a series of targeted attacks on the Chinese working in Pakistan were launched in the 2000s. In spite of the gravity of this matter, China maintained restraint and expressed its concerns to Pakistan privately to prevent a public fallout. Moreover, China realised Pakistan's weakness in its fight against terrorism and gave it a free hand to devise a counterterrorism strategy that suited its national conditions.

This work also finds that China has established vast links with Pakistan's polity, irrespective of their political and ideological orientation. It never supported one group or party over the other and treated all stakeholders equally. The Communist Party of China has signed MoUs with not only mainstream political parties in Pakistan but also with regional and religious parties. This approach was different from that of the US; it also created an image of China as a friend of Pakistan, rather than a supporter of a particular group, party, or ideology. It is under this comprehensive engagement that no matter which political party has ruled the country, or when the army has taken over power, relations with China have remained stable.

China's distinct diplomacy was also reflected in its aid and assistance policy in their economic and defence sectors. From its start in the mid-1960s until the early 1980s, most of China's aid was based on grants. Loans were either interest-free or carried a very low interest rate. Pakistan often made payments in local products which increased its exports. China invested in projects which 'called for minimal investment and brought quick results', provided the best equipment at competitive prices, and trained Pakistani technicians to use them. Chinese experts lived in Pakistan and got salaries according to local standards.[16] In the early 1980s, China's assistance policy began to change from grants to loans. However, Beijing's aid remained important to Islamabad due to its availability, flexible terms, and their having no strings attached to them. Moreover, instead of giving hard cash to Pakistani rulers, China invested in mega projects with a solid impact on the economic development of the country.[17] Projects such as the Karakoram Highway (KKH), Heavy Mechanical Complex (HMC), Pakistan Aeronautical Complex (PAC), nuclear power plants, roads, highways, dams, thermal power projects, cements plants, glass factories, and the most recent, CPEC, are just some examples.

In the defence sector as well, China entered joint production with Pakistan, granted licences, trained Pakistani technicians, and transferred technology. Pakistan gained licenses from China to produce a wide range of weapons such as guns, aircraft (both trainer and fighter), tanks, and anti-tank missiles.[18] Both the countries have jointly developed an advanced aircraft, JF-17, naval frigates, and submarines (under construction). On the other hand, although Pakistan's defence ties with the US had started much earlier, and the two countries had even signed defence pacts, Pakistan could rarely acquire technology from the US in any area.[19] These features of China's policy were distinct from Pakistan's other donors; they created a positive image of China besides strengthening Pakistan's defence in real terms.

Another important aspect of Sino-Pakistan ties, which prevented any negative impact on the relationship, was their dispute settlement mechanism. Mostly guided by China, the two countries have developed a norm to address all their issues privately, away from the public gaze. According to Pakistani analysts, 'Over a period of time, Pakistan and China have learnt how to isolate potential areas of conflict from the larger dynamics of cooperation.'[20] This applies to smaller issues such as the lower quality of Chinese technology (e.g. in railway locomotive) and dumping problems to major concerns such as China's disquiet at militants from Pakistan supporting the separatists in Xinjiang. Perhaps no state-to-state relationship can be free of strife. However, resolving disputes amicably, behind the scenes, prevented unnecessary media attention and pre-empted any negative impact.

A salient feature of the Sino-Pakistan relationship is that both sides have strictly adhered to the policy of non-interference in each other's internal affairs. This policy has remained in force throughout the decades-old relationship. The only available example of China's concern at Pakistan's internal matter was its request to General Zia for clemency for the former Prime Minister Zulfikar Ali Bhutto who was sentenced to death by Pakistan's courts. Even before submitting its request, China termed it Pakistan's internal affair but pleaded Bhutto's case on the grounds of his contributions to Sino-Pakistan friendship. Once Zia rejected the appeal, Beijing did not allow the incident to affect their relations.

Similarly, there is no evidence that China ever dictated Pakistan's internal or external policies. It is particularly significant as China, being a major power and donor, could have used its leverage to expand its interests and influence in Pakistan. This becomes more prominent when compared with US policies towards Pakistan. An analyst states, 'China has observed with interest several upheavals inside Pakistan over the decades. Besides its benevolent interest, China has scrupulously avoided any move or observation that could even remotely be construed as interference in this country's internal affairs.'[21] Pakistan reciprocated in a similar way; there is no incidence of Pakistan's involvement in China's internal matters. Islamabad at occasions acted against international trends to stand by Beijing. As noted: 'the crux of the [China-Pakistan] bond is based on a reciprocal policy of non-interference in domestic issues, and avoiding a clash with each other's core national interests, at least in the public arena'.[22]

TRUST AND RELIABILITY

As a result of these norms being observed over a long period of time, a degree of trust and reliability developed between the two countries. In interviews with scholars from China and Pakistan, these abstract concepts have frequently been mentioned with examples to support them.[23] Thus, Pakistani scholars argue that there is consensus among all political parties, including religious groups and the military, that we must maintain good ties with Beijing. There is no other issue on which the political forces in Pakistan have such a unanimity of views. Islamabad terms relations with Beijing a 'pillar of its foreign policy'. It has become a norm for incoming Pakistani rulers, be it a military general or an elected civilian, to visit China at the first opportunity as a 'tribute' to this 'special' relationship. It is this trust that prompts Pakistani rulers to consult China whenever the country faces a major internal or external crisis.

Likewise, it is on account of decades of its trust that China uses the term 'all-weather' friend only for Pakistan.[24] China maintained uninterrupted relations with Pakistan during the rigorous Cultural Revolution (China cut itself from most the world during this phase), helped Islamabad to resist Western pressures, fulfil all commitments, and transferred technology even in sensitive areas. These factors helped maintain a 'special' relationship.[25] This 'trust' factor was also evident in the defence sector. The three branches of China's armed forces chose Pakistan for their 'first' dealing with a foreign country. For instance, Pakistan was the first foreign country whose army conducted a military exercise on Chinese soil in August 2004; the PLA selected Pakistan to conduct its 'first' ever military exercise on foreign soil; the PLA Navy also chose Pakistan to conduct its 'first' ever naval exercise with a foreign country; the PLAAF conducted a joint air exercise with its Pakistani counterpart, in March 2011, in which it deployed aircraft on foreign territory. China's selection of Pakistan on these occasions shows the level of trust in its ally. Experts of international politics may disagree with the role of these abstract concepts of 'trust' and 'reliability' in the practice of diplomacy, however, Chinese and Pakistani policy makers strongly believe such concepts exist in their relations.

EXPANSION OF COOPERATION

This book also points out that, over a period of time, China and Pakistan have expanded and enlarged the base of their relationship from India-centric and bilateralism to multifaceted and multilateral cooperation. Diplomats of the two countries regularly coordinate with each other on relevant regional and international forums to gain each other's support. The UN platform in particular is the venue of their frequent interaction. In addition, Pakistan's membership to ASEAN Regional Forum (ARF) and in Shanghai Cooperation Organisation (SCO), first as an observer and later as a full member, became possible with China's help. In return, Pakistan backed China for its entry into the UN, for GATT, and for an observer member of SAARC. The expansion of cooperation from bilateral to multilateral forums has enlarged the base and scope of the relationship, and contributed towards its durability.

TWO-WAY RELATIONSHIP

Another important reason for the success of the China-Pakistan relationship is that it is bilateral in nature. It is based on give-and-take in which both sides gain from each other. No doubt, China provided valuable diplomatic, economic, and military assistance to Pakistan; shared technology (even in strategic areas); and built mega projects with a long-term impact on Pakistan's economy. Pakistan's support to China did not match China's assistance in economic terms but was no less significant in diplomatic and political value. In the early 1960s, as Pakistan began developing close ties with China, it defied US pressure and sanctions. Islamabad helped break China's isolation during the early phase of the Cold War, worked for China's seat in the UN, in facilitating Sino-US rapprochement, and building China's links with the Islamic world. At times, Pakistan was China's only window to the non-Communist world. In June 1989, China was once again internationally isolated and became a source of Western criticism. Pakistan defied international sanctions to stand by Beijing. Immediately after those events, Pakistan sent high official delegations to China to express its solidarity. A few months later, it received Chinese premier, Li Peng. This was the first overseas visit of a top Chinese leader since the Tiananmen Square incident. Pakistan continued to back China on crucial issues such as Taiwan, Tibet, human rights, and democracy. This reciprocity contributed to the durability of this relationship.

To a certain extent, Pakistan also cooperated with China in reverse engineering. Being an ally, Pakistan had access to some modern US weapons during the Cold War; it reportedly shared some of them with Beijing. An Indian analyst even claimed that one out of 40 F-16 aircraft Pakistan purchased from the US was transferred or loaned to China. A Chinese scholar even claimed that Pakistan allowed the PRC to look inside the F-16 aircraft,[26] which was the most advanced aircraft that Pakistan had received from the US. It is also reported that Beijing obtained a range of other sensitive technologies which were otherwise denied to China.[27]

Pakistan, which was advanced in centrifuge technology, at some stages might have shared it with Beijing.[28] It is also reported that the Pakistani version of the Tomahawk cruise missile is the product of Sino-Pakistan cooperation in reverse engineering. Prior to 9/11, the US naval ships in the Indian Ocean fired cruise missiles on Taliban hideouts in Afghanistan. Some of them fell on Pakistani territory unexploded, and Beijing was allowed access to them.[29] Given the discreet nature of defence ties, there might be more fields in which the two sides might have cooperated.[30] Pakistan's sharing of technology with China showed the level of its commitment to Beijing. Even though the magnitude of this cooperation was not very high and China no longer required help—as Beijing's own technology has greatly advanced in most areas where Pakistan's help was sought—China valued Pakistan's cooperation which reinforced their bonds. This give-and-take nature of their relationship prevented it from turning into a patron-client equation.

THE ROLE OF ARMED FORCES

The Pakistan military and the People's Liberation Army (PLA) have considerable clout in their respective national affairs, and strategic cooperation is a key factor in their relationship. Some analysts argue that the predominance of the armed forces in the two countries was one of the factors behind the continuity of their relationship.

Pakistan maintains a large army and allocates a huge chunk of its resources to its maintenance due to perpetual confrontation with India. The army has directly ruled the country for nearly 30 years and has remained in power, behind the scenes, in the period it was not holding office. As a result, it has acquired a pivotal role in national security and foreign policy. Although the People's Liberation Army works under the Communist Party, it has a say in the PRC's defence and foreign policies. Since the nature of the Sino-Pakistan relationship was predominantly strategic, the armed forces of the two countries have helped strengthen it. As Fazal maintains:

> A major arena of cooperation which has laid the basis of a close relationship between China and Pakistan has been the defence sector. Since there has been continuity in the military structure of the two countries, therefore, a persistent interaction between them has been having a direct bearing on the continuity in their bilateral relations. Mutually beneficial relations between the armed forces of the two countries have served as an uninterrupted and sustainable factor of continuity in the overall bilateral relationships.[31]

REGULAR EXCHANGE OF VISITS

Another important reason behind the continuity of this relationship are the regular visits by the top leadership of the two countries.[32] Starting from the mid-1950s, the number of visits gradually increased. From the Chinese side, with the exception of Chairman Mao Zedong and Deng Xiaoping, all other prominent leaders have visited Pakistan. From Pakistan's side, since the mid-1950s, almost all rulers—both military and civilian—have gone to China, and most of them, several times.

It was during the mid-1980s, when the incoming Prime Minister of Pakistan, Muhammad Khan Junejo, set a new tradition by choosing China as the first foreign destination for a visit. He labelled it a 'tribute' to friendly relations with the PRC. Many of his successors followed, or tried to follow, this tradition. If China could not become the first overseas destination, it was at least among the first countries Pakistani rulers visited. Pakistani President, Asif Ali Zardari (2008–13), visited China ten times. Since the advent of the new century, the number of visits, especially from Pakistan's side, have increased significantly.

Although visits alone do not make a big difference without concrete measures, they provide opportunities for the two sides to review their relationship on a regular basis, remove any irritant, and add new content in line with changing geopolitical realities. As a former ambassador of Pakistan put it: 'Frequent visits were significant in promoting [a] two-way relationship, especially from the Chinese side. China is a centralised country, decisions made during visits are usually implemented.'[33]

THE ROLE OF THE MEDIA

It is important to mention that the local media in the two countries has also played an important role in shaping a favourable public opinion in their respective countries. From the early days, Chinese media has been controlled by the central government, which directed it to portray Pakistan as a friendly neighbour, highlight its contribution in China's development—especially during its phase of isolation, and showed the positive side of Pakistan's society. As a result, the majority of Chinese interviewed; recalled what Pakistan did for their country rather than vice versa. They regarded Pakistan as a trustworthy friend and an 'iron brother'.[34]

Likewise, the Pakistani media portrayed China as a sincere and reliable friend. It projected the simplicity and commitment of its leaders to their country and people, China's resilience against foreign occupation, and the hardworking nature of its people. Under this goodwill, it has become a norm in Pakistan to remain positive towards China, ignore its negative aspects, and avoid comments on its internal matters. As a Chinese scholar noted, 'The Pakistani media may not have always remained friendly [as Chinese media towards Pakistan] but it was never hostile.' Even after the press and the proliferation of media outlets in Pakistan since the 2000s, China continued to be regarded as a friendly country. As a Western analyst observed, 'The media in both countries have recently assumed an important role in promoting the rhetoric and the image of a strong partnership.'[35]

CONCLUSION

A number of factors collectively provide an explanation for the continuity of China-Pakistan's relationship. Their geographical-proximity, coupled with shared security concerns vis-à-vis India were important components of these ties. The strategic nature of their equations enabled the armed forces on both sides to consolidate their relations, which expanded and enlarged on mutually beneficial terms over a period of time. China provided ample economic, military, and diplomatic support to Pakistan and laid the foundation of an enduring relationship. Pakistan reciprocated by extending support to China, not in monetary terms but by playing a role in procuring a UN seat, breaking its isolation, and improving relations with the US and the Muslim world.

Notes

1. Interviews with Chinese scholars affiliated with different academic institutes and think tanks in China. Some of them also referred to Chinese sayings which stressed upon the need of neighbours.
2. As a result of disintegration in 1971, Pakistan lost its eastern wing; the remaining part continued to hold geostrategic importance.
3. Tourism, Government of Pakistan, <http://www.tourism.gov.pk/geography_pakistan.htm>.
4. Interview with a Pakistani diplomat based in Beijing.
5. Interviews with Pakistani scholars and diplomats.
6. This impression is drawn from reading Chinese statements issued at various occasions in the post-9/11 period.
7. John W Garver, *Protracted Contest: Sino-Indian Rivalry in the Twentieth Century* (Seattle: University of Washington Press, 2001), 189.
8. Shalendra D. Sharma, *China and India in the Age of Globalization* (Cambridge, 2009), 175.
9. These facilities were reduced and possibly totally withdrawn as China's concerns about the support of Pakistani Islamic groups for separatist activities in Xinjiang grew. As a result, many of Chinese students studying in Madrasas were sent back and the remaining were closely monitored by Pakistani authorities. Interview with a Pakistani diplomat, Islamabad, April 2011.
10. Interview with Hasan-Askari Rizvi, Lahore, April 2011.
11. Interviews with Chinese scholars working with think tanks in Beijing and Shanghai.
12. Interview with Professor Riffat Hussain, Chairman Department of Defence and Strategic Studies, Quaid-i-Azam University, Islamabad, April 2011.
13. Christopher Bodeen, 'Pakistan, China set sights on Arabian Sea Link', *The Street* (5 July 2013).
14. Interview with Andrew Small of the German Marshal Foundation of the United States, December 2013. He is the author of *The China-Pakistan Axis: Asia's New Geopolitics* (London: C. Hurst & Co., 2015).
15. As the US refused to sign a nuclear deal with Pakistan, China came forward and supplied much-needed nuclear power plants disregarding the concerns of Washington and the members of the Nuclear Supplier Group (NSG).

16. Yaacov Vertzberger, 'The Political Economy of Sino-Pakistani Relations: Trade and Aid 1963–82', *Asian Survey*, vol. 23, no. 5. (May 1983), 644–5.
17. *The News* (20 May 2011).
18. Stockholm International Peace Research Institute (SIPRI), Arms Transfers Database. Details of Chinese arms transferred to Pakistan can be obtained by entering China US in Supplier and Pakistan in Recipient at <http://armstrade.sipri.org/armstrade/page/trade_register.php>.
19. Stockholm International Peace Research Institute (SIPRI), Arms Transfers Database. Details of the US arms transferred to Pakistan can be obtained by entering the US in Supplier and Pakistan in Recipient at <http://armstrade.sipri.org/armstrade/page/trade_register.php>.
20. Interview with Professor Riffat Hussain, April 2011, Islamabad.
21. Khalid Saleem, 'Pakistan-China ties in focus', *Pakistan Observer* (7 April 2011).
22. Rosheen Kabraji, 'The China-Pakistan Alliance: Rhetoric and Limitations', Asia Programme Paper ASP PP 2012/01, Chatham House (December 2012), 2.
23. The two sides have constantly maintained a robust relationship despite divergent socio-political systems, cultures, and ideologies; and profound changes in domestic, regional, and international system. This was not possible to maintain without trust and reliability.
24. A Chinese scholar explained the origin of the term 'all-weather'. China had close relations with four countries namely, North Korea, Albania, Vietnam, and Pakistan. Beijing provided large scale assistance to these countries. Even though the amount of Chinese assistance to Pakistan was far less than given to other three allies, only Pakistan withstood the vicissitudes of times. Beijing's ties with Pyongyang, Tirana, and Hanoi have undergone different ups and down during the last several decades. Given this context, China uses the term 'all-weather' friend for Pakistan. Interview with Professor Li Xiguang, November 2013, Tsinghua University, Beijing.
25. The most frequent rhetoric used to describe the relationship include 'higher than mountain, deeper than the ocean and sweeter than honey', 'all-weather friendship', 'brothers forever', and 'Chinese can leave the gold not friendship with Pakistan'.
26. Interview with a Chinese scholar and Chief Correspondent of *Guangming Daily*, based in Islamabad, Pakistan.
27. Dipankar Banerjee, 'Not quite a triangular relationship', *The Straits Times* (Singapore, 29 November 1995).
28. Interview with Major General (R) Talat Masood, eminent defence analyst, April 2011, Islamabad.
29. An interview with a Pakistani analyst on the condition of anonymity.

30. It is said that the possibility of covertly slipping technology from Pakistan to China was one of the reasons behind the US reluctance to provide state-of-the-art technology to Islamabad. The US conveyed those concerns to Pakistan at least at unofficial levels. In the most recent case, Pakistan demanded the transfer of drone (a pilotless aircraft) technology, which the US had been using against Taliban hideouts inside Pakistan's tribal areas. In spite of Pakistan's role in WoT, Washington refused such requests.
31. Fazal-ur-Rehman, 'Pakistan's Relations with China', *Strategic Studies* vol. XIX & XX, nos. 4 & 1 (Islamabad, Winter & Spring 1998), 59–60.
32. Former Pakistani military ruler, General Musharraf, while replying to the question of the reasons of stronger relationship between the two sides added that frequent high-level contacts 'matured and enriched' the relationship. *Beijing Review*, vol. 44, no. 22 (May 31, 2001), 8.
33. Interview with a retired diplomat, and a former Pakistani Ambassador to China, Islamabad, July 2014.
34. During field trips to China, the author talked to a wide range of people like taxi drivers, vendors, and shopkeepers, and asked them about Pakistan. Majority of them regarded Pakistan as a friend of China although most of them did not know much about it.
35. Kabraji, 'The China-Pakistan Alliance: Rhetoric and Limitations', 2.

Conclusion

The relationship between China and Pakistan has unique dynamics. It has evolved over a period of time; underpinned by geography and common regional security concerns among other factors. It is a mutually rewarding partnership in which both sides gained from each other. Interestingly, neither China nor Pakistan had apparent intentions to form a relationship, which turned into an entente cordiale. This was an outcome of interrelated developments, in the late 1950s and the early 1960s, which reshaped the regional pattern of alliances bringing China and Pakistan closer to each other. Afterwards, their partnership strengthened their peoples' developed sentimental attachment to each other. By the launch of China's reforms and opening up policy in the late 1970s, the friendship had deepened to such an extent that those reforms did not particularly affect two-way ties. Thereafter, the relationship either grew further or remained stable but did not show any downward trend.

Most existing studies examine the relationship from the geopolitical prism, and put the India-factor as the raison d'etre of this alliance. The argument is based on the origin, a long-held defence-centric relationship, and India's unresolved border disputes with both China and Pakistan. This approach has both merits and short comings.

It is correct that the Sino-Pakistan entente cordiale emerged in the wake of the Sino-Indian border war. Afterwards, the two sides began to coordinate their policies on regional security issues. China eased out of its neutrality towards the subcontinent; it started supporting Pakistan vis-à-vis India and soon emerged as Pakistan's most reliable arms supplier. Not only this, Beijing helped Pakistan in its nuclear and missile programme. All these areas of cooperation are seen in the context of the Indian factor. Since there is no progress in New Delhi's border disputes with Beijing and Islamabad, India remains a constant strategic factor in the Sino-Pakistan entente.

There are two problems with this approach. First, it put emphasis on the Indian-factor while overlooking China's actual role during Indo-Pakistan conflicts. This approach does not assess all the Chinese motives behind arms sales to Pakistan as well as China's changing posture towards the subcontinent. Secondly, it misses other equivalently important factors which played an equally important role in the development of these ties. As a matter of fact, China's most vocal support to Pakistan vis-à-vis India came during the Indo-Pakistan war in 1965. On no other occasion did China show a sign of involvement on behalf of Pakistan. Even during the 1965 war, Beijing twice extended the deadline of its so-called 'ultimatum', enabling India and Pakistan to accept the ceasefire, which they did. As an eminent Indian analyst on China pointed out, China not firing a single bullet at India on Pakistan's behalf is telling. Most of China's support to Pakistan was indirect and came during times of peace. Furthermore, the period of China's strong rhetorical support and free weapons was not very long—from around mid-1960s to late 1970s—it came to an end with the initiation of reforms and the opening up policy. From then onwards, almost all Chinese weapon transfers were based on cash or loan which Pakistan ultimately paid back. For Pakistan, acquiring Chinese weapons remained India-centric but for China, a commercial aspect has also been guiding this policy since the 1980s. In addition to this, if the supply of weapons is any indication, then China is not the only country. Pakistan received large scale US weapons, some of which were of even more superior quality than those of the Chinese.

It also must be mentioned that since the 1980s, Beijing has been taking a relatively balanced approach towards Indo-Pakistan disputes. China's neutrality was evident during the nuclear tests conducted by India and Pakistan in 1998, Kargil in 1999, military standoff in 2001–02, and the Mumbai terrorist attacks in 2008. Keeping in mind the trajectory, China is unlikely to become a part of the Indo-Pakistan conflict. To a great extent, Beijing has separated its relations with Islamabad from its relations with New Delhi, and addresses them independent of each other. As a result, the Indian factor that used to be at the center of relations began to move to the periphery, at least from the Chinese side. The Indian factor will remain relevant to the relationship given India's unresolved territorial disputes with Pakistan and China but its role has changed from what it was during the 1960s.

However, the Beijing-Islamabad partnership has not only remained steadfast but has also expanded and enlarged. In fact, there is much more to this relationship than common hostility towards India. A holistic approach, taking all factors into account, can better explain the rationale of this partnership. A number of other factors generally overlooked have played an equally important role. The major ones being: geographic-proximity, early border settlement, non-interference, the role of the Islamic world, regular visits at top-level, disruptions in US-Pakistan relations which pushed Pakistan closer to the Chinese side, and the role of media and the armed forces of the two countries. Furthermore, China-Pakistan's relationship turned out to be mutually rewarding in which both sides gained from each other. Pakistan received valuable political, economic, and military assistance from China. In return, it contributed in some key areas of China's national security and foreign policy especially during the Cold War. This give-and-take structure of the relationship prevented it from turning into a patron-client equation. The two countries are continuously expanding the relationship; bringing new areas of cooperation within its ambit. Hence, interdependence, expansion, and mutual trust accumulated over decades, making the relationship strong enough to withstand internal and external upheavals.

It seems that China owes equal or perhaps greater credit for maintaining this durable partnership. From the very beginning, it pursued ties with Pakistan from a long-term perspective while keeping in view the permanent factor, geography. Beijing demonstrated patience, restraint, and non-interference; and took an inclusive approach to establish links with Pakistani polity and society regardless of their political, religious, and social orientation. Even though China was a big donor, and in that capacity could have exerted its influence on Pakistan but it did not. There is hardly any publicly available evidence that demonstrates Beijing ever dictating a course of action, pressure, or use of sanctions to compel Pakistan to adopt a certain policy. Instead, China treated Pakistan with equality and respect. Even on the sensitive issue of terrorism (attacks on Chinese workers in Pakistan and some Pakistan-based militant groups' links with Xinjiang separatists), which directly affected China's prestige and internal stability, Beijing showed maximum restraint. In the economic and defence sectors, China not only provided assistance but transferred technology which led Pakistan to gain a degree of self-sufficiency. Whether these characteristics were part of China's overall foreign policy or manifested in relations with Pakistan alone could be measured by studying China's ties with other countries. For Islamabad, these features distinguished Beijing from Pakistan's other allies.

However, the above structure of the relationship existed from the early period of the relationship until recent times. During this phase, the overall relationship was moderate, smooth and stable, and carefully protected by the top leadership of both countries. This phase seems to have come to an end with the advent of new Chinese leadership under Xi Jinping, and the launch of CPEC in around 2013. The relationship has reached a crossroads where it can either grow exponentially, or dilute to a normal state-to-state relationship. China's promise of unprecedented economic assistance, inclusion of CPEC in its Five Year Plan, and unprecedented engagement demonstrates Beijing's heightened interests in Pakistan. This may also modify China's hitherto non-interference policy pushing Beijing to take more active engagement with Pakistan. On the other hand, Pakistan is facing a myriad of challenges; the country has a weak leadership and deteriorating law and order situation. To what extent Pakistan is ready to exploit this huge opportunity presented before it remains to be seen. On the other hand, if China finds its investment at stake, it might review the structure of its relationship with Pakistan.

Some other aspects of the relationship also need attention. Irrespective of effusive rhetoric, the relationship remains far below its actual potential. The strategic dimension remained dominant, especially from the Pakistani side while economic, trade, and people-to-people contacts remained low. Within modest trade, the balance of payments, since the 1970s, has tilted in favour of China and is unlikely to change any time soon. Although China has been reiterating the importance of trade and economic ties, hardly any progress has been achieved in this regard. One of the reasons behind limited economic and trade ties is the fact that Pakistan has only regarded China as a strategic ally, and paid less attention to studying China's economic progress, especially since the reforms and opening up, and how to benefit from it. Even in the age of CPEC, this seems to be the dominant perspective in Pakistan. Until recently, lack of expertise and major studies on China showed Islamabad's casual approach. In a globalized world where regional connectivity, trade, and economic interdependence are superseding strategic considerations, if Islamabad had not paid attention to changing realities and continued with its current approach, it might have slowed down the pace of relations. A change in Pakistan's policy is particularly important since the concepts of 'connectivity', 'trade', and 'economic cooperation' are at the center of China's ambitious 'One Belt, One Road' initiative.

It is also argued that the relationship was started almost on equal footing but has been losing its traditional balance. China's rise to a great power status is almost inversely proportional to Pakistan's weakening power—internal and external. As a result, Pakistan has become a junior partner, while China is taking the driving seat in determining the future direction of the relationship.

Furthermore, it appears that China and Pakistan's claims of having an 'all-weather' friendship are relevant to their bilateral experiences alone but are not valid in wider international arena. It is correct that Pakistan is the only country out of China's other allies with whom Beijing's ties have remained stable. Similarly, no country—big or small—and from the Muslim bloc or the West could supplant China's place in Pakistan's foreign policy. However, if the durability of relationship is indicative, this is limited to China-Pakistan relations. A cursory look at the world scene shows that there are other examples of durable state-to-state relationships. For instance, US relations with its allies in Europe such as Britain, in East Asia with Japan and Taiwan, and in the Middle East with Israel have been equally consistent since their inception. The level of US commitment and assistance to these allies is not lesser than that of China's to Pakistan.

To sum up, a holistic approach, taking all factors together, can help develop a better understanding of the China-Pakistan relationship. Nothing is permanent in international relations nor the Sino-

Pakistan entente. Given the trajectory, mutuality of interests based on geography, and accumulated 'trust', the relationship is most likely to grow further. If CPEC is implemented as conceived, it will take the relationship to new heights.

Bibliography

Newspapers, news agencies, news services, and chronological documents (without reference to specific dates or articles)

'Quarterly Chronicle and Documentation', *The China Quarterly*

'Chronology of Events', *Pakistan Horizon,* Pakistan Institute of International Affairs, Karachi

'Press Clippings', Institute of Regional Studies, Islamabad

AFP

Asia Times

Asian Recorder

Associated Press of Pakistan

Associated Press, The

Aviation Week & Space Technology

Business Recorder, Karachi

China Daily, Beijing

CNTV

Daily Times, Lahore

Dawn, Karachi, Lahore, and Islamabad

Deutsche Presse-Agentur

Diplomat, The, Tokyo

Economic Times, The, Bombay

Express Tribune, The, Karachi

Financial Times, London

Foreign Broadcast Information Service (FBIS)

Indian Express, Bombay

Jang (Urdu Language daily), Lahore

Japan Economic Newswire

Keesing's Contemporary Archives

Morning News, Karachi

Nation, The, Lahore

National Archives, The
Nawa-e-Waqt (Urdu Language daily), Lahore
New York Times, The, New York
News, The, Karachi
Nucleonics Week, New York
Pakistan News
Pakistan Times, Lahore
Pamir Times
People's Daily (both translated and online English version), Beijing
Press Trust of India, The
Straits Times, The
Times of India, The
Tribune, The
United Press International
Voice of America, Washington
Washington Post, The, Washington
Xinhua
Xinhua General News Service
Xinhua General Overseas News Service, The

Interviewees (affiliations at the time of interview)

Acharya, Arabinda. Research Fellow, S. Rajaratnam School of International Studies, Nanyang Technological University, Singapore, February 2011.

Bajpai, Kanti. Visiting Professor, Lee Kuan Yew School of Public Policy, National University of Singapore, Singapore, February 2011.

Basrur, Rajesh M. Professor, S. Rajaratnam School of International Studies, Nanyang Technological University, Singapore, February 2011.

D'Souza, Shanthie Mariet. Research Fellow, Institute of South Asian Studies, National University of Singapore, February 2011.

Fazal-ur-Rehman. Director, China Study Centre, Institute of Strategic Studies, Islamabad, April 2011.

Hussain, Riffat. Chairman, Department of Defence and Strategic Studies, Quaid-i-Azam University, Islamabad, April 2011.

Masood, Talat, Lt. Gen. (retired). Islamabad, April 2011.

Muni, S. D. Visiting Research Professor, Institute of South Asian Studies, National University of Singapore, February 2011.

Rahman, Khalid. Director Institute of Policy Studies, Islamabad, April 2011.

Rais, Rasool Buksh. Professor, Lahore University of Management Sciences (LUMS), Lahore, April 2011.

Rizvi, Hasan-Askari. Former Professor, Punjab University, Lahore, April 2011.

Rong, Zhou. Bureau Chief, *Guangming Daily*, Islamabad, April 2011.

Shahab, Mansoor. Assistant Professor, COMSATS Institute of Information Technology, Abbottabad, April 2011.

Yongnian, Zheng. Director, East Asia Institute, National University of Singapore, Singapore, February 2011.

Zaki, Akram. Former Pakistani Ambassador to China, Islamabad, April 2011.

Zhiyue, Bo. Senior Research Fellow, East Asia Institute, National University of Singapore, Singapore, February 2011.

Interviews in China

Hongqi, Sun. Professor and Head, Pakistan Research Centre, Jiangsu Normal University, Xu Zhou, China, July 2014.

Jianxue, Lan. Associate Research Fellow, China Institute of International Studies (CIIS), May 2014.

Jidong, Chen. Head, Pakistan Study Centre, Sichuan University, Chengdu, China, July 2014.

Khalid, Masood. Pakistan's Ambassador to China, Embassy of the Islamic Republic of Pakistan in Beijing, July 2014.

Shida, Wang. China Institute of Contemporary International Relations (CICIR), July 2014.

Shisheng, Hu. Director Asia and Oceania Studies, China Institute of Contemporary International Relations (CICIR), July 2015.

Tipu, Muhammad Mudassar. Political Counsellor, Embassy of the Islamic Republic of Pakistan in Beijing, July 2014.

Weihua, Wang. Assistant Director, Institute of Foreign Policy Studies, Shanghai Institute of International Studies (SIIS), November 2014.

Xiguang, Li. Head, Pakistan Study Centre, Tsinghua University, Beijing, November 2014.

Zhao, Gancheng. Senior Fellow, Director, Centre for Asia-Pacific Studies, Shanghai Institute of International Studies (SIIS), November 2014.

Main sources

Abbasi, Abdur Razzaq Khan, 'Thirty Five Years of Pakistan-China Relations', *Strategic Studies*, vol. IX, no. 4 (Summer 1986).

Abdul, Sattar, *Pakistan's Foreign Policy, 1947–2009: A Concise History* (Karachi: Oxford University Press, 2006).

Afzal, Rafique, *Pakistan Year Book 1978* (Karachi, Lahore: East West Publishing Company, 1978).

———, *Pakistan Year Book, 1988–1989* (Karachi, Lahore: East West Publishing, 1989).

———, *Pakistan Year Book, 1985–1986* (Karachi, Lahore: East and West Publishing Company, 1986).

Ahmad, Mushtaq, *The Economy of Pakistan* (Karachi: Pakistan Institute of International Affairs, 1950).

———, *The United Nations and Pakistan* (Karachi: Pakistan Institute of International Affairs, 1955).

Ahmad, Naveed, 'Sino-Pakistan Relations (1971–1981)', *Pakistan Horizon*, vol. 34, no. 3 (1981).

Ahmar, Moonis, 'Sino-Soviet Detente and its Impact on Asian Security', *Central Asia* (1990).

Ahrari, M. Ehsan, 'China, Pakistan, and the "Taliban Syndrome"', *Asian Survey*, vol. 40, no. 4 (2000).

Aijazuddin, F. S. (ed.), *From a Head, through a Head, to a Head: The Secret Channel between the US and China through Pakistan* (Karachi: Oxford University Press, 2000).

———, *The White House & Pakistan: Secret Declassified Documents, 1969–1974* (Karachi, Oxford: Oxford University Press, 2002).

Akhtar, Shaheen. 'Pak-China Economic Relations: Forging Strategic Partnership in the 21st Century', *Regional Studies*, vol. XIX, no. 3 (Summer 2001).

Alam, Shah, 'Iran-Pakistan Relations: Political and Strategic Dimensions', *Strategic Analysis* (October–December 2004).

Ali, Ghulam, 'China: Emerging Partner of Saarc', *Defence Journal*, vol. 11, no. 4 (November 2007).

———, 'China's Deepening Engagement with Pakistan on Counter-terrorism', *Central Asia Caucasus Analyst*, vol. 12, no. 10 (26 May 2010).

———, 'China's Seat in the United Nations: An Analysis of Pakistan's Role', *IPRI Journal*, vol. IV, no. 2 (Summer 2004).

———, 'Sino-Pakistan Relations since 9/11', in Shen, Simon; Blanchard, Jean-Marc F. (eds.), *Multidimensional Diplomacy of Contemporary China* (Lanham: Rowman & Littlefield, 2010).

———, 'Wen Jiabao's Visit to India and Pakistan Reinforces Stability and Neutrality', *East Asia Forum* (21 January 2011).

Ali, Mehrunnisa, 'China's Diplomacy during the Indo-Pakistan War, 1971', *Pakistan Horizon*, vol. 25, no. 1 (1972).

———, 'Soviet-Pakistan Ties since the Afghanistan Crisis', *Asian Survey*, vol. 23, no. 9 (1983).

Arif, K., *China-Pakistan Relations: Documents 1947–1980* (Lahore: Vanguard Books, 1984).

Athwal, Amardeep, *China-India Relations: Contemporary Dynamics* (New York: Routledge, 2008).

Atique, Fauzia, 'Pakistan's Foreign Policy: A Quarterly Survey', *Pakistan Horizon*, vol. 38, no. 4 (Fourth Quarter 1985).

Ayoob, Mohammed, 'Pakistan's Relations with China: A Study in the Coincidence of Objectives and the Convergence of Interests', *China Report*, vol. 5, no. 1 (1969).

Azeemi, Haris Raqeeb, '55 Years of Pakistan-China Relationship', *Pakistan Horizon*, vol. 60, no. 2 (April 2007).

Banerjee, P. K., 'China in India and Pakistan', speech to the United States Congress, Congressional Record (Washington DC, 13 June 1966), <http://www.dawn.com/news/1170986/pakistan-seabed-territory-grows-by-50000-square-kilometres> (Pakistan's EEZ extended).

Barnds, William J., 'China's Relations with Pakistan: Durability Amidst Discontinuity', *The China Quarterly*, no. 63 (1975).

———, *India, Pakistan, and the Great Powers* (London: Pall Mall Press, 1972).

Barnds, William J., Lawrence Ziring, Ralph J. D. Braibanti, and W. Wriggins, *Pakistan: The Long View* (Durham: Duke University Press, 1977).

'Benazir Bhutto on Pak-Chinese Ties', *Beijing Review*, vol. 32, nos. 7 & 8 (1989).

Bernstein, Thomas P., 'Between the Stools?: US Policy towards Pakistan during the Carter Administration', *Asian Survey*, vol. 22, no. 10 (October 1982).

Bhalla, Madhu, 'Geopolitics of Economic Relations', in Swaran Singh (ed.), *China-Pakistan Strategic Cooperation: Indian Perspectives* (New Delhi: Centre De Sciences Humaines, 2007).

Bhattacharjea, Mira Sinha, 'India-China-Pakistan: Beyond Kargil—Changing Equations', *China Report*, vol. 35, no. 4 (1999).

Bhattacharya, Abanti, 'The Xinjiang Factor', in Swaran Singh (ed.) *China-Pakistan Strategic Cooperation: Indian Perspectives* (New Delhi: Manohar; New Delhi: Centre De Sciences Humaines, 2007).

Bhatty, Maqbool A., 'Impact of Sino-US Relations on Security Situation in South Asia', *National Development and Security*, vol. 6, no. 1 (1997).

———, 'Sino-Pakistan Relations: Future Prospects', *National Development and Security*, vol. 4, no. 4 (1996).

Bhola, P. L., *Pakistan-China Relations: Search for Politico-Strategic Relationship* (Jaipur: R.B.S.A. Publishers, 1986).

———, 'Sino-Pak Relations in the Emerging New World Order', *Indian Journal of Asian Affairs*, vol. 7, no. 2 (1994).

———, 'Sino-Pakistan Economic Relations (1950–1983)', *South Asian Studies*, vol. 19, no. 1 (1984).

Bhutto, Zulfikar Ali, *Foreign Policy of Pakistan; a Compendium of Speeches Made in the National Assembly of Pakistan 1962–64* (Karachi: Pakistan Institute of International Affairs, 1964).

———, *Myth of Independence* (Karachi: Oxford University Press, 1969).

———, 'Pakistan—and China?' *Survival*, vol. 5, no. 5 (September–October 1963).

Burke, S. M., *Pakistan's Foreign Policy: An Historical Analysis* (London: Oxford University Press, 1973).

Butt, Muhammad Ijaz, 'Chinese Aided Development Projects in Pakistan', *Central Asia*, no. 48 (2001).

Chaudhri, Mohammed Ahsen, *Pakistan and the Great Powers* (Karachi: Council for Pakistan Studies, 1970).

———, 'Pakistan's Foreign Policy: A Quarterly Review', *Pakistan Horizon*, vol. 32, no. 2 (April 1989).

———, 'Pakistan's Relations with the Soviet Union', *Asian Survey*, vol. 6, no. 9 (1966).

Cheema, Pervaiz Iqbal, 'Significance of Pakistan-China Border Agreement of 1963', *Pakistan Horizon*, vol. 39, no. 4 (1986).

———, 'The China Threat: A View from Pakistan', in Herbert, Yee, Storey, Ian (eds.), *The China Threat: Perceptions, Myths and Reality* (London; New York: Routledge, 2002).

'China, Pakistan Foster Cooperation', *Beijing Review*, vol. 35, no. 42 (1992).

'China, Pakistan Woo Closer Ties', *Beijing Review*, vol. 37, no. 50 (1994).

'Chinese Media Coverage of the Kargil Conflict', *China Report*, vol. 35, no. 4 (1999).

Choudhury, G. W., *India, Pakistan, Bangladesh, and the Major Powers: Politics of a Divided Subcontinent* (New York: Macmillan, 1975).

———, 'Reflections on Sino-Pakistan Relations', *Pacific Community*, vol. 7, no. 2 (1976).

Cooley, John K., *Unholy Wars: Afghanistan, America and International Terrorism* (Sterling, VA: Pluto Press, 1999).

Cultural Information Office Embassy of the People's Republic of China in Pakistan, *News Bulletin* (13 May 1974).

Curtis, Lisa, 'China's Credentials on the Global Stage at Stake in the Current Crisis in Pakistan', *Jakarta Globe* (27 May 2009).

Dillon, Michael, *Xinjiang-China's Muslim Far Northwest* (London & New York: Routledge, 2009).

Du, Youkang, 'South Asian Security and its Impact on China', *China Report*, vol. 37, no. 2 (2001).

Dumbaugh, Kerry B. (ed.), *Exploring the China-Pakistan Relationship*, Roundtable Report (Alexandria, VA: Centre for Naval Analyses, June 2010).

Dutta, Sujit, 'China and Pakistan: End of a "Special Relationship"', *China Report*, vol. 30, no. 2 (1994).

Fair, C. Christine, 'Pakistan in 2011: Ten Years of the "War on Terror"', *Asian Survey*, vol. 52, no. 1 (2012).

Fani, Muhammad Ishaque, 'Pak-China Security Relations and Mutual Ventures', *JRSP*, vol. 46, no. 2 (2009).

Faruqui, Ahmad, 'China Card Could yet Trump Musharraf', *Asia Times*, vol. 25 (May 2002).

———, 'The Complex Dynamics of Pakistan's Relationship with China', *IPRI Journal*, vol. 1, no. 1 (Summer 2001).

Fazal-ur-Rahman, 'Pakistan-China Economic Relations: Opportunities and Challenges', *Strategic Studies*, vol. XXVI, no. 2 (Summer 2006).

———, 'Pakistan-China Relations in a Changing Geo-Strategic Environment', *Strategic Studies*, vol. XXII, no. 2 (Summer 2002).

———, 'Pakistan-China Relations: The Shadow of Kargil and 9/11', in Shiping Tang, Mingjiang Li, Acharya, Amitav (eds.), *Living with China: Regional States and China through Crises and Turning Points* (New York: Palgrave Macmillan, 2009).

———, 'Pakistan's Evolving Relations with China, Russia, and Central Asia', in Akihiro Iwashita (ed.), *Eager Eyes Fixed on Eurasia: Volume 1: Russia and its Neighbors in Crisis* (Sapporo: Slavic Research Centres, Hokkaido University, 2007).

———, 'Pakistan's Relations with China', *Strategic Studies*, vols. XIX & XX, nos. 4 & 1 (Winter & Spring 1998).

———, 'Prospects of Pakistan Becoming a Trade and Energy Corridor for China', *Strategic Studies*, vol. XXVII, no. 2 (Summer 2007).

———, 'Targeted Attacks on Chinese: Myth and Reality', *Strategic Studies*, vol. XXVII, no. 4 (Winter 2007).

———, 'Traditional and Emerging Areas of Strategic Cooperation between Pakistan and China', *Strategic Studies*, nos. 2 & 3 (Summer & Autumn 2009).

Fitzpatrick, Mark (ed.), *Nuclear Black Markets: Pakistan, A. Q. Khan and the Rise of Proliferation Networks, a Net Assessment* (London: IISS, 2007).

Garver, John W, *China's Decision for Rapprochement with the United States, 1968–1971* (Boulder, CO: Westview Press, 1982).

———, 'China's Kashmir Policies', *India Review*, vol. 3, no. 1 (2004).

———, *Protracted Contest: Sino-Indian Rivalry in the Twentieth Century* (Seattle: University of Washington Press, 2001).

———, 'Sino-Indian Rapprochement and the Sino-Pakistan Entente', *Political Science Quarterly*, vol. III, no. 2 (1996).

———, 'The Future of the Sino-Pakistani Entente Cordiale', in Michael R. Chambers (ed.), *South Asia in 2020: Future Strategic Balances and Alliances* (Carlisle: Strategic Studies Institute of the US Army War College, 2002).

Government of Pakistan, *Joint Communiqués: January 1968–December 1973* (Islamabad: Ministry of Foreign Affairs, 1973).

Government of Pakistan, *National Assembly Debates*, vol. III (1973).

Gupta, Sonika, 'Role of Political Culture', in Swaran Singh (ed.) *China-Pakistan Strategic Cooperation: Indian Perspectives* (New Delhi: Centre De Sciences Humaines, 2007).

Hagerty, Devin T., 'India's Regional Security Doctrine', *Asian Survey*, vol. 31, no. 4 (1991).

———, 'China and Pakistan: Strains in the Relationship', *Current History*, vol. 101, no. 656 (2002).

Haider, Ziad, 'Baluchis, Beijing, and Pakistan's Gwadar Port', *Georgetown Journal of International Affairs*, vol. 6, no. 1 (2005).

———, 'Sino-Pakistan Relations and Xinjiang's Uighurs: Politics, Trade, and Islam Along the Karakoram Highway', *Asian Survey*, vol. 45, no. 4 (2005).

Hali, S. M., 'Pak-US Vs Pak-China Relations', *Pakcolumns*, <http://www.pkcolumns.com/2010/07/14/pak-us-vs-pak-china-relations-by-s-m-hali>.

Hanns-Seidel-Stiftung, *Proceedings of the International Conference on China and Emerging Asian Century, September 27–28, 2005* (Islamabad: Institute of Strategic Studies in collaboration with Hanns Seidel Foundation, 2005).

Hartpence, Mathias, 'The Economic Dimension of Sino-Pakistani Relations: An Overview', *Journal of Contemporary China*, vol. 20, no. 71 (2011).

Hilali, A. Z., 'China's Response to the Soviet Invasion of Afghanistan', *Central Asian Survey*, vol. 20, no. 3 (2001).

Hongyu, Wang, 'Sino-Indian Relations: Present and Future', *Asian Survey*, vol. 35, no. 6 (1995).

Hussain, Mushahid, *Pakistan's Politics: The Zia Years* (Lahore: Progressive Publishers, 1990).

———, 'Pakistan-China Defense Co-operation: An Enduring Relationship', *International Defense Review*, vol. 26, no. 2 (February 1993).

Jain, R. K., *China, Pakistan and Bangladesh* (New Delhi: Radiant Publishers, 1978).

______, *China South Asian Relations: 1947–1980,* vol. 1 (New Delhi: Radiant Publishers, 1981).

______, *China-South Asia Relations: 1947–1980*, vol. 2 (New Delhi: Radiant Publishers, 1981).

Jetly, Rajshree, 'Sino-Pakistan Strategic Entente: Implications for Regional Security', ISAS (14 February 2012), *Working Paper* no. 143.

Kapur, Haris, 'China's Relations with India and Pakistan', *Current History*, vol. 57, no. 337 (September 1969).

Kardon, Isaac B., 'China and Pakistan: Emerging Strains in the Entente Cordiale', *Project 2049 Institute* (Arlington, Virginia, 25 March 2011).

Karim, Arshad Syed, 'China after Mao', *Pakistan Horizon*, vol. 39, no. 2 (1986).

Kaushik, B. M., 'The Indian Nuclear Test, China & Pakistan', *China Report*, vol. 10, no. 4 (1974).

Kennedy, John F., *The Strategy for Peace* (New York: Harper and Row, 1960).

Khan, Mohammad Ayub, *Friends, Not Masters: A Political Autobiography* (Islamabad: Mr Books, 2001).

______, 'Pakistan Perspective', *Foreign Affairs,* vol. 38 (July 1960).

Khan, Roedad (ed.), *American Papers: Secret and Confidential India, Pakistan and Bangladesh Documents 1965–1973* (Oxford: Oxford University Press, 1999).

Khan, Sulmaan Wasif, *Muslim, Trader, Nomad, Spy: China's Cold War and the People of the Tibetan Borderlands* (University of North Caroline Press, 2015).

Khan, Sultan Muhammed, 'Pakistani Geopolitics: The Diplomatic Perspective', *International Security*, vol. 5, no. 1 (Summer 1980).

Kher, Aparna, 'Pakistan in China's Arms Trade', in Swaran Singh (ed.), *China-Pakistan Strategic Cooperation: Indian Perspectives* (New Delhi: Centre De Sciences Humaines, 2007).

Kim, Samuel S. (ed.), *China and the World: Chinese Foreign Policy Faces the New Millennium* (Colorado: Westview Press, 1998).

Kissinger, Henry, *On China* (London: Penguin, 2011).

Kumar, Sushil, 'Towards an Asian Power Cycle: India, China and Pakistan', in Kanti Bajpai, Mattoo, Amitabh (eds.), *The Peacock and the Dragon:*

India-China Relations in the 21st Century (New Delhi: Har-Anand Publications Pvt Ltd, 2000).

Kumar, Sumita, 'The China-Pakistan Strategic Relationship: Trade, Investment, Energy and Infrastructure', *Strategic Studies*, vol. 31, no. 5 (September 2007).

Lee, Itamar, 'Deepening Naval Cooperation between Islamabad and Beijing', *China Brief*, vol. 9, no. 13 (24 June 2009).

Levi, Werner, 'Pakistan, the Soviet Union and China', *Pacific Affairs*, vol. 35, no. 3 (1962).

Mahmood, Khalid, 'Economic Dimension of Pakistan China Relations', in *Proceedings of One-Day International Seminar on Pakistan-China Relations in Changing Regional and Global Scenario* (Jamshoro: Area Study Center for Far East & South East Asia, University of Sindh, 29 September 2005).

Mahmud, Khalid, 'Sino-Pakistan Relations: An 'All-Weather' Friendship', *Regional Studies*, vol. XIX, no. 3 (Summer 2001).

Major Powers and South Asia (Islamabad: Institute of Regional Studies, 2004).

Malik, J. Mohan, *China and India: Great Power Rival* (Boulder, CO: First Forum Press, 2011).

———, 'Dragon on Terrorism: Assessing China's Tactical Gains and Strategic Losses after 11 September', *Contemporary Southeast Asia*, vol. 24, no. 2 (2002).

Mangi, Lutfullah, 'Pakistan and China: An Excellent Model for Relations between Neighbouring Countries', *Contemporary International Relations*, vol. 20, no. 6 (2010).

Mehrotra, O. N., 'Sino-Pak Relations', *China Report*, vol. 11, nos. 5 & 6 (1975).

———, 'Sino-Pak Relations: A Review', *China Report*, vol. 12, no. 5 (1976).

Military Balance: 1970–1971 (London: International Institute for Strategic Studies, 1972).

Ministry of Foreign Affairs, Pakistan, 'Agreement between China and Pakistan for the Purchase of Ten Ships from Pakistan', *Foreign Affairs Pakistan*, vol. V, nos. 9 & 10 (September–October 1978).

______, 'Exchange of Letters on Trade Mark between Pakistan and China on 26 July 1979', *Foreign Affairs Pakistan*, vol. VI, no. 7 (July 1979).

______, 'Trade Protocol between Pakistan and China; April 21, 1979', *Foreign Affairs Pakistan*, vol. VI, no. 4.

Mishra, Keshav, *Rapprochement across the Himalaya: Emerging India-China Relations* (New Delhi: Kalpaz Publications, 2004).

Montagno, George L., 'Peaceful Coexistence: Pakistan and Red China', *The Western Political Quarterly*, vol. 18, no. 2 (1965).

'Musharraf Reaffirms Pakistan-China Ties', *Beijing Review*, vol. 43, no. 4 (2000).

Mustafa, Zubeida, 'China's Policy Towards Pakistan', *Pacific Community: An Asian Quarterly Review*, vol. 5, no. 1 (1973).

______, 'Pakistan's Foreign Policy - A Quarterly Survey', *Pakistan Horizon* 35, no. 4 (1982).

______, 'The Sino-Pakistan Border: Historical Aspect', *Pakistan Horizon*, vol. 15, no. 2 (1972).

Narayan, Raviprasad, 'China and South Asia, July–December 1999: A Chronology', *China Report*, vol. 36, no. 2 (2000).

______, 'China and South Asia, January–June 1999: A Chronology', *China Report*, vol. 36, no. 1 (2000).

Ni, Yanshuo, 'Corridor of Cooperation: Pakistan is Increasingly Becoming China's Most Important Partner in Asia', *Beijing Review*, vol. 49, no. 13 (2006).

'Pakistan Prime Minister Visits China', *Beijing Review*, vol. 41, no. 9 (1998).

'Pak-China Relations in the 21st Century: Regional Situation, Security, Economic & Trade Cooperation', *Policy Perspectives*, vol. 1, no. 1 (Islamabad: Institute of Policy Studies).

Proceedings of the Two-Day Seminar on Pakistan-China Relations, 2011: Year of Friendship January 11–12, 2011 (Islamabad: Institute of Strategic Studies, 2011).

Prospects of Peace, Stability and Prosperity in South Asia (Islamabad: Institute of Regional Studies, 2005).

Rais, Rasul Bux, *China and Pakistan: A Political Analysis of Mutual Relations* (Lahore: Progressive Publishers, 1977).

Rajan, D. S., 'China: Revisiting the 2005 Friendship Treaty with Pakistan'

(10 December 2006), <http://www.southasiaanalysis.org/%5Cpapers21%5Cpaper2058.html>.

Rajput, M. Akram, 'Soviet-Pakistan Relations', *Pakistan Forum*, vol. 3, no. 12 (1973).

Ram, Mohan, 'Karakoram Highway', *Economic and Political Weekly*, vol. 13, no. 26 (1978).

Raman, B., 'All Eyes on Gilani's Visit to China' (16 May 2011), <http://www.southasiaanalysis.org/%5Cpapers45%5Cpaper4493.html>.

———, 'Counter-Terrorism: India-China-Russia Cooperation', *China Report*, vol. 40, no. 2 (2004).

Rashid, Ahmed, 'The Taliban: Exporting Extremism', *Foreign Affairs*, vol. 78, no. 6 (November–December 1999).

Rizvi, Hasan-Askari, *Pakistan and the Geostrategic Environment: A Study of Foreign Policy* (New York: St. Martin's Press, 1993).

Sekhar, D. Varaprasad, 'Civilian Technology Transfers', in Swaran Singh (ed.), *China-Pakistan Strategic Cooperation: Indian Perspectives* (New Delhi: Centre De Sciences Humaines, 2007).

Sen Gupta, Bhabani, *The Fulcrum of Asia: Relations among China, India, Pakistan, and the USSR* (Delhi: Konark Publishers, 1988).

Sherwani, Latif Ahmed, *India, China and Pakistan* (Karachi: Council for Pakistan Studies, 1967).

———, 'Review of Sino-Pakistan Relations (1981–85)', *Pakistan Horizon*, vol. 39, no. 1 (1986).

Singh, Gurnam, 'China and the Indian Ocean Region', *China Report*, vol. 20, no. 3 (1984).

———, 'Pakistan's China Policy: Causal Considerations 1960s', *Punjab Journal of Politics*, vol. 6, no. 2 (1982).

———, *Sino-Pakistan Relations: The Ayub Era*, 1st ed. (Amritsar: Guru Nanak Dev University Press, 1987).

Singh, Swaran, *China-South Asia: Issues, Equations, Policies* (New Delhi: Lancers Books, 2003).

———, 'Introduction', in Swaran Singh (ed.), *China-Pakistan Strategic Cooperation: Indian Perspectives* (New Delhi: Centre De Sciences Humaines, 2007).

———, 'The Kargil Conflict: Why and How of China's Neutrality', *Strategic Analysis* (October 1999).

Sinha, Satyabrat, 'The Strategic Triangle: India-China-Pakistan', *China Report*, vol. 40, no. 2 (2004).

'Sino-Pak Cooling Off?', *Economic and Political Weekly*, vol. 3, no. 8 (1968).

'Sino-Pakistan Ties: Turning Forty', *Beijing Review*, vol. 34, no. 22 (1991).

Small, Andrew, *The China-Pakistan Axis: Asia's New Geopolitics* (London: C. Hurst & Co., 2015).

Song, Deheng, 'Li Peng Tours Three South Asian Nations', *Beijing Review*, vol. 32, no. 47 (1989).

'Speech by the Chinese premier Mr Geng Biao at the banquet given by CMLA, June 16, 1978', *Foreign Affairs Pakistan*, vol. V, nos. 5 & 6 (May–June 1978).

Stebbins, Richard P., *The United States in World Affairs 1961* (New York, 1962).

Stern, Jessica, 'Pakistan's Jihad Culture', *Foreign Affairs*, vol. 79, no. 6 (November–December 2000).

Sutter, Robert G., *Chinese Foreign Policy after the Cultural Revolution, 1966–1977* (Boulder, CO: Westview Press, 1978).

Thornton, Thomas Perry, 'Between the Stools? U.S. Policy Towards Pakistan During the Carter Administration', *Asian Survey*, vol. 22, no. 10 (1982).

Wirsing, Robert G., 'In India's Lengthening Shadow: The US-Pakistan Strategic Alliance and the War in Afghanistan', *Asian Affairs: An American Review*, vol. 34, no. 3 (2007).

———, *The Enemy of My Enemy: Pakistan's China Debate* (Honolulu, Hawaii: Asia-Pacific Center for Security Studies, December 2003).

Wolpert, Stanley, *Zulfi Bhutto of Pakistan: His Life and Time* (Oxford: Oxford University Press, 2007).

Wriggins, W. Howard, 'The Balancing Process in Pakistan's Foreign Policy', in Lawrence Ziring, et al. (eds.), *Pakistan: The Long View* (Durham, NC: Duke University Press, 1977)

Yasmeen, Samina, *Pakistan's Relations with China, 1947–1979,* Islamabad Papers (Islamabad: Institute of Strategic Studies, 1980).

———, 'Sino-Pakistan Relations and the Middle East', *China Report*, vol. 34, nos. 3 & 4 (1998).

'Yang's Two-Nation Tour Successful', *Beijing Review*, vol. 34, no. 451991.

Yuan, Jing-dong, 'India's Rise after Pokhran II: Chinese Analyses and Assessments', *Asian Survey*, vol. 41, no. 6 (November–December 2001).

Yunus, Mohammad, *Reflections on China: An Ambassador's View from Beijing* (Lahore: Services Book Club, 1987).

Main Websites

Federation of American Scientists
Institute of Asia Pacific Studies
Institute of Peace and Conflict Studies
Ministry of Foreign Affairs of the Islamic Republic of Pakistan
Ministry of Foreign Affairs of the People's Republic of China
Pak Akhbar
Pakistan Aeronautical Complex

Index